GREGOTTI & ASSOCIATES
THE ARCHITECTURE OF URBAN LANDSCAPE

Guido Morpurgo (Milan, 1964), PhD in Architecture and Urban Design, was trained at the Polytechnic University of Milan, where he is currently visiting professor of Architectural and Urban Composition.

An associate in the Gregotti Associati studio between 2000 and 2008, he has worked on national and international projects and competitions, in particular in Shanghai, where the redevelopment of the area of the former British concession in Waitanyuan and the new city of Pujiang are notable examples.

He has published articles and essays on the works of Gregotti & Associates, including the monographs *Gregotti Associati 1953–2003* (Skira Rizzoli, Milan 2004) and *Gregotti & Associates: The Architecture of Urban Design*, (Rizzoli, New York, 2008), and edited the volumes *Fragments of Constructions* (Skira, Milan, 2001), *Headquarters Pirelli Real Estate* (Skira, Milan, 2005), *An Intelligible Order: Gregotti Associati Banca Lombarda New Headquarters* (Skira, Milan, 2007), *Festschrift per gli ottant'anni di Vittorio Gregotti* (Skira, Milan, 2007).

Since 2006 he has been co-owner of Morpurgo de Curtis ArchitettiAssociati studio, creators of the Milan Holocaust Memorial (cfr. Biraghi M., Micheli S., *Storia dell'architettura Italiana 1985–2015*, Einaudi, Turin, 2013).

Art direction and layout
Dario Zannier

Translation
Colin Parmar

First published in the United States of America in 2014
by Rizzoli International Publications, Inc.
300 Park Avenue South
New York, NY 10010
www.rizzoliusa.com

Originally published in Italy in 2014
by RCS Libri S.p.A., Milan

The publisher would be pleased to hear from rightsholders
of any unidentified iconographic sources.

2014 2015 2016 2017 / 10 9 8 7 6 5 4 3 2 1

ISBN: 978-0-8478-4284-1

Library of Congress Control Number: 2014941195

Printed in China

Guido Morpurgo

Gregotti & Associates

The Architecture of Urban Landscape

RIZZOLI NEW YORK

New York · Paris · London · Milan

CONTENTS

ACKNOWLEDGMENTS

I would first of all like to thank Vittorio Gregotti, incomparable *maître a penser*: this new book offers yet another chance to share with him themes and topics pertaining to architecture as a disciplinary culture and the history of ideas of which his thoughts are an integral part, while benefiting from the same inexhaustible intellectual energy and matchless intensity that I have been able to take advantage of daily over the many years I have spent working in the Gregotti Associati studio.

Very special thanks go to architect Augusto Cagnardi for his ability to convey the sense of the experience of architecture as a life form and his unreserved passion for this profession.

My personal debt to Michele Reginaldi, to his talent as architect and artist, is further deepened: this special occasion is to be added to the many adventurous experiences in architecture and the many future hopes shared with him.

To all three, I owe the same gratitude for having reaffirmed their faith in me, entrusting me with the opportunity and the responsibility of putting together this new volume on their work.

I would also like to thank architect Pierluigi Cerri, cofounder of the Gregotti Associati studio, for his kind and intellectual help.

Particular thanks must go to Franco Purini for agreeing to write the concluding text that rounds off this book.

Within the Gregotti Associati studio, I dedicate friendship and acknowledgment to architect Sergio Butti: without his constant devotion it would not have been possible to collect, select and organize the iconographic and documentary materials that make up this work. Affectionate thanks also to Emanuela Monarca and Mariangela Moiraghi for their patience and capacity for collaboration, gifts that I have appreciated for many years and which I have once again been able to avail myself of.

I would also like to remember Cristina Scalabrini of Rizzoli Milano and Gloria Nantz of Rizzoli New York for their efficiency and organization.

Thanks also to Colin Parmar for the attentiveness and quality of his work in the none too easy task of translation.

I offer my thanks to Dario Zannier for the care and commitment he has shown in defining the graphical part of the project and the elaborate design of the book, as well as for the friendship that he has once again shown me.

To Annalisa de Curtis, whose talent as an architect I take advantage of every day, goes my permanent gratitude for many things, too many to list here, and to which I add thanks for her keen advice and patient reading of my texts.

FOREWORD

Vittorio Gregotti

This is the second volume dedicated to our studio's projects and buildings in its sixty-two years of activity; it concerns the projects and constructions of the past seven years.

It must be said from the start that this period coincides with the seven years of the economic crisis, the result of very debatable management by the powers that be in financial capitalism of the possibilities that globalization, despite the enormous practical and ideological difficulties, has also offered to architectural culture. This also has a negative effect on the crisis that has been afflicting architectural culture and its most popular relationships with the media for more than thirty years through its predominant position of positively reflecting the state of affairs, beyond a few rare and laudable attempts to critically relate with the state of affairs and to search for a future as a necessary possibility.

What we would like to ask ourselves with this publication is whether, despite many errors and imperfections, we have managed to give meaning to the responsible bias in our point of view, albeit in the complicated condition of the contemporary culture of architecture as art, which now competes only with postmodern academicism; to give a meaning to our willfulness to conceive the project as a creative modification, as a quest for fragments of truth able to critically interpret the reality of the present with all its contradictions and offer moderate order (but against all censorship) without sacrificing the opportunities given by an imagination capable of perceptions that can face up to the specificities of our craft and the rules constructed by the project, compared with the conditions offered by the precious diversity of site cultures, built from history and the desires of positive variations, to be interpreted critically.

Each of these projects (even, and often especially, those recorded in the register of works) has its own story, which it would be nice to tell rather than present. A story of uncertainties and difficulties, often complex affairs and failures, sometimes complicated clashes with interests and objectives quite different from those we consider a part of architecture as an artistic practice. Our intentions, sometimes capable, even in their contradictions, of arousing, we hope, offers of a necessary possibility and new and special questions, are often very difficult to make coincide with these.

All this is matched up against our studio's long and complex history, which began, as I have mentioned, more than sixty years ago and which I am the senior and continual witness to.

Even though it is perhaps projecting today's way of thinking onto it, it seems to me that right from the start, our studio has offered a series of research directions, which have been maintained, albeit with different interpretations, throughout our long journey. Some of them can be distinguished, first of all by the idea of the value of collective work, driven both by the teachings of Walter Gropius's Bauhaus and by my own personal direct experience in the field as a young man; then by the interest in all three aspects of our work, architecture, planning, and product design, and the ever more complex relationship between them; also by the indispensability of work around the theory of the project in various forms; of teaching, writing, and participation in international debates and journal proposals; finally, by belonging to the tradition of that new form of cutting-edge experience of the first thirty years of the twentieth century, represented by critical internationalism we practice, with continuity since the 1950s, and shared by an interconnected part of my generation, with a positive critique of the inheritance of the modern movement and, as far as Italy is concerned, starting with the teachings from experience of the two generations of rationalists before us, to whom we owe a great debt, despite all the specific differences.

The differences in interpretation of the ideal themes and of the craft of that tradition developed over time, as our own work bears witness to, with various different centers: firstly around the themes of relationship with the history and culture of places and their contexts, then to passionately contribute towards the themes of participation and the highest hopes of politics reclaiming the direct capacity, with no ideological dependency, of architectural language to propose ideals of new social organizations of freedom and justice; and then on the questions raised by the relationship between city and surrounding areas, with an obvious interest in the theme of constructing hypotheses around urban planning, especially in regards city outskirts and their chance of becoming authentically "city," with all their social and functional complexity and, since the 1970s, considering the anthropogeographical landscape as structural material for the project.

This second volume aims especially to show how these interests confront the theme of globalism, against all forms of colonialism and commercial and folk-stylistic self-colonialism, but also shows the differences between cultures and what each one can offer the globalized world as unique and profound experience. These may be very great differences like those that distinguish European from Chinese culture, differences that arise from the overlapping of different cultures such as in North Africa, subtle differences such as those that distinguish the regions of European nations.

We know that it is a difficult and ambitious challenge, but we believe that, with our studio's experience, it can be met, against the use of the precious and ever-changing resources offered by the impalpable techniques and communications we often elevate to mythical status and which confuse aims with tools, content, and values. Against quantity mistaken for greatness, against the extension of the notions of creativity as false inventive liberty applied to every human activity, against temporary novelty and for the continuation of architecture as metaphor for everlasting works.

I must add that the stylistic continuity of our language has never been for us a condition in tackling a project theme: if the result shows continuity of formal language, this arises from the continuity of the principles confronted by the coming into being of means and problems, from the belief that it is precisely the essence of specificity of our craft that makes exchanges with other artistic practices (and I mean practices, not techniques) indispensable, thus making necessary the dialogue with the other disciplines and human experiences.

That leaves me with the pleasure of thanking the numerous people who have collaborated, directly and indirectly, with our studio, starting with all my various partners (Meneghetti, Stoppino, Viganò, Nicolin, Matzui, Reginaldi, Cerri, Cagnardi) and associates. To them, I owe the best results of our work and some passionate discussions, which gave rise to such results. Their names and their various responsibilities can also be found in this book. Finally, I would like to thank architect Guido Morpurgo, who edited this and the previous volume with the same passion and critical capacity with which he participated in our work for many years.

INTRODUCTION
ARCHITECTURE OF URBAN LANDSCAPES:
THE THEORY AND PRACTICE OF CONSTRUCTING A PROJECT

"And while the history of ideas sought, by deciphering texts to reveal the secret motions of thought [its slow progression, its struggles and relapses, the obstacles it has overcome], so the level of 'things said,' in particular, comes into being: the condition of their appearance, the forms of their accumulation and succession . . . the discontinuities that punctuate them."

Michel Foucault[1]

Anthropogeography as a connection between nature and culture through landscape, basing the construction of the environmental whole on man. Landscape interpreted as subject to an inalienable and continual construction/reconstruction, in order to offer different possibilities and relationships in the dialectic between new interventions and structures settled in the historical dimension. Landscape as an architectural form of territory, which reveals the permanence of the deepest anthropological matrices. These are the foundations that make up the common basis of the projects undertaken by the Gregotti Associati studio from 2008 to 2014 and presented in this book, which is the ideal follow-up to the earlier work *The Architecture of Urban Design*.[2] The projects and works carried out reelaborate on the principle of geography as voluntary environmental morphology, a tendency at the root of an idea of landscape, which, especially in Vittorio Gregotti's experience, runs through more than sixty years of architectural work. The scale of intervention, themes, and places are brought together under the idea of a project rooted in culture and the experience of the modern, a project of resistance to the postmodernist ideology that in architecture "one declares oneself against context, against history, against urban design, in favor of the idea of the generic city, as the sum of inflated competitive objects."[3]

The architecture of the urban landscape and, more broadly speaking, of the anthropogeographical landscape, represents the synthesis of a working method begun with the "inaugural" projects of the '60s and '70,[4] the crossover of the dimensional and relational scales, able to reinterpret the profundity of its aesthetic and utilitarian meaning in terms of its "complex experience,"[5] to be accomplished through modification, integrating natural features into urban design, open spaces,

infrastructure, and buildings. It is an idea of the city and the overall inhabitable environment whose utopian component coincides with the fact that it is a form of interpretation of reality, a neoenlightenment redefinition of the world through architecture.

The studio's work over the past seven years has developed into a geography of sites provisionally grouped into three territorial spheres: North Africa, China, and Europe. These are a combination of environmental zones and cities that offer variations on the Gregottian understanding of form of territory, of "landscape as history,"[6] according to a dual condition: relative to the visible landscape, usable-measurable, and as the result of the complex interaction between the "invisible structures" represented by the ideas that preside over the formation of concentrated and sprawling urban archipelagos, of cultivating systems, as well as by knowledge and practices; with meanings deriving from the succession of societies. The three regions of the world identified as areas where the project could be applied represent an anthropogeographical triad, which seems problematically to epitomize some of the fundamental and urgent issues that architecture as an artistic and social practice is nowadays expected to respond to.

In the infinite space of the North African landscape, in view of the demand for new settlements able to rebalance the flow of migration, to offer sedentary conditions to nomadic populations and, at the same time, to grace capital cities with symbolic and identity-building works, the new cities and institutional buildings planned by the studio elaborate on the extreme theme of the relationship with the desert as a condition of radical confrontation between the artificial and the natural. Here, architecture becomes a sort of total landscape, which seems to ideally fulfill the principles introduced by Vittorio Gregotti in the late 1960s with the publication of *Il territorio dell'architettura*,[7] corresponding with his decision to effect a "formal technology of the anthropogeographical landscape," which produces alterations in the physical environment through the "logic of interference with great size." The complex relationship between project and history is structured through "contextual interaction": the city as a construction principle of inhabitable space is transposed onto a new horizon of operability represented by the "settlement principle . . . an act of foundation renewed each time as well as a revealing of the historical surroundings." Assuming the morphological dynamic of territory, Gregotti introduces a new form of design interpretation for geography of the environment, which produces the reading of "territory, in its physical manifestation, as an archaeological structure that nonetheless requires neither restoration nor completion. The city is no longer the privileged seat of *mémoire*, the built environment is no longer the sea in which one can dive for some wonderful fishing. The themes of 'preexisting environmental features' have made a leap in scale which involves an entire design methodology and the politics underlying it."[8]

These are ideas and concepts that, from the following decade onward, were further developed in the operational dimension of action that modifies the sites, thanks to the contribution of Augusto Cagnardi. It is a research pathway that, in the overview of a disciplinary instrumentation, which has by now become inefficient in the face of the challenge of complexity, inaugurates a new methodology of regulation of urban development. The relationship between master plan and project plan[9] is a diagonal procedure that crosses the scales of architecture, town planning, and territorial development planning in an integrated form.

Within this perspective of the foundation of a theory and practice of the architectural project, today the interpretation—or rather the archaeology of the very meaning of the contemporary landscape, an anthropogeographical text characterized by its own signs and traits—goes beyond the reiteration of the redeeming sense of its albeit necessary preservation and estimation as cultural heritage. Just as when faced with the general inability to understand the contemporary urban phenomenon, it does not consider it sufficient to adhere to the aesthetics of the "residual," a supposed "third landscape"[10] represented by abandoned areas, problematic in-between spaces in search of direction, subject to a process of renaturalization (and contemplation?). Anthropogeographical landscape architecture opposes the apotheosis of "*Bigness*," the unconditional surrender to the aesthetics of "*Junkspace*," which represent the annihilation of any relationship between history and urban identity.[11] On

the contrary, the principle of interaction between architecture and context, between the need for specificity and the urgency of establishing a relationship with the overall physical environment, becomes, through these projects, a condition for cultural belonging, opposed to the dissipation of quality and the articulation particular to the uses of urban space, to the meanings of geographical space and the characters of its own historical stratification.

And it is for these reasons that the projects collected in this book, despite the differences in location, scale, and typology relative to the structural diversity of the three environmental areas, have a demonstrative value in common: they still represent, in their reciprocal morphological concatenations, discontinuity and spread over time, a possibility of facing contemporaneity from within architecture. They seem to confirm the fact that the relationship between history and urban identity, between "destiny and character" (in the sense proposed by Walter Benjamin), can continue as the foundation for the interpretation of the physical and cultural conditions posed by the multiplicity of contemporary landscapes.

But these projects are modifying topographies deriving, in the first instance, from direct experience of the places. They are, indeed, "lived geographies,"[12] receptacles of meaning and experience that, as such, become objects of articulate narrations, both as architectural texts—projects and completed works—and as literary texts: reports, dissertations, revisions, tales.

Corresponding to the project as the place of research in architecture, therefore, is a conceptual dimension founded on that which Leonardo Benevolo defines as a "complementary rapport between writings, projects, and built works"[13]: the theory and practice of the construction of the project.

Reflection on things said in the form of narration, a flair for building a complex relationship between practice and theory, then, opens a new chapter in Gregotti & Associates' long "treatise," made up of projects, works, constructions, books, specialist journals, use of the media, lectures, and conferences, following an antiregulatory stance, which, especially in these recent projects, can be found in various forms in the marriage of rules and linguistic pluralism.

Thus the planning commitment in China as an attempt to establish a dialogue between new formations and physical and cultural foundations to generate interaction in Asian postmetropolitan landscapes also has a literary result in Cagnardi's accounts and reflections, dizzying close-ups of the mechanisms regulating the decisions and methods by which Chinese urban development is promoted, written during his frequent returns from an ever more indecipherable Shanghai to a Europe that, seen from that special observatory, perhaps seems even further from China itself.[14] And the measure of that distance and that difference between Western and Chinese cultural traditions becomes a tool with which to interpret ten years of work, an experience summed up by Gregotti in a narration that, analyzing Chinese architecture today compared with its own history, dissects the present to find a new place for the cultural heritage of European modernity, which the studio's projects, especially those for the new cities, transpose onto the horizon of Asian hypermodernity.[15]

One of the central themes in the development of the latest generation of projects, that of the principle of morphological variation, also has a specific translational space in Michele Reginaldi's amazing and extremely dense *cahiers de dessin*, which, enveloped in consecutive turns of a single conceptual, instrumental, expressive, and artistic kaleidoscopic spiral, gather together the swirl of summary exercises of drawings and constructions making up the "depository of morphological reflection."[16] His personal research on development procedures, variation, and expression of architectural form is a sort of perpetual process, metamorphic activity, which runs deeply through the projects presented in this book.

Right from the start, the principle of the relationship between rules and their variations affects the whole genealogy of Gregotti & Associates' works and projects, an event recalled in its complexity and intricacy in the essay by Franco Purini, which introduces the final chapter of this book: a complete, partly illustrated list of Gregotti & Associates' works from 1951 to 2014. This glance through the studio's various articulations highlights the cultural style and the development procedures of an entire design enterprise, which, even in the cases presented in this book, is represented by various scales of activity while maintaining a structural

(and perhaps untimely[17]) consistency, in principles and outcomes, with the identity of an overall work.

Research on new possible outcomes of urban morphology is based, especially in the projects for new cities and settlements, on the variation of the orthogonal grid principle as the basic layout, a rule and at the same time a regulatory form open to the multiple variations in the relationship between built-up areas, open space, and green areas, roads and pedestrian routes and infrastructure. A stable structural principle, and one that is at the same time capable of adapting the urban form according to the specific relief conditions, even produces artificial voluntary geographies, new measures of the anthropogeographical landscape to be created by digging and moving earth, intersecting with infrastructural routes, with specific materials such as water (networks of navigable canals and artificial lakes), the removal and repositioning of earth on the various different levels of inhabitable space.

This morphological research intervenes in the definition of architecture as a variation of the family of forms of building types, according to specific assembly procedures, in order to attain, on the basis of original geometric shapes, variations, continuous germination and regeneration of the relationship between type, use, and meaning, as articulation in a sort of combinatory grammar of their linguistic-expressive forms, but also as a representation and plastic characterization of their compositional elements; as an excavation in plastic volumes; the articulation and alternation of the spatial sequences within the buildings through generative sections; repetition-variation of the partitioning elements and composition of elevations, but avoiding aesthetic myth-making, the creation of iconic spectacles and anything that might stretch the visual simulation of architectural representation.

The result of this morphological and conceptual succession of modifications, upsets, and removals is programmatically summarized in the collection of the projects and works completed and developed in recent years in the problematical "European Archipelago." Even in the temporal cross-section, the graduated traversal offers a broad record which always recalls the idea of architecture in relation to the historical dimension of cities and landscapes. Indeed, it is "from the very example of the city and architecture that it can be affirmed that the historical terrain is at once the foundation and the fundament of all architecture, a terrain which leaves us free and responsible for any direction we wish to take in order to construct the possible other."[18]

This permanent exercise in design literature, facing the difficulties of the construction of real works, even in their temporal discontinuity, in relation to the nature of the physical and cultural materials always identified with a condition of the long duration of the works and the relationships that they create with the context, as well as on the sense of correspondence between structure and architectural form, has been confirmed in recent years in a particularly dense sequence of theoretical contributions by Gregotti. Six chapters on the subject of the risks to architecture of mixing up one's own ends and means in the interchangeability of the visual arts,[19] of losing oneself in the production and reproduction of the images and consequently of the need to reconstruct one's own boundaries in relation to the other disciplines[20]; of overcoming the dimension of the refusal to consistently interpret the modification of the present[21], of elaborating the conditions of the relationship between architecture and postmetropolises[22] in order to be able to overcome the inability to correctly tackle the issue of meaning in architecture in relation to the uncertainties and simulations of the contemporary,[23] rediscovering one's own foundations and specificities, well beyond the fiction and subversion offered by the idea of the sublime "as identifying with the culture of globalized financial capitalism."[24]

Together with the projects he has developed with various partners, associates, and a great many collaborators and assistants in university courses, which have taken place over time, his writings as a critical interpretation of reality are themselves a foundation and hold a very special place in the history of architecture as a specific discipline with its own instruments and methods, representing an extraordinary and permanent lesson, first and foremost for students of architecture, to whom this book is dedicated.

1 Foucault, M., *L'Archéologie du savoir*, Éditions Gallimard, Paris, 1969.

2 Morpurgo, G., *Gregotti & Associates: The Architecture of Urban Design*, Rizzoli, New York, 2008.

3 Gregotti, V., *Incertezze e simulazioni*, Einaudi, Turin, 2012.

4 I refer in particular to the ZEN district (incomplete) and the Science Departments of the University of Palermo (1969); the project for the University of Florence (1971); the University of Calabria (1972, only partially realized) and the detailed plan for affordable housing in Cefalù (1976–1979).

5 D'Angelo, P. (ed.), *Estetica e paesaggio*, Il Mulino, Bologna, 2009.

6 Tosco, C., *Il paesaggio come storia*, Il Mulino, Bologna 2007.

7 Gregotti, V., *Il territorio dell'Architettura*, Feltrinelli, Milan 1966

8 Tafuri, M., *Le avventure dell'oggetto: Architetture di Vittorio Gregotti*, in id. *Vittorio Gregotti: Progetti e architetture*, Electa, Milan, 1982, p. 14.

9 Cagnardi, A., *Master Plan and Project Plan*, in Morpurgo, G., *Gregotti & Associates: The Architecture of Urban Design*, cit., pp. 146–155.

10 Clément, G., *Manifesto del terzo paesaggio*, Quodlibet, Macerata, 2005.

11 Koolhaas, R., *Junkspace*, Quodlibet, Macerata, 2006.

12 Tosco, C., *Petrarca: Paesaggi, città, architetture*, Quodlibet, Macerata, 2011.

13 Benevolo, L., *La sottile magia del lavoro d'equipe*, in "Corriere della Sera," 24 July 2008.

14 Cagnardi, A., *Ritorni da Shanghai: Cronache di un architetto italiano in Cina*, Allemandi, Turin, 2008.

15 Gregotti, V., *L'ultimo hutong: Lavorare in architettura nella nuova Cina*, Skira, Milan, 2009.

16 These are the volumes edited by Bruno Pedretti: *Officina morfologica: Le costruzioni di Michele Reginaldi* (2001); *Quaderni senza parole: Il disegno di Michele Reginaldi* (2005); *Michele Reginaldi: Disegni e costruzioni* (2005); all published by Bolis Edizioni.

17 The term *untimely* is used here in the sense intended by Friedrich Nietzsche in his *Unzeitgemässe Betrachtungen* "Untimely Meditations" (1873–1876); thus it implies not a sort of failed contemporariness, but rather the construction of a different future through the criticism of that which is "contemporary," in the sense of sharing in the values currently dominant in architectural debate and activity.

18 Gregotti, V., *Incertezze e simulazioni*, cit.

19 Gregotti, V., *L'architettura nell'epoca dell'incessante*, Laterza, Rome-Bari, 2006.

20 Gregotti, V., *Contro la fine dell'architettura*, Einaudi, Turin, 2008.

21 Gregotti, V., *Tre forme di architettura mancata*, Einaudi, Turin, 2010.

22 Gregotti, V., *Architettura e postmetropoli*, Einaudi, Turin, 2011.

23 Gregotti, V., *Incertezze e simulazioni*, cit.

24 Gregotti, V., *Il sublime al tempo del contemporaneo*, Einaudi, Turin, 2013.

NORTH AFRICA
TOTAL LANDSCAPE ARCHITECTURE

[Architecture is a] great subject truly, for it embraces the consideration of the whole external surroundings of the life of man; we cannot escape from it if we would so long as we are part of civilization, for it means the molding and altering to human needs of the very face of the Earth itself, except in the outermost desert.

William Morris[1]

Confronting the vast horizons of the desert, zero grade background conditions for any possible architecture, despite specific differences in site and scale, is the central theme of a research specialization common to the case studies illustrated in this section: investigating the limits of possible modification of context and landscape, of their use and significance, through urban design.

The reasons for this shift in the spatial problems of architecture to a geographical scale seem to be rooted in the tradition of Utopian thought. Reworked as an ideal foundation and method orientation for the transformation of any workable context, including the outermost desert, the plan for a new urban landscape is represented in the proposals developed for North Africa as a concrete Utopia. Based on settlement models mindful of the continuous construction of cities on existing physical remains, designs, and ideals ingrained in historical urban experience, it represents the idea of the progressive function of the project culture, which leads back to the Utopia itself within the confines of the discipline, extended to cover a new graduated and conceptual dimension of "architectural territory."[2] But the Utopian component of these proposals is also laid out in the interpretation of the dominant material, consisting of physical conditions and contemporary cultural characteristics, represented by a society that, even through the "odyssey of resentment"[3] dramatically expressed by popular protest, seeks the collective representation of its own needs and hopes.

Migratory phenomena in particular, being a fundamental element of morphological thrust, offer the opportunity for the planning of a new city, especially as against the expansion of conditions of urbanization, which mark the acute and excruciating detachment from historical towns and the geographical horizon—as in the case of the recent developments on the outskirts of Algiers, structurally lacking in agglomeration and quality, being expanded due to continual immigration from the south of the country. It is in these non-sites that the memory of the identity of places is erased and their founding landmarks are lost. They distance cultures from that pervasive geographical structure, which, even in terms of historical meaning, is still their primeval backdrop and fundamental testimony: the Sahara and its mythical stories of human experience.

The possibility that the plans for the new Algerian cities offer for steering the geography of the desert landscape—the symbolic place of belonging for nomads—toward other meanings corresponds to an idea of the guided change of certain territorial unities. It strives for consistency that coincides with a multipolar urban system, redefining the relationship between nature and culture, and takes stock by revitalizing the relationship between civilization and boundless geographical space. At once unique and "ancient" because it is knowingly rooted in a historical culture, as testified for example by the habitational structures of the M'zab,[4] the ordered group of new cities is proposed as an alternative way of inhabiting for a possible future social organization: the option of sedentism offered to the Bedouin population by the Algerian government.

Studies carried out for the first nucleus of four new cities along the 2,700 km of the Algerian section of the Trans-Saharan Highway put forward the idea of codifying a modular settlement principle: simple, repeatable, and extendable.

Adaptable to the relief and the specific details of each individual local neighborhood, the environmental morphology created by the orthogonal grid envisions the formation of base nucleus of 6,000 inhabitants, extendable to 24,000. The model implies progressive, but at the same time self-limiting, urbanization, which introduces an advanced methodological and morphogenetic principle, establishing a specific relationship between project and context: the "transformation of the appearance of the landscape over time."[5] The modification of fragments of desert into partially self-sufficient settlements (agricultural areas and bioclimatic protection zones are planned) develops with the progressive realization of urban fabric made up of housing, small shops, workshops, and services positioned at the center, as in the traditional models of the medina and the casbah.

The historical dimension as planning material, the idea of context as symbolic surroundings and the recognition of the principle of identity of place are also the foundations on which the proposal for the new city of El Ménea, Algeria and the cultural hub that is the new 6th of October City, Egypt are built. Marking the boundary between the basically abstract and infinite space of the desert and the new inhabitable place, the plans for these extreme voluntary geographies are objectified in settlement patterns, which are both evocative of ancient establishments found in North Africa and structurally organized for the benefit of a real and possible present. Here the idea of landscape is inseparable from the critical interpretation of the environmental morphology as "human geography: modification of the natural landscape by people, with symbolic works whose quality transcends the topicality of the goals of transformation."[6] In the new city founded east of Cairo, the confrontation with the desert takes place through the triangulation between the urban grid system with a large oasis at its center, the three main pyramids of the Giza plain, and, opposite them, the archaeological area of Saqqara, linked in a diagonal visual alignment. The trailing edge of the Sahara that, from the Libyan desert, wedges itself right in the city of Cairo thus becomes the object of a sort of "neo-enlightenment" physical and cultural remeasuring between human-geographical regions: architecture is "total landscape," an expression of the encounter between ancient and modern civilizations.

In the case of individual buildings, too, the unifying element is the idea of a geography that is continually reestablished on the basis of dialogue with the sites, be they urban, as is the case with the plans for the former French protectorate area of Rabat (Royal Academy of Arts and National Museum of Archaeology and Earth Sciences), or suburban, like the two institutional buildings in Algiers, designed to create a context where there are no longer any points of reference. Here the site offers a chance to create intentional relief: a platform that sums up the idea of an evocative landscape, a mythical place, withdrawn from nonetheless immanent urban expansion: an oasis. Whether a void dug into the solid form[7] of a tower grafted onto a remolded artificial ground (Ministry of Land-Use Planning and Environment) or a system of sliding blades that reconstruct an ideal mineral stratification (Regulatory Authority of Post and Telecommunications), these projects insist on the need to provide the city with symbolic elements that give it an identity, so that the construction of the whole environment can be based on architecture.

    The idea of human geography as the measure of a region/landscape finally finds an objective result in the realization of a project that had been ongoing for fifteen years: the construction of two stadiums in Morocco. The writing of the plans is a dialogue with the desert as context, focusing on the principle of enclosure as founding act. The adaptation between artifice and site takes place, in the case of Agadir, with the skyline of the Atlas mountains, through an artificial hill/modern Herodium[8] and, in the case of Marrakech, an interpretation of the walls of the ancient medina: landscape is delimitation.[9]

Bird's-eye view of the project for the new city of El Mènea, Algeria

1 Morris, W., Exerpt from *Prospects of Architecture in Civilization*. Speech given at the London Institution on March 10, 1881.

2 Gregotti, V., *Il territorio dell'architettura*, Einaudi, Turin, 1966. See in particular Chapter 1 "Materiali."

3 Cioran, E.M., *Histoire et utopie*, Éditions Gallimard, Paris, 1960. Italian edition: Adelphi Edizioni, Milan, 1982, pp.75–100.

4 Cfr. Ravéreau A., *Le M'Zab une leçon d'architecture*, Sindbad-Actes Sud, 2003.

5 Gregotti, V., *La forma del territorio*, in *Edilizia Moderna*, no. 87-88, 1966, p.1.

6 Gregotti, V., *Il territorio dell'architettura*, cit.

7 For a more in-depth study of this topic, see Purini, F., *The Solid in the Void*, Morpurgo, G. (edited by), "Headquarter Pirelli Real Estate", Skira, Milan, 2005, pp.122–137.

8 For a description of the Herodium, see Bourbon, D., *Designing the Earth: The Human Impulse to Shape Nature*, Harry N. Abrams, Inc. , New York, 1995.

9 In the sense understood by Georg Simmel in *Brücke und Tür*, Koelher, Stuttgart, 1957.

Gregotti Associati International
(A. Cagnardi, V. Gregotti, M. Reginaldi)
Partner: S. Benkirane
With: P. E. Colao, M. Destefanis
(Associates), C. Castello
Lighting design: P. Castiglioni

The area that is the subject of the international tender is located in the far north of some sloping ground, occupied by a city park that includes a large villa of historical importance for the city of Rabat.

The purpose of the new museum is to document and tell the story of this territory, forged by the geological gap between Europe and the rigid African plate, and its encounter with man. The theme has been tackled starting with the idea that the building can find its own roots in the depths of the earth.

This principle of belonging to the earth is regulated via an architectural device that, with a total footprint of over 15,000 m², creates a "voluntary geography" through the articulation of a geological stone base with sloping terracing, leaving several patios located at strategic points that assumes the role of elements of comparison and commensuration with the surrounding park. A system of pedestrian ramps makes the terracing reachable, and with its greenery it forms a variously articulated modern stone rampart.

The part of the new building looking out over the city center is more markedly monumental in scale, being formed from the triangulation between two adjacent towers and a large glass structure in the background. Marking the entranceway for the public, the towers draw on the urban terrain, which is modified to form two sloping embankments slowly connecting with the city plan, which is to be reorganized next to the current crossroads, to make space for the drop-off point for buses, taxis, and public transport. The part of the section dedicated to the Quaternary period is the element marking the end of the building toward the historic villa, whose roof is modeled on the opposite slope to that of the sloping surface of the park.

The two towers house the two stairways that lead up from the foyer to the outside terraces and down to the auditorium. The stairs are illuminated from above and protected by a large perforated-metal superstructure, as well as by horizontal grilles, which act as sun shields. These two structures are veritable signposts to the museum, and at their center can be seen the overhead lighting system for the foyer and the route leading to the exhibitions.

The foyer leads directly to the ticket office, the information area, the waiting areas, the prayer room, the documentation center, the cloakroom, the toilets, and the bookshop. It is also possible to get to the lower floor where the auditorium with toilets and additional halls are located.

Access to the teaching areas and their relative terraces is free, while access to the temporary exhibition halls is controlled during events. Access to the museum halls (and the cafeteria) is controlled from the foyer.

Arriving from the parking lot (6,400 m² on two stories), there is a direct link to the foyer and the ticket office. From the same boulevard there is also access to the entrance reserved for the authorities, which leads straight down to the foyer or into the park.

There is also access from the foyer down to the floor where storage and services for research and scientific classification of exhibition materials are located. Around the two central patios are located the museum management.

The staff entrances and parking lots are located to the east on Roosevelt Avenue, next to the covered loading bay for museum material and temporary exhibitions, which is on a level directly connected with that of the storerooms.

The large entrance hall, which leads on to the museum visit, has a high ceiling with long balconies along the sides and mainly overhead lighting. The introductory space, dedicated to Moroccan history and geography as a whole, is organized in such a way as to give visitors a view of its contents from above.

The area dedicated to the illustration of geological eras is arranged in such a way as to increase the sensation of going underground and is characterized by a tetrahedrally coffered false ceiling in concrete.

The two-story space, which leads out into the open and contains a large dinosaur skeleton, invites visitors to move up to the space dedicated to the Quaternary period housed in the large external structure, which, facing directly north, is covered on its southern face with photovoltaic panels. This space offers the public two exits directly into the green area.

The central hall constitutes the ideal synthesis between prehistory and history, and is visible from the various areas arranged in succession along the route of the visit, which is also connected to the surface by a series of built structures and open spaces located throughout the park.

1.
Plan of the basement (parking lot and service and support areas)

2.
Plan of the ground floor (exhibitions)

3.
Plan of the first floor (animation workshops and activities for the public)

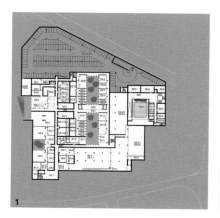

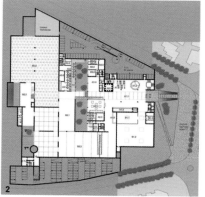

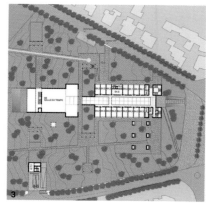

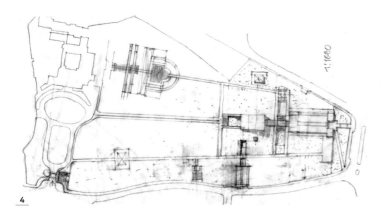

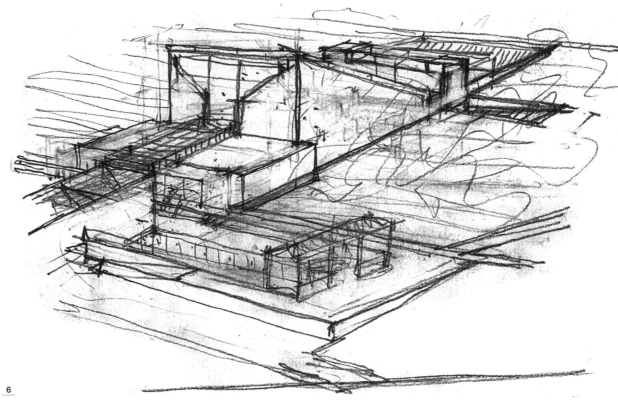

6

4.
Study sketch of the overall plan of
the new intervention in relation to
the existing villa

5.
General planimetry/volumetry
(orthophotography montage)

6.
Study sketch of the overall volume of
the intervention

7.
General view from the northwest

8

9

8.
General easterly profile

9.
Longitudinal section east

10.
Transverse section of the entrance hall

11.
Nighttime view of the main entrance from the square

10

11

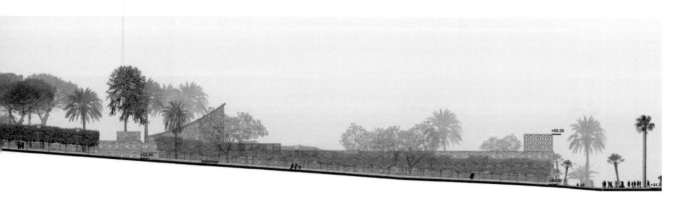

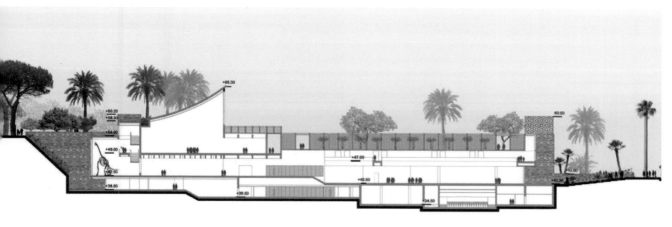

From the large square space with a tiered ceiling, which houses bronzes and sculptures from archaeological digs, visitors enter a large hall divided into four sections dedicated to artifacts dating to later than the seventh century and covered by a low vaulted ceramic-lined brick ceiling. From here the visitor exits into the entrance area, passing in front of the museum shop.

Finally, going up around 300 m, one arrives at the historic villa, which, once restored, will be able to house a restaurant, the headquarters of the Friends of the Museum society, and spaces for special events and have the possibility of independent access via its own original gateway.

12.
The Hall of Times with *Atlasaurus* skeleton

13.
The entrance hall

MARRAKECH FOOTBALL AND ATHLETICS STADIUM
1999–2011

With the Kingdom of Morocco's bid to host the FIFA World Cup in 2006, the Association Morocco 2006, together with the Ministry of Sports, invited international tenders for eight football and athletics stadiums. The group of designers composed of Gregotti Associati International and Sâd Benkirane was invited to participate for the stadiums in Casablanca, Agadir, and Marrakech, receiving first prize for the last two.

Marrakech Stadium, in the process of being completed, is situated in the north of the city, in a non-urbanized area beyond the Palmeraie, toward the first foothills of the Atlas Mountains. As in Agadir, the project was developed on the basis of a study of the morphological and environmental characteristics of the site. In this case, the context offered the possibility of reflecting the local architectural tradition, regarding in particular the relationship between interiors and exteriors, light and shadow, public and private, as well as the use of color.

Gregotti Associati International
(A. Cagnardi, V. Gregotti, M. Reginaldi)
Partner: S. Benkirane
With: S. Azzola, S. Butti, I. Chiarel, P. Colao, M. Pavani (Associates), F. Campello, A. Cotti, S. Ferrari, A. Minguzzi

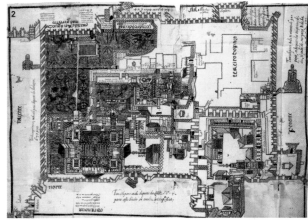

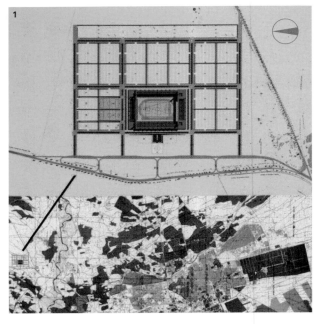

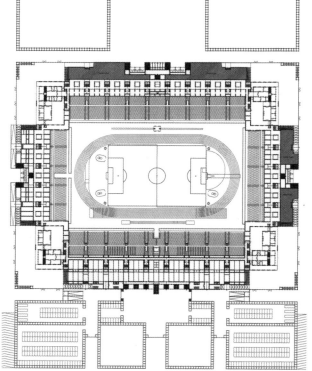

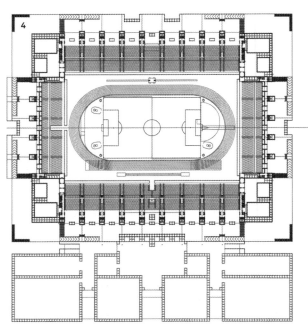

1.
Territorial setting and general planimetry

2.
Historical map of Marrakech

3.
General plan of the ground floor

4.
General plan at +2.70 m

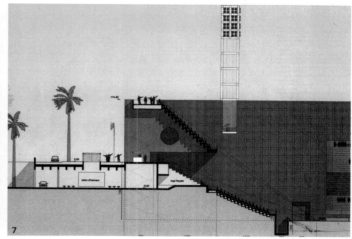

The three main points of the proposal were the characterization of the site as an oasis in continuity with the Palmeraie; the use of an urban morphological structure, which recalls the ancient walled settlement of the historical city; and an introverted organization of the spaces, similar to that of the local architecture, which, developed around central patios, contrasts an extreme richness of materials and colors on the inside with the austere simplicity of the exterior.

The stadium is thus identified as a sort of enclosure marked out by the two large transverse walls that contain the stands punctuated by access towers, which enliven its linearity with shadows.

For climatic reasons, the roofing of the east–west stand is in this case made up of tensile structures and Teflon sheets, which allow ventilation, while the north–south stand has metal roofing resting on a large lintel, under which are the head terraces.

The structure fits into a regular framework punctuated by alignments of palm trees and sloping embankments, where even the parking lots are integrated in a traditional-style landscape design.

5.
General view

6.
View of the ancient city walls of Marrakech

7.
Typical transverse section of the tiers

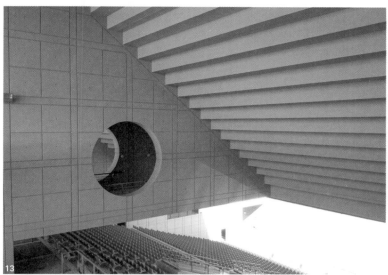

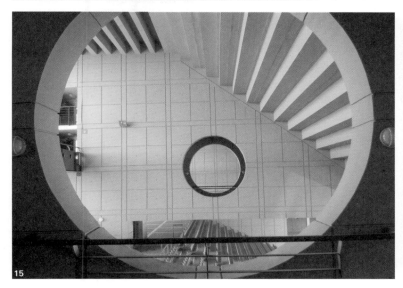

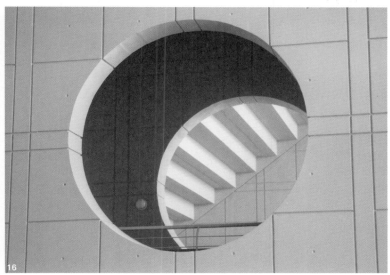

8.
View of a corner tower

9.
Longitudinal connecting bridge, between the first and second levels of the tiers

10.
Detail of a corner tower

11.
View of the tiers from one of the corner towers

12.
View of the double row of tiers in the eastern sector

13.
Detail of the overhanging supporting structure of the second level of the tiers

14.
View of the gym

15 and 16.
Details of the openings in the walls holding up the tiers

AGADIR FOOTBALL AND ATHLETICS STADIUM
1999–2014

Gregotti Associati International
(A. Cagnardi, V. Gregotti, M. Reginaldi)
Partner: S. Benkirane
With: S. Azzola, S. Butti, I. Chiarel,
P. E. Colao (Associates), C. Calabrese,
M. Pani, C. Scortecci, S. Wenzel

The stadium, currently being finished, is situated on the north side of the city of Agadir, whose hinterland is strongly ridged and looks arid and rocky. The project establishes a close dialogue with the geography of the place, deriving the structure and the architectural conformation from its morphology.

Recalling the Berber tradition of sourcing construction materials on site, thus redesigning the place of the settlement itself, the new stadium is set out like another ridge in the terrain. This morphological architecture is an artificial hill that integrates with the land thanks to a system of reinforced embankments faced with terraces made from cement and dark red gravel.

The project offers many advantages, such as being earthquake-proof, the adaptability of the terraced structure to the steep slope of the land, the reduction of the above-ground built parts, and secure access and outflow systems along the embankments.

The fact that it rains very little there means that the best roofing for the stands is a brise-soleil made from slats of wood painted white, while the internal space is characterized by the strong use of color, also for signaling purposes, in contrast to the natural hues of the external ballast marking out the presence of the sports ground in the environment.

1, 2, and 3.
Study sketches

4.
General planimetry

5.
General plan at +18.90 m

6.
General view from the desert

7.
General bird's-eye perspective view

8.
View of the double arcaded loggia
that crowns the stadium

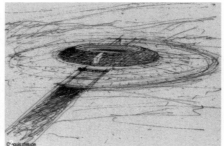

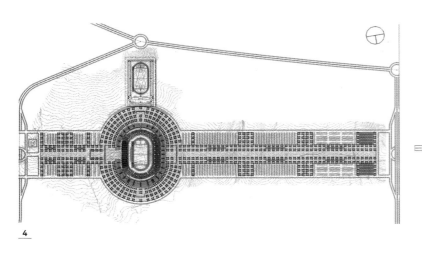

4

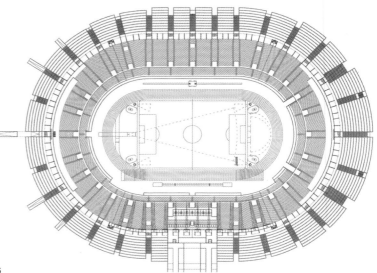

5

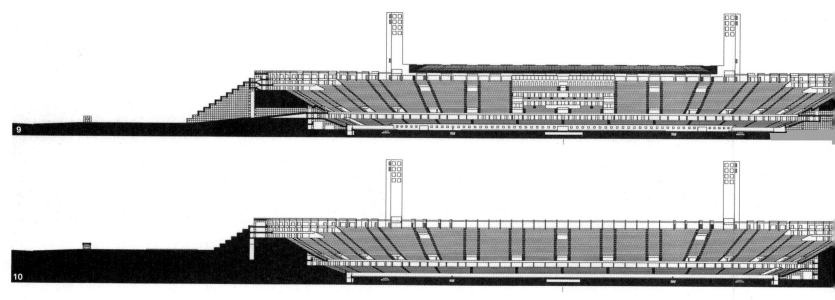

9 and 10.
Typical cross section

11.
Detail of the artificial hill (exterior wall) built by a system of reinforced embankments clad in concrete and dark red steps

12.
General view toward the main entrance area

13.
Detail of the exterior wall with an emergency exit

14.
General view of the internal basin

15.
View of the VIP stand

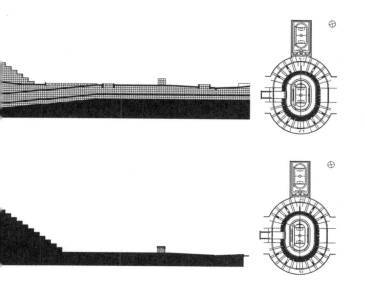

Gregotti Associati International
(A. Cagnardi, V. Gregotti, M. Reginaldi)
Partner: S. Benkirane
With: P. E. Colao, M. Destefanis
(Associates), C. Castello,
E. Lucchini-Gabriolo, J. Muzio,
M. Parravicini, P. Ronchi, C. Scortecci

The location chosen as the headquarters for the new Royal Academy of Arts is on the northern edge of the city park where the governor of the former French protectorate, Louis Hubert Lyautey, had his villa built in 1925 by the architect Albert Laprade according to a general plan proposed by Henri Prost in 1916. This building represents an illustrious attempt to link European art deco with the local tradition. The new building, which is the subject of an international tender, relates to the preexisting villa in two ways: on the one hand, it is situated on the side of the park overlooking the Medina and the sea; on the other hand, it projects the stylistic richness of the villa, consisting of the intertwining of closely adjacent constructions, which cross over in both directions, on various levels, its proximity and extensions alluding to the complexity of ancient urban systems and their very particular habitability consisting of shade, large interior spaces, and the coziness of studying and living.

The new architectural complex, whose total footprint is 6,500 m², must see in the greenery of the park (and in the theme of its restoration) an opportunity to reinterpret the downward slope of the land and the definition of its borders, offering the new architect a rich series of viewpoints.

On the inside, the theme is that of reconciling the need for future flexibility of use with the architectural definition of some principal spaces, the recognizability of the parts, the multiplicity of entrances and their definition, and the various levels of habitability that must allow the grouping of types of activity in the various areas and the public's controlled access to them during exhibitions and theatrical shows.

The choice of materials is oriented toward exploiting a still thriving tradition of craftsmanship: ceramic, wood, stucco, stone, plaster, historically natural materials. Also planned is the use of grilles to protect from the sun, delineating half-open spaces, and the presence of water.

Looking toward Lyautey's villa, the volume of the new building is reduced and does not exceed a height of 6 m, thus allowing a view of the old town and the sea from the ground floor of the villa, while on the opposite side, the open courtyard, which can be reached from the exhibition space, is lower than the surrounding ground level, thus facilitating a direct relationship with the park.

The two long facades overlooking Marrakech Avenue and the royal palace lead up to the main entrance of the new building along their transverse axis, while the central northeast/southwest road running through the park (open only to service traffic) links the Lyautey residence (whose historical entrance has been maintained) and the new building with Rue Chellah, which leads to the historic town center of the Medina.

1.
Study sketch of the ground-floor plan

2.
View from the arcaded loggia of the existing villa (photomontage)

3.
Study sketch first-floor plan

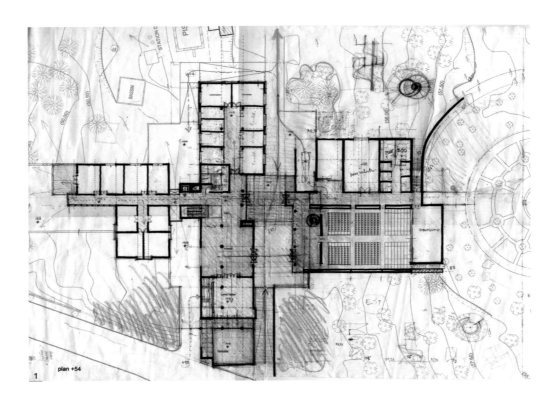

plan +54

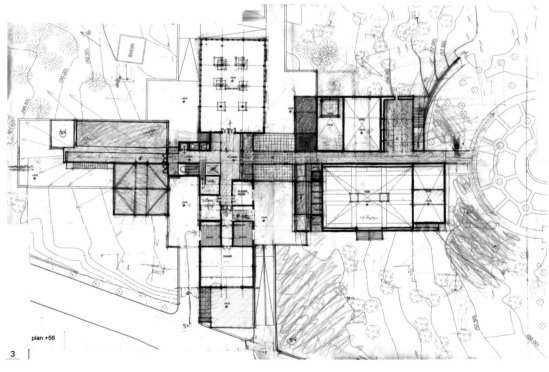

plan +58

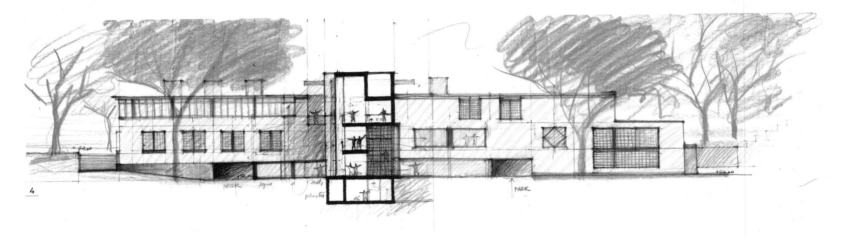

4.
Study sketch of the front with the cross section of the retail space above the main entrance

5.
General bird's-eye view from the north (model)

6.
View of the westerly entrance (model)

7.
View from the north (model)

8.
General bird's-eye view from the east (model)

9.
Access route to the entrance hall

10.
Retail space outside the main entrance

11.
View of the southeast corner

Gregotti Associati International
(A. Cagnardi, V. Gregotti, M. Reginaldi)
With: G. Donato (Associate),
A. Boccacci, C. Calabrese, C. Castello,
E. Lucchini-Gabriolo, M. Parravicini,
P. Seria, S. Zauli

The project for the eastern part of the city toward the center of the new 6th of October City occupies an area of 55 feddan (about 23 ha.), presenting a strategic geographical position to the southwest of the Egyptian capital: situated between Cairo and the Nile valley, it faces the area of the pyramids, the archaeological site of Saqqara and the northern edge of the desert.

The new settlement, designed to offer housing and services to new inhabitants, as well as businesses, accommodation facilities, and other services for cultural tourism, is based on a regular grid structure and arranged around a vast central public green area. Open gradually to the east toward the Sahara, it is characterized by a set of gardens, geometrically laid out both within each garden and between gardens, with places to rest, amuse oneself, and eat, according to North African and Asian tradition.

The central green space borders on a small artificial lake to the west, at the center of which is located a tall signalling element, which reveals a hub of attraction made up of an island aquarium.

The broad eastern edge of the city, facing onto the desert, is characterized by the presence of a vast area of about 40,000 m² designated for cultural uses and directly accessible by car from the road. It includes one open-air and one 2,000-seat covered multifunctional theater area, a library, a conference center, and a museum space.

This group of collective activities sits on a 6-m-high square foundation, which includes services and parking and is the central reference point in this part of the green space. It faces toward the pyramid complex, which can be seen from it, finding its ideal reference axis in the diagonal alignment of the three monuments.

The total built-up space of the new settlement is subdivided into two parts structured on a system of fifty-five square blocks of 123 × 123 m (center-to-center distance 140 × 140 m), of which fifty are for residential use. The urban network is defined by 17-m-wide roads for cars and pedestrians, with room for two 3.5-m lanes plus two 5-m-wide pavements, thus allowing for bus stops off the road, tree planting along the road, and a possible future cycle lane, as well as the footpath.

As for the pedestrian roads, they have space at the center for temporary parking and for the passage of service and emergency vehicles. The consistent cross section of the roadways allows for future flexibility in how they are used.

1

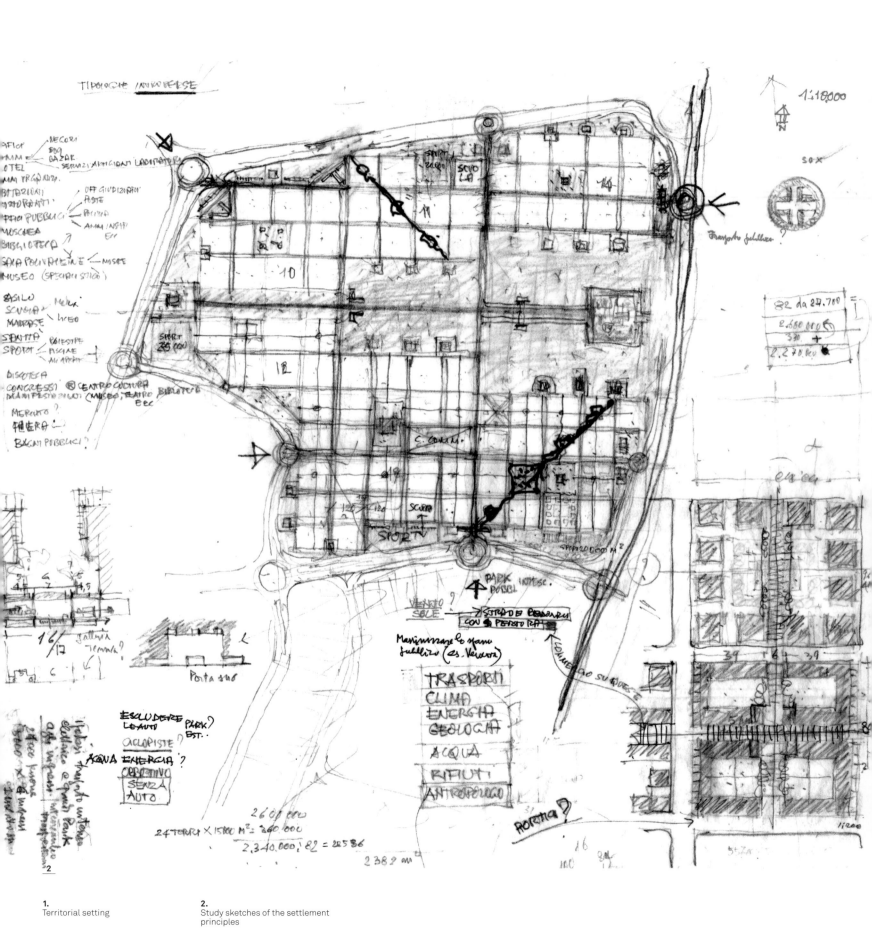

1.
Territorial setting

2.
Study sketches of the settlement
principles

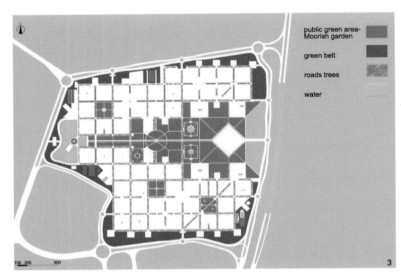

public green area-
Moorish garden

green belt

roads trees

water

3

100 200   500

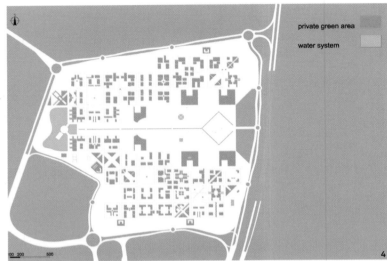

private green area

water system

4

100 200   500

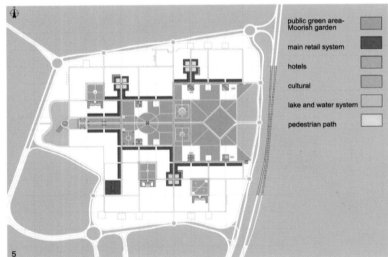

public green area-
Moorish garden

main retail system

hotels

cultural

lake and water system

pedestrian path

5

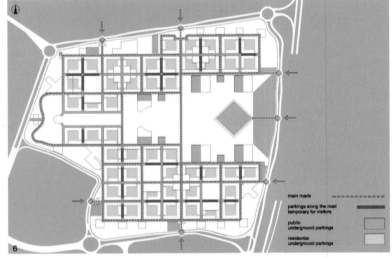

main roads

parkings along the road
temporary for visitors

public
underground parkings

residential
underground parkings

6

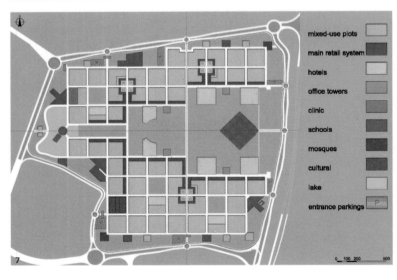

mixed-use plots

main retail system

hotels

office towers

clinic

schools

mosques

cultural

lake

entrance parkings

7

0   100 200   500

8   Hotel system

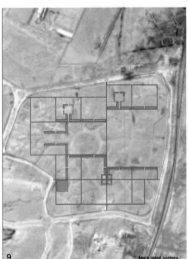

9   Main retail system

The layout of the lots allows for the variability and functionality of the buildings there. As well as the three green central blocks, the new settlement is marked by the presence of three squares of 80 × 80 m, each with its own character, located on the axes of the four surrounding blocks.

The tree-lined edge of the settlement protects the urban environment from the outside road system surrounding it. Local traffic is connected with the surrounding roads via six main entrances and one service entrance for the cultural center, which is also open to outside visitors. Each entrance is served by a public car park which is part of the interchange system, allowing connections between external public transport and public transport within the settlement.

The residents' private parking lots are located below each block and also aboveground, along the arterial routes.

The area between the external blocks and the connecting roads will be characterized by dense and tall vegetation, the presence of buildings located at the ends of their respective internal roads, and sports facilities next to the schools (from nursery school up to various types of high school).

On the edge of the large green area within the settlement are ten 72-m-tall buildings housing offices and large hotels. The foundations are designed to allow these buildings to be connected to the front system (north and south) of the internal blocks. These are distinguished,

12

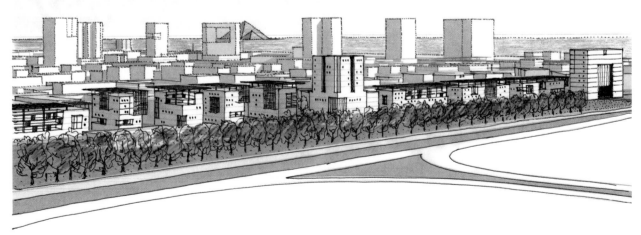

13

12.
General bird's-eye view
13.
Study sketch of the southeast edge

14.
General nighttime view from the west
15.
Shopping square
16.
Tree-lined street

as in the four squares within the blocks, by the presence of mixed usage with business and services.

In general, businesses are freely located (unless there is a high-level mall, which could also include other services such as multiplex cinemas, gyms, etc.). Their ground-floor distribution with a constant height of 4.5 m allows the upper floors to be used either for residential purposes or for various services. There are also two special blocks used as a clinic and a small-scale resort hotel.

The blocks will have either four or six aboveground stories, with colonnaded covered areas, distinguished by large overhangs guaranteeing protection from the sun for the footpaths and the public area of the road.

The development of the project introduced special building regulations regarding the height of buildings, the dimensions of the overhangs and the bow windows, the measure of the distances between buildings, and provisions and rules concerning traffic, parking, and infrastructure services (electricity, water, sewage, trash collection, etc.).

The integration of all these elements of building regulations with a large public and private green area, a global density of 0.8 m²/m², the moderate average height of the complex as a whole which allows the block areas to be 50 percent built up, the presence of various uses for the urban space and the provision of services, together with a series of provisions aimed at regulating the system of traffic, parking, and public transport, identify the new 6th of October City within a framework of getting back to the roots of the local settlement tradition and the human-geographical identity of the place.

EL MÈNEA, ALGERIA
PLAN FOR THE NEW CITY
2011

Gregotti Associati International
(A. Cagnardi, V. Gregotti, M. Reginaldi)
Partners:
Ecosfera S.p.A. (F. Nissardi)
Landscape design: BEREG, Algiers
Renewable energies project:
BE.ETB, Batna
Transport and environmental
studies: CNTC, Boumerdès
With: I. Chiarel, P. E. Colao,
M. Destefeanis, T. Macchi Cassia,
C. Pirola, M. Trovatelli (Associates),
C. Castello, C. Scortecci

The tender for the foundation of the new city is based on the decision to locate it according to the horizontal plane of the Sahara, on a plateau 40 m above the floor of the valley on which the original El Mènea, long transformed into a *palmeraie*, stands. The position of the existing city in a fold of earth recalls the history of human settlement in the desert, with sites chosen according to the greatest likelihood of finding water and creating oases, thus making a stable human presence possible.

The new settlement, which will lie alongside the motorway RN1, the Trans-Sahara Highway, flanked by a railway line crossing the whole country from north to south, will be supplied by a new aqueduct.

Between the two settlements will be the natural space of the desert, a sloping plane linking the differing altitudes of the two centers, extending in a north–south direction within the geographical space of the Sahara. These natural surroundings will be traversed by connections between the area situated in the fold and the new area on the plateau.

The idea is to create a settlement able to compete with the old one, responding to the requisites outlined in the call to tender: to cope with the unevenness of the area caused by the location of the population and businesses (9 percent of the population inhabits 87 percent of the area); the realization of services, transport, and communal facilities to allow for better use of the area's resources and a consequent raising of employment levels and a modernization of the economy; and enhancement and protection of natural and cultural heritage. These objectives of a general restructuring of Algeria can be attained thanks to the new infrastructure system of the Trans-Sahara Highway.

In the context of complete territorial reorganization, the project for the new city of El Mènea constitutes an important urban system as it represents a national hub able to help counteract the phenomenon of urban drift to the Mediterranean coastal cities.

The urban structure of the new settlement is arranged as a linear city, by nature extendable. Running alongside the Trans-Sahara Highway, it is arranged as a residential center, an active center of food production from farming, and a logistical and multimodal platform for the southeastern region of the country. Its physical boundaries are represented by the relief of the terrain on the southeastern side of the plateau, which also acts as a natural windbreak.

The total urban layout is arranged on a linear grid based on the principle of giving special importance to public spaces and communal facilities, elements that govern the location of the businesses that will be situated there. The shape, following the line of the crest that forms the edge of the plateau, is organized according to three main territorial sectors: to the northwest is a broad strip of palm grove standing between the new settlement and the RN1. The densely planted area and the new city are separated by a minor road, a sort of external link road itself having an empty buffer strip, which distributes the connections to the Trans-Sahara Highway along the whole length of the settlement.

1

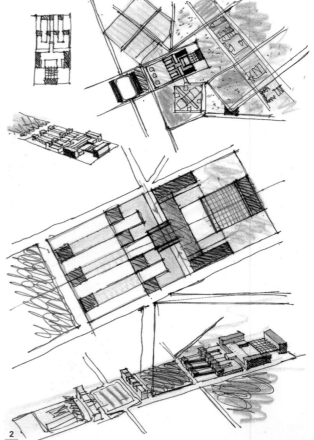

2

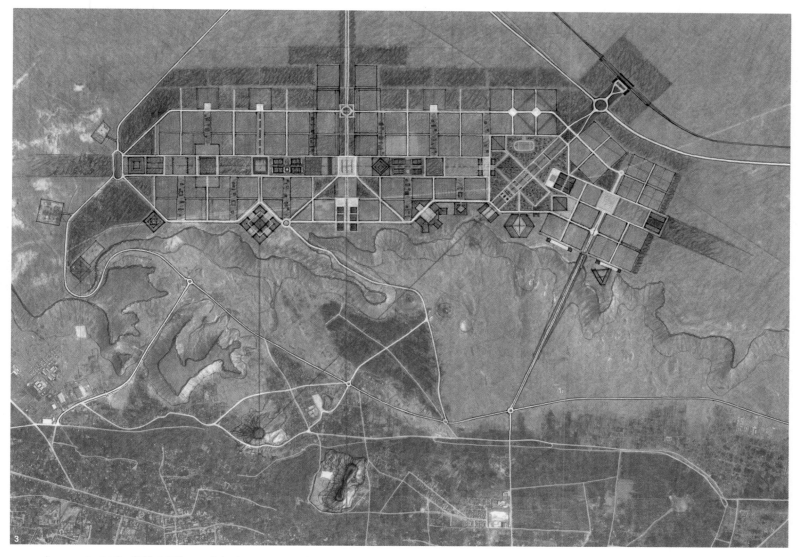

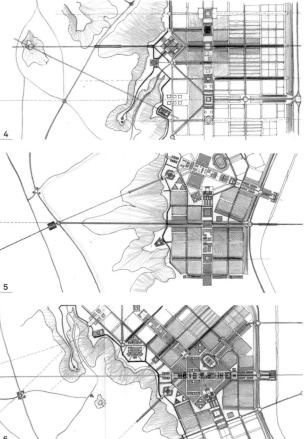

The main body of the new city is organized on an orthogonal grid made up of *insulae*: large *quadras* of various different typologies and uses. The first of these is in the northwest, overlooking the link road, and is destined for horticulture and as a further mediation element between the local territory and the urban environment. The *quadras* making up the low-density residential area, of two to three stories aboveground, will be compact, but will nevertheless allow for the houses and private gardens to be arranged according to a design based on the principle of morphological diversity.

A central green axis will run the entire length of the city. This linear park, punctuated by communal facilities and services, also brings together the three points that connect with the RN1, affording opportunities to create specific ground plans to form a transverse axis, at the center of the settlement, dedicated to the service industry and, in the southeast, to a vast public green area, which will house a university campus complete with competition-level sports facilities, including a large stadium. On the eastern edge, bordering on the strip of desert lying between the preexisting settlement and the new one, preserved as a geological buffer zone, are the main communal facilities, including a mosque and the connections between the two cities.

1.
Territorial setting

2.
Study sketches of the university

3.
Study sketch of the final version of the general urban system

4.
Study sketch of the settlement system of route No. 2

5.
Study sketch of the settlement system of route No. 5

6.
Study sketch of the settlement system of route No. 4

7.
Study sketch of the settlement
principle (preliminary version)

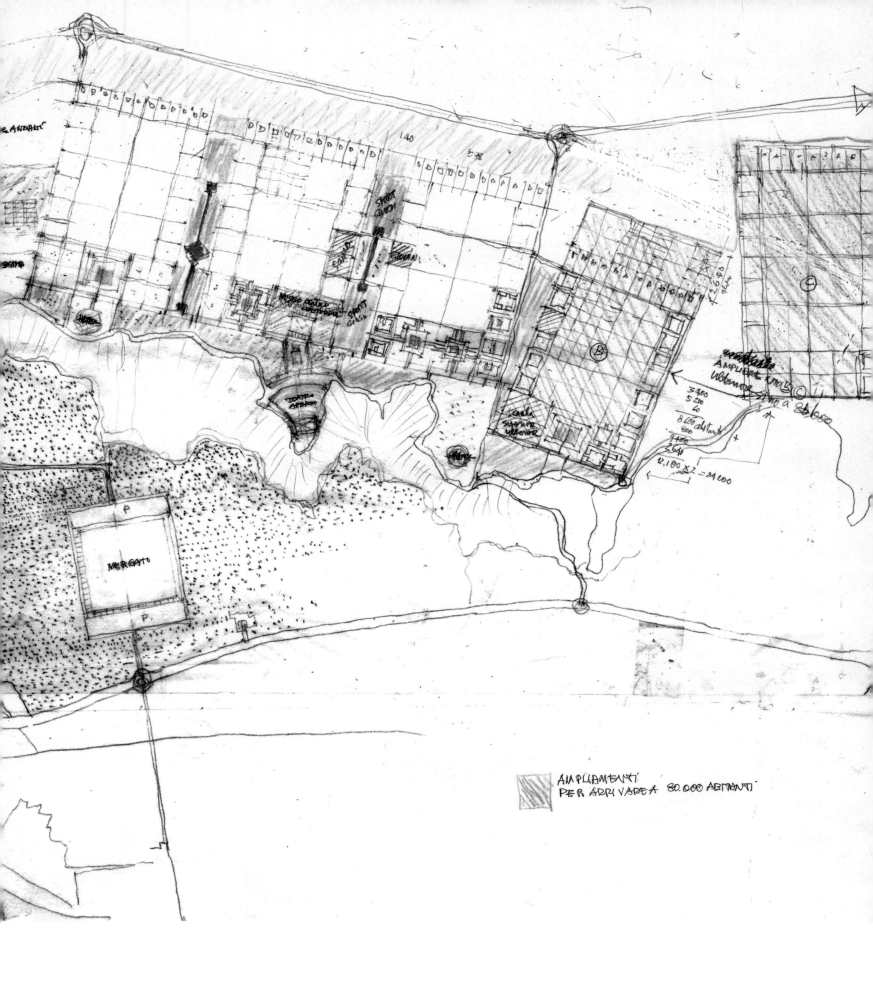

AMPLIAMENTI
PER ARRIVARE A 80.000 ABITANTI

39

8.
Bird's-eye view of the central road

9.
General view from the northwest

10.
General nighttime view from the southwest

NEW CITY OF SIDI ABDALLAH, DOUÉRA, ALGERIA
NEW HEADQUARTERS OF THE MINISTRY OF LAND-USE PLANNING AND ENVIRONMENT
2011

Gregotti Associati International
(A. Cagnardi, V. Gregotti, M. Reginaldi)
Partner: Ecosfera S.p.A. (F. Nissardi)
With: C. Calligaris, P. E. Colao,
M. Destefanis, G. Donato, T. Macchi
Cassia, M. Trovatelli (Associates),
M. Parravicini, P. Ronchi, C. Scortecci

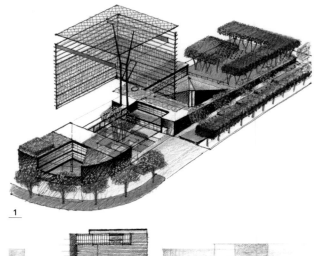

1

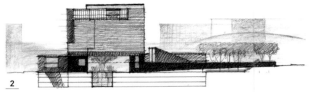

2

The tender project for the headquarters of the Ministry of Land-Use Planning and Environment is part of the development plan of the new city of Sidi Abdallah now being built on a 2,000-hectare parcel of land, 30 km southwest of the capital city, on the edge of the Douéra basin. The international tender was an important chance to relate the new public building to a nascent urban context, structured by a system of blocks of varying population density, services for the inhabitants, and public institutions. The new context offers the potentialities and complexities typical of historical North African cities, but without the limitations derived from excessive crowding and overpopulation. Public space and its landscape features will be particularly important within a system oriented on the whole toward sustainable development.

The area dedicated to the ministry's new headquarters is located on a small hill, delimited by three roads, which will have to be flattened in order to build the underground parking lot required in the plans (on three levels, each 4,200 m^2). The geological nature of the land is basically clayey, and the local relief seems to have already been largely modified by the presence of roads that define the borders of the general urban design of the place.

The hill itself inspired the morphological structure of the project: the proposal is to remodel it in an ideal way as new urban ground, a green bastion to house public functions and the general reception. The clay itself is used as a building material and, transformed into terra-cotta, it becomes the common element uniting the built facades and bolsters, reinforcing the sense of the new construction belonging to the land and the local building traditions.

The ground support system is structured around a sequence of courtyards and terraces that are all accessible at different levels. A series of themed gardens characterizes the system of integration with the earth, thus forming a new landscape that is both natural and urban. Finally, there are a series of small shady squares sloping down along the main road and ending with the square leading to the ministry entrance. This landscape base thus recalls the original hill and sustains the architectural mass of the building.

In general, the layout of the building follows the urban-sector regulations regarding buildings being set back 15 m from the main road and is distinguished as being virtually cubic.

The northeastern parts of the base form an L-shaped block, defining the urban front looking out over the main road and underlining the importance of the square in front, which reconnects the site of the new ministry with the general road network of the new city. These two wings of the building house the offices that are thus located in the best position in terms of both orientation and sun.

The terra-cotta elements proposed for these two facades are held up by two pillars of gigantic order, split in two and positioned within the hall. These signal stelae reinforce the building's special character, making it recognizable within the urban environment.

1 and 2.
Study sketches of the graft system of the core in the basement

3.
Study sketch of the council hall

4.
Study sketch of the facade

5.
Ground-floor plan

6.
First-floor plan

7.
Second-floor plan

8.
Typical floor plan

9.
Typical longitudinal section of the council hall

10.
Nighttime view

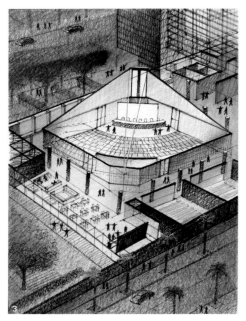

3

4

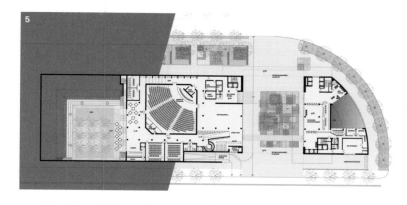

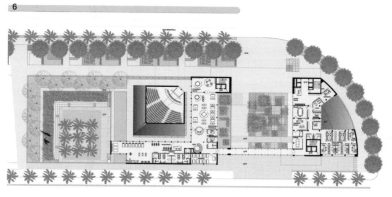

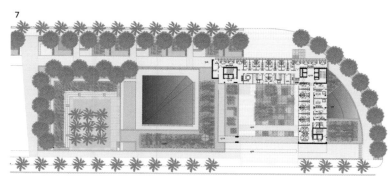

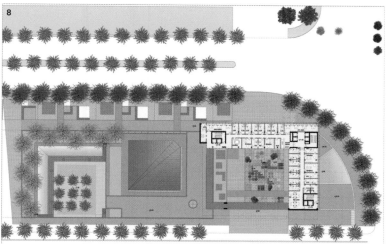

The facades are characterized by a double-skin system formed of the brise-soleil made up of clay "leaves" placed vertically to optimize the protection from the sun, which is very important given the northeast and northwest exposures, but at the same time able to guarantee an unencumbered view toward the new city.

The southern face is characterized by an analogous system of light elements but placed horizontally, weaving a protective fabric to shield the central green courtyard from direct sunlight. The horizontal positioning of the plates allows a direct view out to the pond.

This structure is also designed to carry the system of photovoltaic panels, which will contribute significantly to the building's energy supply.

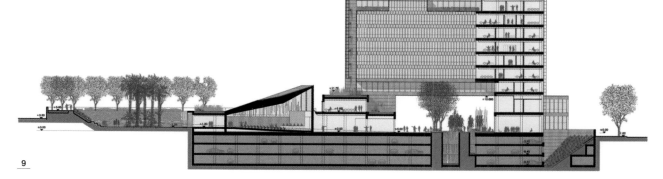

The central and more morphologically important nucleus is made up of the full-height hall, which is the main entrance to the building. It is a sort of large cubic space, semitransparent and hollow, which represents the institutional and urban value of the new ministerial headquarters.

The interior of the hall is characterized by the presence of a "green core," a nucleus that reflects the idea of bioclimatic quality, an emblem of the ministry's commitment to the environment, architecture symbolically composed of earth and greenery, and becoming a metaphorical oasis. A centrally placed waterfall retraces the three floors occupied by the underground parking lot, bringing to mind underground springs. The sound of running water and the cool environment contrast with the outside environment, which is dry with the noises of the city as a background. It is planned that vegetation will grow up the walls of the hall thanks to a special attachment system and the presence of natural light and controlled air, encouraging the image of this space as a bioclimatic green lung for the whole building.

The internal distribution system is organized around the hall/oasis with the two entrances required by the tender program: one directly accessible from the main road for the minister and delegations, while access for staff and the public is via the south entrance.

In the west wing are areas reserved for the minister and delegations. The assembly is made up of a semicircular hall seating 500 with separate, independent access for the minister, the various delegations, the speakers, and the public. There will also be halls that holds fifty people, a multipurpose space, a temporary exhibition space, a cafeteria, and services for the public.

It will also be possible to reach the building's common services via the wide stairway leading from the entrance area to the forum. These include a library and media center, halls for staff training, a gym, and related support areas.

The offices are distributed over nine floors. An aerial walkway crosses the central square at the height of the first floor, ensuring an internal connection between the offices and the forum, which is located on the other side of the central green hall.

The top two floors, occupied by the minister's offices, are characterized by a system of terraced green recesses which distinguish this part of the building and make its arrangement more complex.

Together, the accessible green terraced areas ideally connect these spaces with the large green patio, characterizing the superstructure as a sculptural form encasing the large glazed hall.

11.
Study sketch—southwestern view

12.
Study sketch of the inner zone of the central structure

13.
Longitudinal section

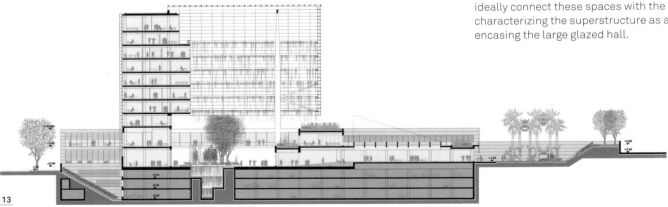

13

14.
Study sketch—southeastern
view

15.
View of the core from above

16.
Detail of the entrance area

Gregotti Associati International
(A. Cagnardi, V. Gregotti, M. Reginaldi)
Partner:
Ecosfera S.p.A. (F. Nissardi)
COSIDER Engineering
With: P. E. Colao, M. Destefanis,
T. Macchi Cassia (Associates),
M. Parravicini

The competition project for the new headquarters of the Regulatory Authority of Post and Telecommunications concerns a lot in the business quarter of Bab Ezzouar, on the outskirts of the Algerian capital.

Service-industry zones are concentrated in the area, housing the headquarters of important national, international, and civil-service companies, as well as commercial spaces serving people and businesses, and a large park. The surroundings, characterized by individual freestanding buildings and therefore lacking a recognizable identity, inspired the idea to bring the entire quarter to a new level of urban quality through the construction of new buildings, designed as a morphological system able to integrate the expressive and symbolic value of a public institution, together with the generation of new relationships between the buildings themselves and open spaces.

The position and dimensions of the lot, in relation to the opportunities offered by the functional program, constitute the defining conditions of the building's form, in terms of fitting into the quarter, the general urban composition, and the architectural definition of the image.

The shape of the lot, long and narrow and bordered on two sides by the urban park, guarantees views far from the physical mass of the new building, lending it a plastic structure based on the succession, superimposition, and combination of blocks in a staggered row, with different heights, which assume different degrees of prominence depending on where they are seen from. This solution, compared with the more traditional tall, compact buildings present in the area, allows for an articulated building to be laid out that develops longitudinally, a sort of artificial horizon that reforms the perception of the whole quarter.

The variable conformation of the building is regulated by a sort of gradient governing its development: laid out over eleven floors aboveground and three below, it is made up of four elongated rectangular blocks placed next to each other to form an integrated body with sections and heights varying from 6 to 48 m.

The position of the building on the ground creates a close relationship between internal and external space and between the external space and the surrounding area. To the northwest is the entrance foreground, which forms an

1.
Urban setting in the Bab Ezzouar area

2.
Nighttime view

3.
Typical transverse section

4.
Study sketch of the general volumetric layout

5.
Axonometric sketch of the internal layout of the entrance hall

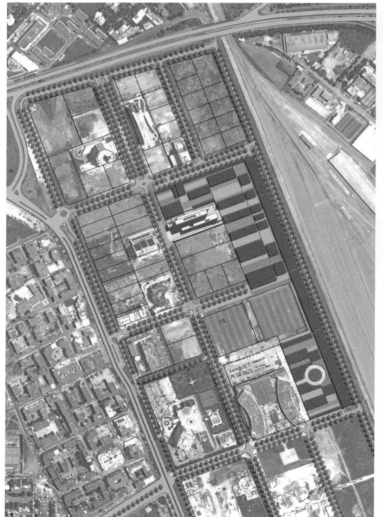

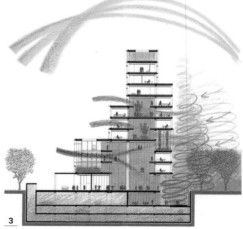

extension of the road network, underlining the link between the building and the quarter. The generous dimensions of the entrance form a large, deep portal that emphasize the verticality of the building.

The ramps leading into the underground parking lot and the service road running the length of it separate the building from the southwest edge, which is an area destined for future construction.

Entry to the internal areas of the building is via a square to the south. Delimited by the park, a stairway leads to a sunken courtyard overlooked by a restaurant and other service spaces for staff.

The southern limit, along the edge of the public park, is marked by a hollow in the ground: a patio with landscape characteristics, reinforced by the presence of water flowing from the perimeter wall of the park, which, together with the vegetation, answers the need to create a bioclimatic space. Facing northeast, it is also well-placed regarding exposure to the sun and prevailing winds. The large openings at the side allow for heat exchange with the building. The transition between interior and exterior, between the public space of the park and the private space of the patio, constitutes the physical separation needed between an area open to the public and the area for the private use of the new building.

The arrangement of the building into parallel linear elements also reflects in the interior the urban organization of the Bab Ezzouar quarter, based on the subdivision of elongated lots.

On the ground floor, a corridor three floors high visually connects the square in front of the entrance to the north and the park in the south. In keeping with Algerian tradition, the central nucleus of the building is a large hall over 18 m high, from the ground floor up to the two two-story-high halls, one above the other, located in the upper levels. The different environments are distributed around this nucleus: spatiality, the strong presence of natural light, diffused or filtered according to the orientation, the open or protected views of the outside, the choice of materials and the use of color all reflect the quality that characterizes the patios and the local architectural tradition in general.

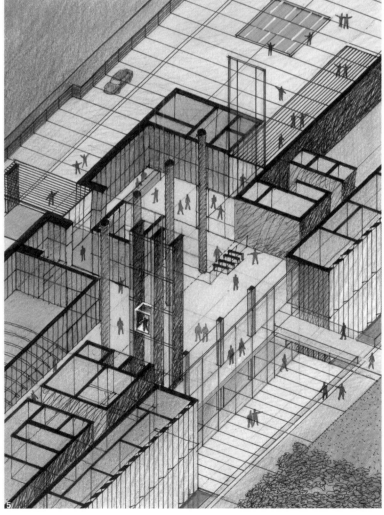

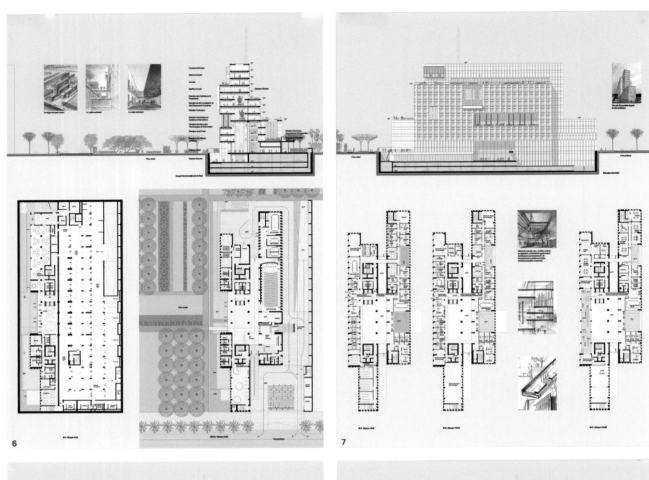

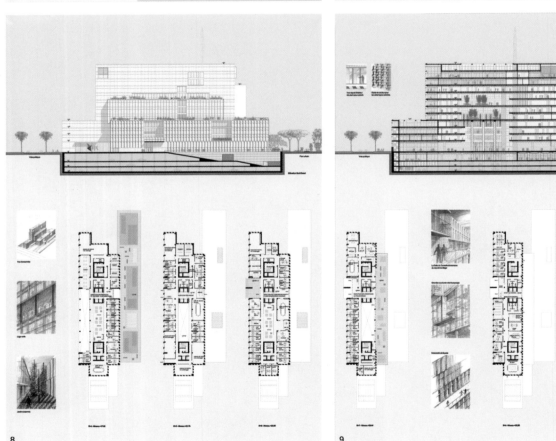

6.
Study sketches; transverse section looking southward; basement plan (parking lot); ground-floor plan

7.
Northeast face; study sketch of the view from the main road; plans of the first, second, and third floors; study sketches

8.
Southwest face; study sketches; plans of floors four, five, and six

9.
Longitudinal section east; plans of floors seven, eight and nine

10.
Southeast face; southwest face; plans of floors ten and eleven; transverse section, plan, and overall view of the council hall

11.
Detail of the facade; typical office with colored ceramic panels; study for the matching of ceramic facing elements; details of how the facing is attached to the facades; northwest face

12.
View of the entrance hall

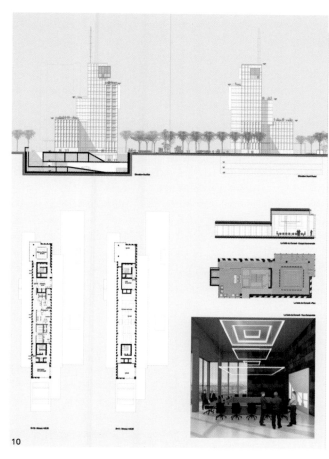

10

11

The system, designed for the composition of the architectural image as a whole, revises the tradition of the *mashrabiyya*: latticework enclosing the external openings and allowing natural forced ventilation and a view from the inside out. The element providing shade is a vertical dihedral in self-cleaning prefabricated concrete, made from a mixture of cement and white marble, which, with the addition of chemical additives, maintains its pure white color over time.

The sequence of the elements making up the sunscreens is obtained through a rhythm of solids and voids on a 75-cm frame. This modular system allows the morphological variations to be inserted into the facades: big windows, bow windows, empty spaces, and observation decks. At the same time, thanks to the play of light and shade, the latticework of the trihedra intensifies the crumpled effect of the facades, which become a sort of large bas-relief that resembles the North African sculpted plaster technique.

A part of each block is treated with a dominant color—green, blue, yellow, and red—so that each one, with its variations in tone and intensity throughout the day, intensifies the recognizability and location of the building within the quarter.

The public park, in the form of a linear woodland, as well as constituting a heat-mitigation element, is also an opportunity to mediate the rapport between the new building and the railway to the south. The principle on which it is organized is based on the counterpoint between clumps of vegetation and clearings, which establishes a form of visual interpenetration between the building and the park itself and, at the same time, its organic oneness with the quarter, underlining its public and institutional role.

12

AZIRIR, GORGES D'ARAK, MARABOUT MOULAY H'SSAN, AND AMGUEL, ALGERIA
MODULAR CITIES ON THE TRANS-SAHARA HIGHWAY
2011

Gregotti Associati International
(A. Cagnardi, V. Gregotti, M. Reginaldi)
Partner: Ecosfera S.p.A. (F. Nissardi)
With: P. E. Colao, M. Destefanis,
T. Macchi Cassia (Associates),
C. Castello, E. Lucchini Gabriolo,
C. Scortecci

The plan for four new cities of 24,000 inhabitants in an area of 450 hectares each, along the Trans-Sahara Highway, the so-called "road of African unity" (opened in 1973), which winds its way for more than 2,700 km over ancient caravan routes, fits into a general plan by the Ministry of Planning to reorganize Algeria. The formation of a network of cities made up of twenty-four new settlements represents a multipolar urban system that is integrated into the framework of infrastructural renovation, the reorganization of the universities, the relaunch of industrial sites, and a new national food-farming policy.

The formation of new modular settlements, made possible by the completion of a new aqueduct, is based on the idea of offering the Sahara's nomadic pastoral population, mostly Arabs, Berbers, and Bedouins, the chance to become sedentary. The decision to locate the settlements of Azirir, Gorges d'Arak, Marabout Moulay Hassan, and In Amguel along the almost 700-km stretch of the Trans-Sahara Highway linking In Salah

(population 35,000) and Tamanrasset (population 92,000), and heading on toward Niger, was based on the principle of "stabilizing the Bedouin population by regulating and reducing urban drift to the cities of the north, especially by young people."

The experimental project for the formation of an integrated system of the four newly founded cities is based on the reinterpretation of the historical components, the anthropological characteristics, and the geographical peculiarities that characterize this part of the Sahara, so as to develop its natural and cultural heritage through a strategy of rebalancing resources, residential structures, and services for the population. For this reason, the sites were chosen on the basis of their proximity to an existing center or existing infrastructure, or for their historical and landscape interest. The placement of the settlements was also chosen on the basis of a principle of equidistance (140 km), so that they

Azirir

Gorges d'Arak

Marabout Moulay H'ssan

Amguel

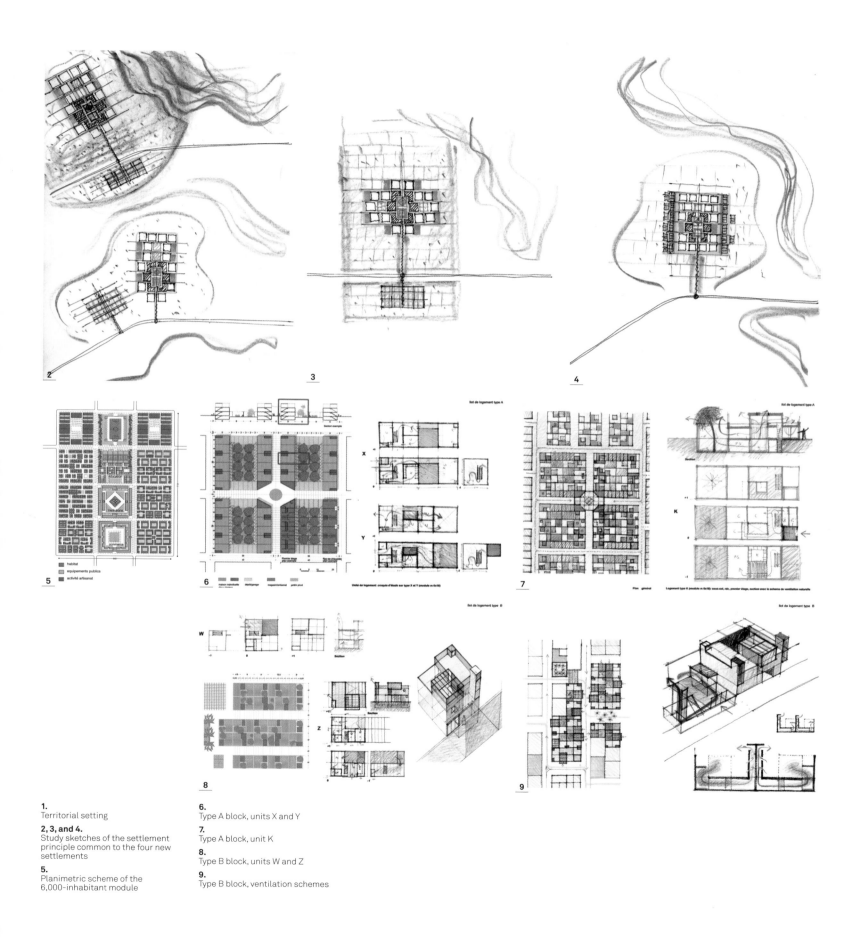

1.
Territorial setting

2, 3, and 4.
Study sketches of the settlement principle common to the four new settlements

5.
Planimetric scheme of the 6,000-inhabitant module

6.
Type A block, units X and Y

7.
Type A block, unit K

8.
Type B block, units W and Z

9.
Type B block, ventilation schemes

10.
Planimetric scheme of the
24,000-inhabitant module,
solution A

11.
Planimetric scheme of the
24,000-inhabitant module,
solution B

are all easily reachable from one another both by the inhabitants and by the population of the existing villages in the relative territorial sectors.

The modular settlement principle shared by the new cities means that, in any given situation, a principle of variability and adaptability to the geomorphological conditions of very different landscapes can be brought into force. The sites of Azirir and Gorges d'Arak are characterized by the notable presence of geological gorges with strong iconic value; Marabout Moulay H'ssan contains an important archaeological site; Amguel is close to a mineral extraction site and next to an airport.

Each new nucleus is a module composed of an urban fabric able to house 6,000 inhabitants, a sort of base city expandable to a population of 24,000.

The residential fabric was designed as a new architectural and urban interpretation of the particular characteristics associated with the traditions of the tribal group resident in the western region of the Sahara, such as the Saharawi, and in south-central Algeria, such as the Tuareg Kel Ahaggar, and was planned according to the principle of unifying a series of base modules through prefabrication. These units allow a certain flexibility of use, for example offering the possibility to use the garages initially as animal shelters, giving nomads the chance to make the transition to a sedentary lifestyle through the progressive integration of Bedouin families, according to an idea of sustainable modernization.

The distribution of the habitations is organized around recurring modules of 36 × 36 m making up twelve units of 100 m² each (with a family of five to six people), distributed on two levels plus an underground story, with a private garden, roof terrace, and protected space. The unit includes storage space and a garage for vehicles, carts, and bicycles. The habitation type incorporates the principles of natural ventilation (terraces, gardens, orientation of ventilation openings, chimneys, earth tubes, etc.), and the use of the underground room during the hottest periods.

The settlement principles of the Medina and the Kasbah are the reference point for the organization of the urban structure of the new settlements: made up of housing and craft and commercial space arranged around covered, air-conditioned central areas where essential urban services are concentrated.

Of particular importance is the distribution of greenery, both at the level of individual habitation units arranged around patios and private gardens, and as a general public green area, through the reconstruction of oases, protected bioclimatic zones, which are dedicated to the cultivation of plants and vegetables and stock raising, as well as waste recycling and the production and supply of renewable energy.

Considering the relative distance between one city and another, each has been designed to contain basic services (school, shops, basic health care, religious and recreational structures, and local government) and at least one regional service (higher education, complete health-care unit, national administration, and airport).

The basic module for a population of around 6,200 inhabitants is organized on a primary grid of 12-m-wide roads, which generates twelve modules of 162 × 162 m. The four main modules constitute housing; two are dedicated to productive activities (around 160,000 m²) and six to natural habitat, with the possibility of small shops and businesses nearby.

The secondary road system is dedicated to pedestrians and cyclists, for light transport and access to individual dwellings. This second system supplies the necessary variations to organize the *insulae* according to their position within the general system. The internal routes of the *insulae* have a communal central space (30 × 30 m) unifying community life among the blocks, with the possibility of small shops and workshops.

Parking areas are located on the edges of the settlement, as well as those dedicated to each residential unit.

As for the basic configuration of the settlement, the overall area, which includes the bioclimatic buffer zone and agricultural production, is approximately 200 hectares.

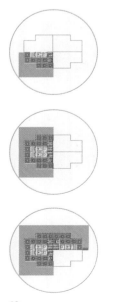

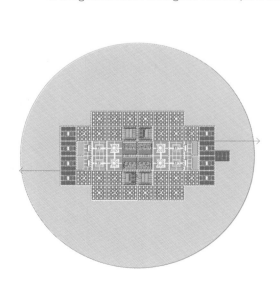

10

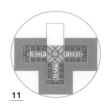

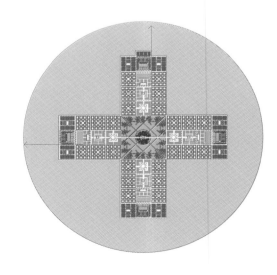

11

12.
Planimetric scheme of the new
settlement of Azirir

13.
Planimetric scheme of the new
settlement of Gorges d'Arak

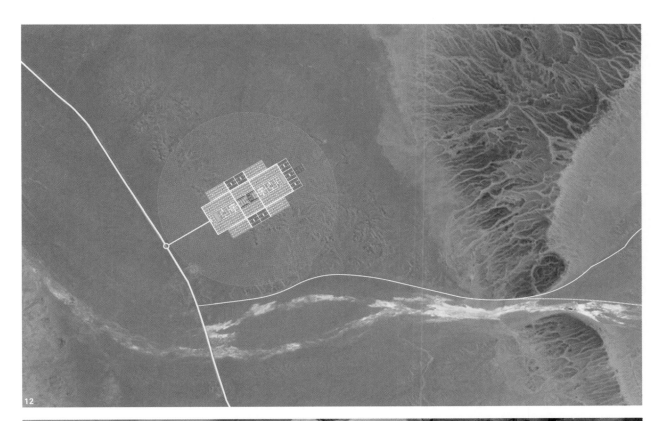

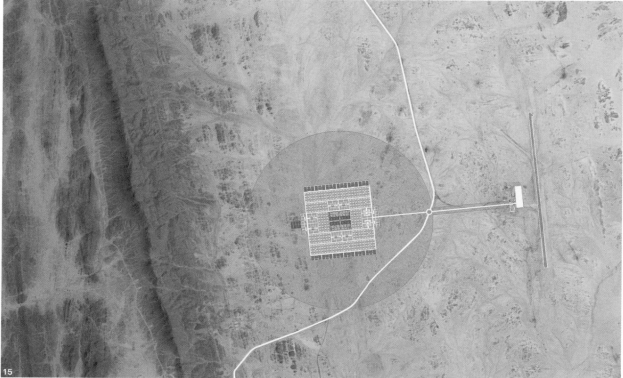

14.
Planimetric scheme of the new
settlement of Marabout

15.
Planimetric scheme of the new
settlement of Amguel

16.
Bird's-eye view of the new settlement
of Gorges d'Arak

17.
New settlement of Azirir: the built-up
area and the oasis (photomontage)

CHINA
FOUNDATIONS AND FUNDAMENTALS:
INTERACTIONS IN POSTMETROPOLIS LANDSCAPES

Gebrochen auf dem Boden liegen rings
Portale, Giebeldächer mit Skulpturen
Wo Mensch und Tier vermischt, Centaur und Sphinx,
Satyr, Chimäre – Fabelzeitfiguren.

Heinrich Heine[1]

The search for interactions between a new civil condition of urban design as a possible form of landscape architecture of collective interest and the structural fragmentation of the postmetropolitan whole represents the ideal foundation uniting the projects developed in Gregotti & Associates' second phase of activity in China.

With the consolidation of the realization process of Pujiang new town,[2] the chance to further develop the working methodology elaborated over ten years of competitions and direct appointments of varying scope and complexity takes the form of experimentation and proposals in this new phase. They are promoted by the government and private or semipublic companies, for specific solutions and urban development models for a settlement geography made up of the "scattered totalities"[3] characteristic of postmetropolises, especially Shanghai and its catchment area. Characterized by a condition of permanent transition, a lack of structure in their public spaces, the reduction of the urban environment to a juxtaposition of urbanized areas with no architectural quality or differentiation in use, crisscrossed and often torn apart by fluxes imposed by the pervasive presence of transport infrastructure and by construction giants founded on the extraneousness of neocolonialism, contemporary Chinese hypercities offer many fields for possible experimentation, but ever fewer occasions for objective transformation, which is focused and aware of the context.

The interpretation of the urban and territorial environment as a "nonsite"[4]—left over from the presence of these conditions of urban disintegration, derived from the instability of the overall morphological structure and the precariousness of the structurally transforming physical and cultural elements—produces a substantially unique human-geographical landscape. Spread out over an often inexplicable range of relationships, this new areal city requires a complex experience of its spaces through a transformational project, which orients it toward an urban form that is once again intelligible and workable for architecture.

Particularly important are projects that, starting with the theme of the architecture of infrastructural connections, propose strategies for a general redesign of the environmental and urban morphology, where built-up areas of varied dimensions succeed on another on a huge scale, in an apparently irresolvable "vertigo of the unlimited,"[5] as in the case of the Zhuhai Coast.

As incessant postmetropolitan development sanctions the loss of the very idea of identity and is too often oblivious to the ancient and colonial city's cultural foundations, there is a corresponding consolidation and stratification of the social divide, at once imposed and voluntary, which creates ever more widespread, sprawling, and insurmountable ghettos.[6]

Even in the face of this new geography of cultural and physical fragmentation, which implies a new form of social division and segregation, the methodology of urban design adopted in the cases presented is based on the experimentation of settlement principles, which are diversified but united by the idea of articulating the rapport between the new constructions and their physical and cultural foundations. These can be found in the settlement rationale of the historical urban structures, which, having survived the processes of elimination and radical substitution typical of the contemporary Chinese urban phenomenon, are still depositories of memory, form, and ideas (as in the case of Zhoujiajiao and Suzhou).

But establishing foundations also means being able to introduce a new possible design for open space where there is no trace or memory, just plots to be filled by the model development principle still in operation in the Chinese postmetropolis: the skyscraper city. In an attempt to give meaning and urban value to these sites with no points of reference, the urban ground project can then be laid out in the design for a great adaptable platform, housing spaces and services of high public usability (Expansion of the Pudong financial district).

The integrity of the project process as a modifying action able to cross all dimensional and relational scales presides especially over the design of settlement structures based on the development of some of the consolidated, almost "codified," project principles during the well-established design experience in China.

The idea of contrasting the fragmentation of Chinese territorial unities with the theme of the permanence of urban design as a stability strategy sees the principle of morphological variation as a condition of identity for the urban order and for architecture, elucidating their use and the expression of their cultural character. This idea of a morphology of living, a cultural geography founded on the crossing of the various operational scales—from area, to city, to architecture—constitutes at once a concrete working methodology and a theoretical design practice. It is a working reflection that acts on the significance of present and potential places to reconsider the role the architect can still play to fulfill the conditions of habitability of urban contexts in the most extreme and indecipherable postmodernism.

Morphological variation, therefore, means keeping open the comparison with the reasons for architectural foundations, be they still observed at the sites—the ancient Chinese settlement forms— or ideals, through the critical updating of references. Urban design then, with its numerous variations and successions, becomes a field for experimentation, which generates morphological metamorphoses according to changes in usage, activated by the successive phases of the numerous and often contradictory Chinese urban development programs.

This process, which reduces the distance between a project and its feasibility, derives, then, from the possibility of expressing the morphological characters of the sites in a new condition of duration, where the design process and meaning are identified with each other within a unitary expressive language, able to represent a new "human-geographical figurativeness."[7]

In this sense, too, the projects developed for China from 2008 to 2014, all without concrete results except for the beginning of construction on Pujiang's Central Belt, are bearers of a demonstrative motion whose validity seems to be extendable to the general theme of reconstruction of an idea of areal and urban form, where architecture can assume a recognizable meaning only if it relates to rules that reveal their own content as archetypes of foundations.

In this perspective, the Chinese postmetropolis that transposes the mythology of globalized finance, consumerism, and communication into nonspaces still seems interpretable through urban design, which ultimately represents a shift not only in disciplinary meaning but also in more broadly humanistic meaning "of a resolution of 'mythology' in the space of history."[8]

1   Lying broken on the ground all around / Portals, gabled roofs with sculptures, / Where man and beast mix, Centaur and Sphinx, / Satyr and Chimaera: figures from a fabled time
    Heine, H., *Für die Mouche*
2   See Gregotti, V., *L'ultimo hutong: Lavorare in architettura nella nuova Cina*, Skira, Milan, 2009 and Morpurgo, G., *Gregotti & Associates: The Architecture of Urban Design*, Rizzoli, New York, 2008, Realignments 1999–2007 chapter.
3   Gregotti, V., *Architettura e postmetropoli*, Einaudi, Turin, 2011.
4   Ponte, A., *Il non sito*, in *Casabella*, no. 597–598, January–February 1993, pp.102–104.
5   Eco, U., *The Infinity of Lists: An Illustrated Essay*, Rizzoli, New York, 2009.
6   For a discussion of the phenomenon of the urban divide, see the study by Calame, J. and Charlesworth, E., *Divided Cities: Belfast, Beirut, Jerusalem, Mostar, and Nicosia*, University of Pennsylvania Press, Philadelphia, 2009 and preface to the Italian edition of that work, Città divise, Medusa Edizioni, Milan, 2012.
7   Gregotti, V., *Il possibile necessario*, Milan, 2014.
8   Benjamin, W., *Das Passagen-Werk*, Suhrkamp Verlag, Frankfurt-am-Main, 1982. Italian edition by Agamben, G., *Parigi capitale del XIX secolo: I «passages» di Parigi*, Einaudi, Turin, 1986.

Project for the Zhuhai coast, Zhuhai, China.
General view from the north.

Gregotti Associati International
(A. Cagnardi, V. Gregotti, M. Reginaldi)
Partner: Tianhua Architecture
Planning & Engineering Ltd.
(X. Huang)
With: C. Calligaris, I. Chiarel,
G. Donato, G. Gramegna (Associates),
C. Calabrese, F. Campello, C. Castello,
M. Corsico, S. Ferrari, B. Medini,
S. Zauli

Zhujiajiao is an ancient settlement built on the water. It has a rich architectural and urban heritage, which grew up along a dense network of canals. The main waterway is the canal running from east to west, the obligatory route for commercial transport between the rice-growing area around the lake and nearby Shanghai.

A five-span stone bridge connects the two banks of the main canal. The village was developed in ancient times along smaller canals, both to the north and to the south. In the southern area, the canals flow through a vast lagoon. The whole area is crisscrossed by ancient canals with the double function of communication and irrigation of the paddy fields, in which the flow of water is controlled by locks. The largest canals were opened up recently to allow for cargo shipping and tourism.

The urban structure of the historic nucleus is organized in such a way that the pedestrian routes are parallel to the canals and within the curtain of buildings facing them. The area was built up according to the principle of the juxtaposition of one- or two-story houses with gardens normally at the back or in front of the canals. In the southern section of the old city, a quarter has recently been built and is made up of parallel autonomous buildings, reproducing the standard and repeated model characteristic of all recent developments in Chinese cities.

1.
Territorial setting

2.
Urban setting

3.
General planimetry of the intervention

4.
Planimetry of the area of the lake with the hotel on the artificial island

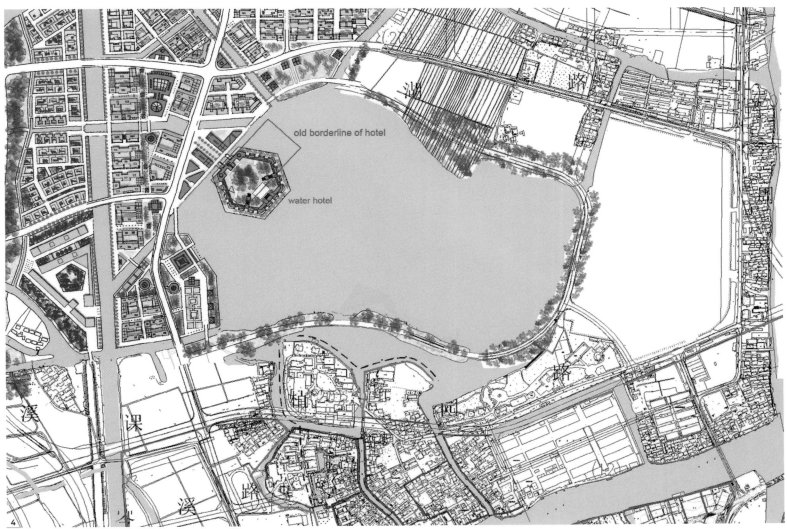

old borderline of hotel

water hotel

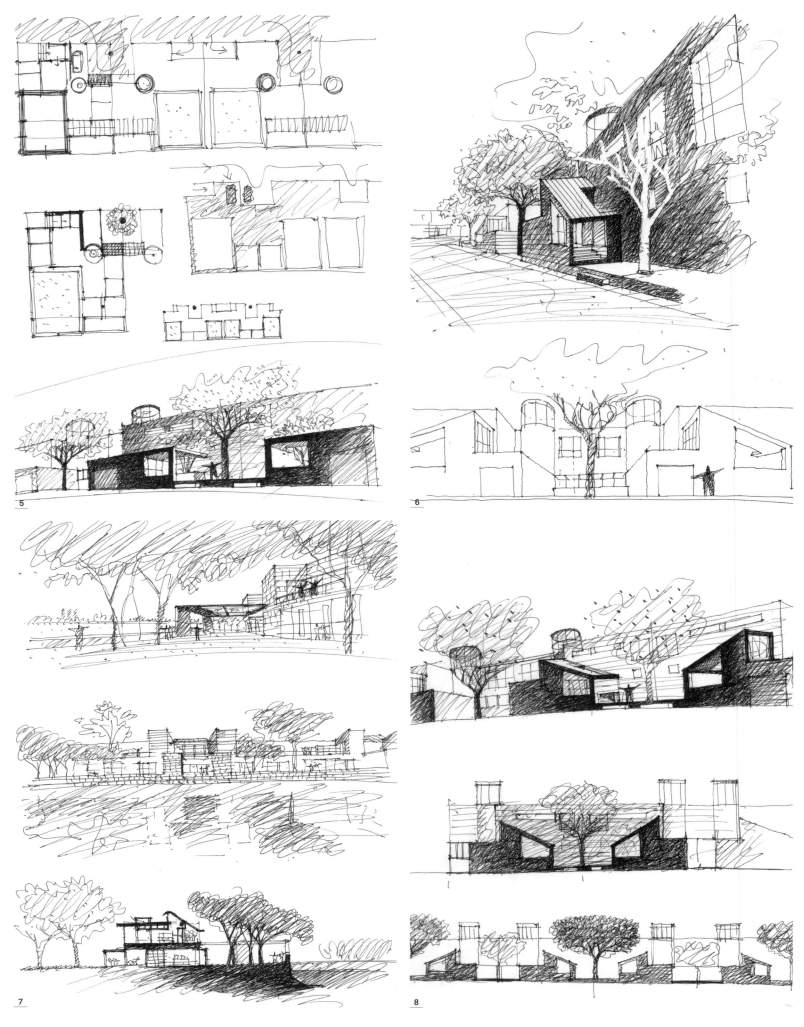

5

6

7

8

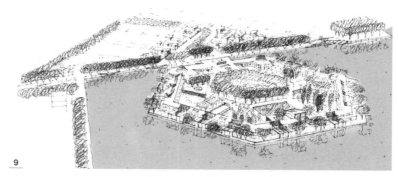

The proposal for the urbanization of the Citic area, adjacent to the center of the old city, is based on the consideration that the structure of the ancient city and the new villas around the lake are not sufficient to build a new kind of urban fabric in which new and old are integrated in a single unifying form. The common matrix might be represented by the system of artificial islands built in the lagoon upon which the main body of the city is organized and, in general, by the idea of offering continuity for the special settlement principle, which is characteristic of a city built on the water. In the new system, the canals can be reused for public transport, thus returning to the lake its role of great natural landscape element and link between the ancient center and the new zone of urban expansion.

The project thus introduces the idea of forming a new center that integrates the historical center, around which not just housing but also service activities, even of a special nature, will be based, as required by the new importance assumed by this city in a phase of strong development.

The possibility of accessing the new center via water offers an alternative to the direct access to the old center. The existing city is currently accessed after crossing a recently built part of the city, completely autonomous in terms of the morphological characteristics of the urban context, and so unable to meld with the ancient city built on the water.

The urban fabric introduced by the proposal is made up in large part of a new housing system, based on three model settlement principles.

The first kind consists of two-story urban villas, characterized by the main body of the building extending inward into the block, leaving the service road at the back. This principle allows a precise configuration of the external face and protects the privacy of internal gardens. The spatial modulation of individual cases can produce a variety of inhabitable areas as well as a diverse system of facades overlooking the canal. This kind of settlement typology contrasts with the model of the individual house, through the idea of forming a fabric of filled-in areas (habitations) and spaces (gardens and canals), according to the principle of the excavated solid, or a single unitary and morphologically consistent building, an analogy with the example of the historic center of Zhuijiajiao.

5, 6, 7, and 8.
Study sketches of the buildings for low-density single habitations (urban villas)

9.
Axonometric study of the hotel on the octagonal artificial island

10 and 11.
Study sketches for a footbridge over a navigable canal

12, 13, and 14.
Study sketches for footbridges

15.
Nighttime prospective view of a medium-density zone. In the foreground, the local shopping center.

16.
Study sketch for a medium- and high-density district

17.
Study sketch for low-density buildings (semidetached townhouses)

15

A second type of housing is the townhouse of three to four stories, which allows a greater building density and alignments along the main roads and canals. These buildings can include retail sales services and small service spaces on the ground floor.

The third type is represented by tall buildings (eleven floors), which create visual reference points and condense the urban landscape of the new settlement. They are positioned in areas where wide open views are guaranteed, thus reinforcing their role as landmarks.

There is also a special element in the spatial arrangement of the system of islands that make up the new settlement proposal. This is represented by a hotel complex, itself an octagonal island, which is to be built as an autonomous element in the lake, joined to the shore by a connection to the north–south road layout that serves the whole area.

16

Gregotti Associati International
(A. Cagnardi, V. Gregotti, M. Reginaldi)
Partner: Tianhua Architecture
Planning & Engineering Ltd.
(X. Huang)
With: S. Butti, C. Calligaris,
M. Destefanis, G. Donato, T. Macchi
Cassia (Associates), C. Castello

The international consultation concerns an area of around 850,000 m², in a central location in the financial district of Lujiazui, the business zone of Pudong. The urban scene is undergoing a rapid transformation in which there are many empty lots, and it is characterized by a large number of isolated and self-referential tall buildings, most of which were built in the 2000s. With respect to this pending complex architectural context, the project (first prize), which concentrates on the integration of the new eastern financial zone of Lujiazui within Shanghai's vast financial district, establishes a compact morphological configuration able to incorporate the future towers in a coordinated urban design. The proposed settlement system revolves around a network of public spaces extending on both sides of the preexisting and monumental Century Boulevard, the main east–west artery serving the entire area, imposing an orthogonal grid that regulates the plan of a city core, a center for tertiary businesses with adjoining services and residential areas, formed from towers integrated into a new urban morphology.

Pedestrian roads, squares, tree-lined avenues, and waterways keep the built-up areas in line along the grid, which is punctuated by blocks conceived as bases for the towers that will stand 20 m high with rooftop gardens. Containing services, shops, and various facilities, the bases ensure that community life is highly accessible to the city

floor, avoiding the formation of the residual spaces lacking identity normally produced by the isolation of skyscrapers. The towers, rising up from the bases, will thus be able to assume forms rich in architectural variety that respect an urban structure well defined by the blocks and their alignments on the roads.

This idea of a city of skyscrapers, measured on the ground with elements on a human scale and proportions adapted to social life, is entrusted to three large malls or parallel avenues, over 70 m wide, with the city mall (a series of furnished squares) at the center and a water mall and a green mall at the sides, crossed by a tree-lined avenue in front facing the river.

The urban design also has the objective of merging four general levels and making them coexist: the pedestrian city at ground level; the lowest level (-7.5 m) where service roads, technical areas, and parking, and also a commercial promenade along the new canal, are located; the level of the blocks (+20 m) where there is a further green layer; and finally the various levels of the towers that rise above the blocks.

The project for the new, mostly tertiary zone involves the support of an integrated infrastructure: two underground motorways and five underground railway lines, which limit traffic jams, ensuring that 150,000 people will be able to use the area simultaneously.

1.
Urban setting in the Pudong area.
On the left, the Huang-pu river.
In the center, Century Boulevard

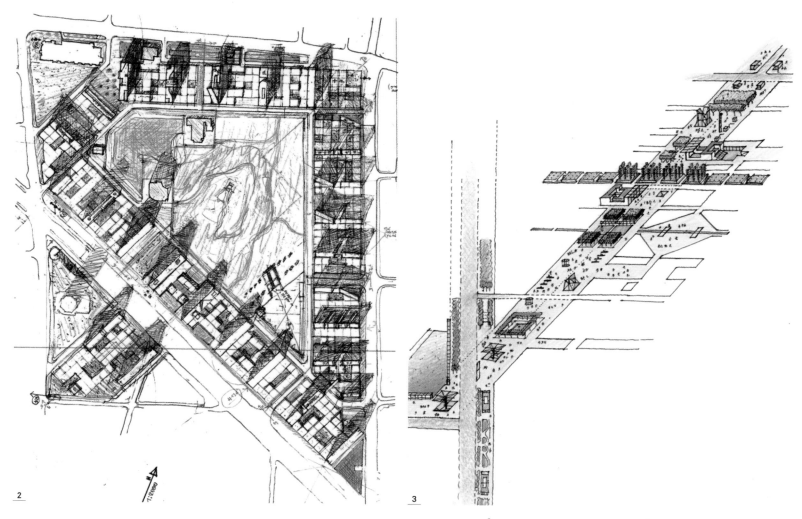

2

3

2.
Planimetric-volumetric sketch of the
first solution (skyscrapers arranged
within an extensive public park)

3.
Study sketch for a tree-lined avenue

4.
Nighttime prospective view of the
final solution (parallel avenues)

5.
Concept sketch of the system of
parallel avenues

4

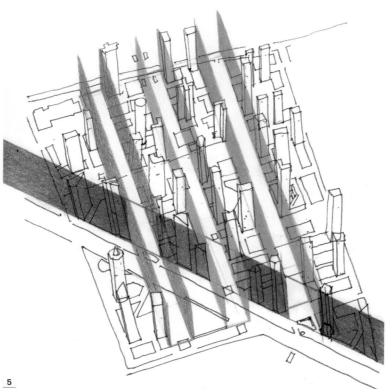

5

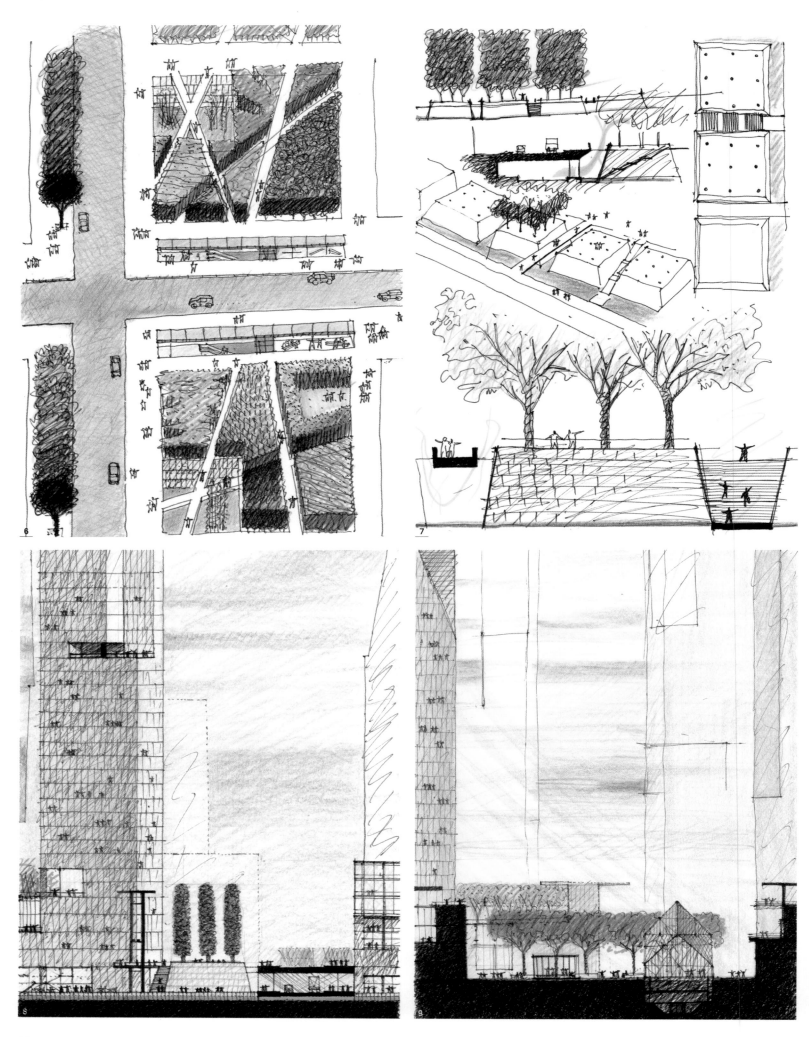

6, 7, 8, and 9.
Study sketches for a pedestrian avenue, with green areas and public services at different heights

10.
General daytime view from the east: at the center of the picture is the system of three pedestrian avenues, distinct from the preexisting road network around the edges of the project area

11, 12, and 13.
Prospective views of the three avenues: the public spaces are the morphological foundation of the area, orienting the layout of the skyscraper bases, which can then develop in their own way in terms of size and character

Gregotti Associati International
(A. Cagnardi, V. Gregotti, M. Reginaldi)
Partner: Tianhua Architecture
Planning & Engineering Ltd.
(X. Huang)
With: I. Chiarel, G. Donato
(Associates), A. Boccacci,
C. Calabrese, C. Castello,
M. Parravicini, C. Scortecci, P. Seria,
S. Zauli

The site involved in the competition for a new town is a triangular area of 5.7 km^2 situated in the western part of the city of Suzhou, 6 km from the city center. The area is defined by three large arterial roads: Provincial Road 230 to the east, Tai Lake Avenue to the south, and Kaulum Mountain Road to the north. The project takes into account the general master plan, which envisions a greenbelt as a regulatory element in territorial interaction, and as a buffer zone between the great Tai Hu Lake and a recently built quarter. Furthermore, it is envisioned that the center of the new settlement will be situated in the southwest, alongside a small lake.

The existing infrastructure system will not be modified, while for the new settlement a layout is proposed in keeping with the principles of an eco-city.

It has also been requested that the scale of the city and its urban landscape be inspired by those of small European cities.

The site is crossed by a dense network of small canals, along which various country villages are organized. In this flat area, the only geographical relief is a hill about 70 m high, which separates the site into two sections. The main section borders a technology park in the west, while the smaller section is surrounded by countryside and is connected with the urban system leading toward the tertiary structures situated on the shores of the small lake within the future town.

The planned infrastructure and public transport system are aimed at guaranteeing the connection between the new town and the historical center of the ancient city of Suzhou.

The plan proposed is not conceived as a typical master plan, but as a newly conceived design based on the idea of an eco-city connected with its surroundings, able to reveal its own urban structure through its connections with the nearby areas, the built landscape, and the sequence of public spaces, and reattributing a role to the hill rising from the plain.

The urban design organizes the new town within the green area as a settlement system made up of nine distinct "community villages" surrounded by woodland and connected to each other by local roads, which in turn are connected with the nationwide road network. Each urban community is served by a road network based on *quadras* of about 100 × 100 m, which delimit the blocks in order to condense the urban fabric. Each block contains residential units of variable density: villas, four-story townhouses, six-story buildings, and, occasionally, groups of tall buildings.

Both the size of the community villages and their settlement typology can be combined into different variations, thus allowing flexibility and adaptability. The proposal is based on the following principles:

Respect for environmental characteristics
The project interprets the spirit and the presence of the main human and geographical elements of the surroundings: Tai Hu Lake, the handling of its shores, its potential in terms of leisure-time activities. It also underlines the differences in ground level, with particular reference to the central hill and its potential as a panoramic viewpoint for the whole settlement, and also the fact that the settlements are spread out, their scale defined by buildings of limited height. The central position of the hill offers the chance to integrate the plateau into the central level of +20 m and to reuse an existing quarry as an open-air botanical garden.

Green areas and water
The city of Suzhou boasts great historical gardens of exceptional quality. In the new town, the green areas reflect the settlement principles governing this region and the nature of its environment. This means green areas that, apart from the particular role played by the hill and the sports facilities, are distributed among and made available to the various community villages.

1 and 2.
Territorial and urban settings

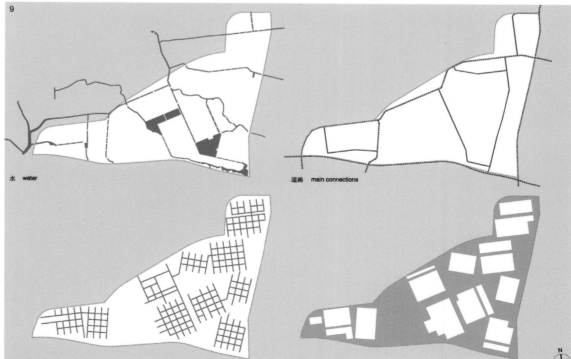

水 water

道路 main connections

内部结构 network

开放空间 open spaces

3, 4, and 5.
Views of the recurring aspects of the historical residential fabric along the navigable canals

6.
Existing community villages/new community villages

7 and 8.
Schematic comparison between neighborhoods occupied by preexisting villages and the system of proposed areas of reaggregation and expansion

9.
Village structure: water; main connections; road network; open spaces

It is also envisioned that the canal system will be used as much as possible according to its present layout, which can be improved both in terms of purification and regeneration of the water. The project envisions two new catchment areas for water treatment, one connected with the main service center and the other in the southeastern corner.

One particular theme is represented by the greenbelt provided by the existing plan, which divides the settlement in two along Tai Hu Lake. In order not to block access to the lake for the residents of the new town, the creation of a small marina connected with it is proposed.

New construction and the restoration of existing buildings

One of the founding principles of an eco-district is the salvaging of existing buildings. In the case of Suzhou, the value of the existing urban system is in its fragmentation and the interconnectedness of the built sections in "community villages."

In the new settlement, the old houses may offer an alternative lifestyle opportunity to new residents, as well as a special chance to obtain a piece of heritage, which can be restored with special functions.

Furthermore, it is precisely the principle of "community village" that the project has assumed as the founding element of the new settlement structure. The built space

is laid out in such a way that the network of canals is maintained as an element closely tied in with the open space, in which the system of rural green areas is partly substituted by urban green areas: two different systems crossing over and overlapping—that of the urban villages, open toward the green areas, and that of the system of green spaces and water enriching the spaces that have residential and urban functions.

The resulting built-up area of all the community villages is around 2,600,000 m² for housing and 435,000 m² for the mixed-function block, representing the main center of the new town. The nonbuilt area is greater than 50 percent.

Service infrastructure

With a view to saving energy, for each community village it was proposed that the distribution network of the air-heating systems be centralized, using production processes able to guarantee good performance (starting with geothermal energy). For waste treatment, a system of waste separation is envisioned, perhaps making use of a pneumatic handling system.

Public services

Public services in the new settlement are envisioned on three different levels: services for each community village (trade, security, etc.); services for groups within the communities (education, settlement services); and general

10.
Concept design study
11.
Green area and water scheme
12.
Road network scheme
13.
Pedestrian and cycle network scheme

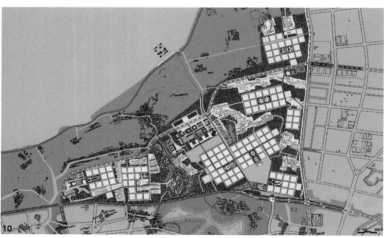
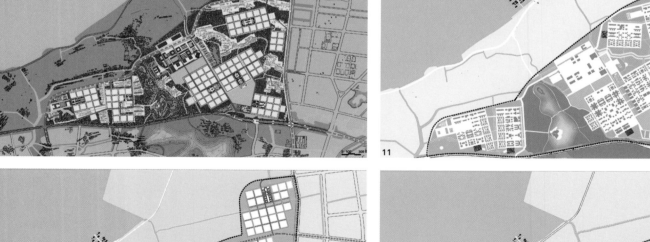

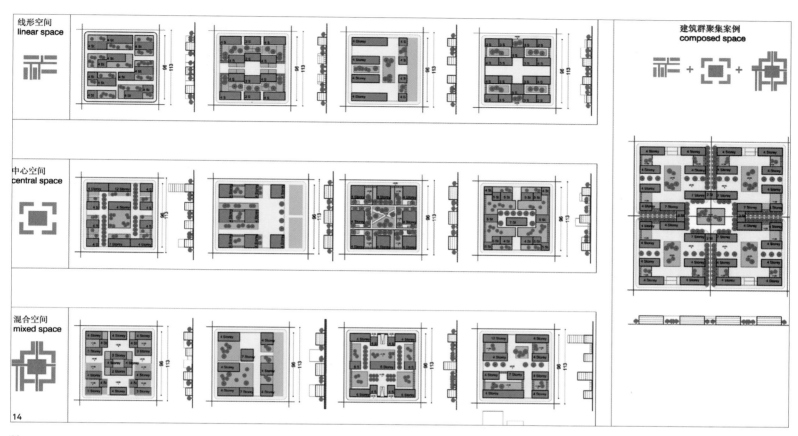

14.
Example of plot layout

15, 16, and 17.
Example of plot layout—linear
space: planimetric schemes and
views

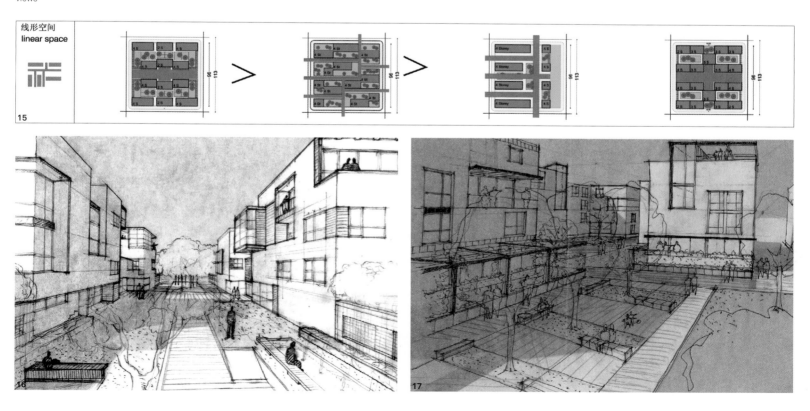

urban services able to meet the needs of the population (cinemas, theaters, concert halls, shopping centers, restaurants, public service structures, tourist services, local health services).

Alternative energy sources

An area of 10,000 m² has been reserved for each community for the production of alternative energy through solar power, with a peak production capacity of about 1,400 Kw each. These areas may be developed architecturally in various ways: as the roof of a large parking lot, the provision of the area for open-air markets, or for greenhouse cultivation.

Public transport

A particularly important aspect of an eco-district is obviously an efficient and nonpolluting public transport system, well enough developed to reduce car use to a minimum, guaranteeing connections on a broader scale between the whole city; the planned underground railway and the railway; airport, and regional motorway hub.

18, 19, and 20.
Central space: planimetric schemes and views

21, 22, and 23.
Mixed space: planimetric schemes and views

24 and 25.
Views of eco-town center

26 and 27.
Views of village type 2

中心空间
central space

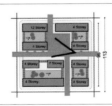
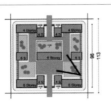
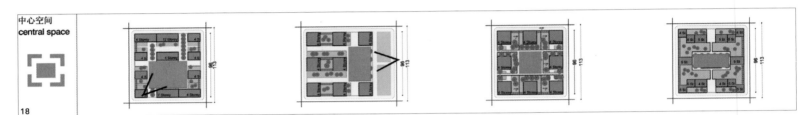

18

19

20

混合空间
mixed space

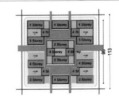
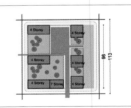

21

22

23

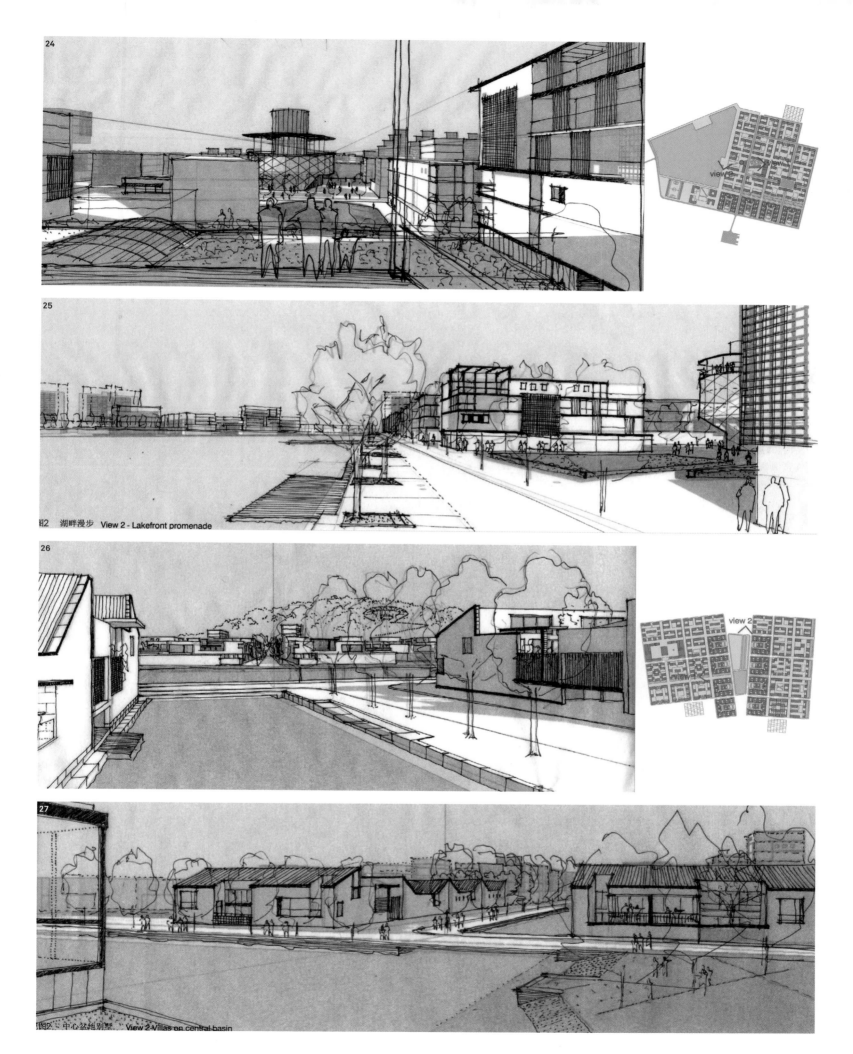

图2　湖畔漫步　View 2 - Lakefront promenade

图2　中心盆地别墅　View 2 - Villas on central basin

ZHUHAI, CHINA
PROJECT FOR THE ZHUHAI COAST
2009

Gregotti Associati International
(A. Cagnardi, V. Gregotti, M. Reginaldi)
With: C. Calligaris, I. Chiarel,
M. Destefanis, T. Macchi Cassia,
M. Trovatelli (Associates),
G.A. Giannoccari,
E. Lucchini-Gabriolo, B. Medini,
M. Parravicini, P. Ronchi, C. Scortecci,
S. Zauli

The competition project concerns the layout of around 50 km stretch of coastline in the recently created city of Zhuhai. Located in the southern province of Guangdong, in the southeast of the country, it is within the so-called Pearl Gulf, a triangle of water whose corners are formed by Macao, Hong Kong, and Guangzhou. The area around the region of Macao is characterized by numerous islands and a small mountain chain rising between 400 and 500 m. Since the sea is shallow, the coast can be continually extended for building, due to the restrictions on building in the mountain chain imposed by the 2001–2020 Territorial Plan.

Construction along the coast consists of a sort of shoreline of tall buildings arranged discontinuously and separated from the mountains that sweep down to the sea. The discontinuity of the buildings means that the undulating natural landscape can be seen in the background. The alternation between the verticality of the buildings, the natural green promontories, and the undulating green backdrop offers a rich variety of views in which nature is still present in places and becomes an important feature of the urban scenario.

The complex and extensive territorial setting has been handled by organizing the coastal layout in terms of the new layout for the coastal motorway, which, by linking up with the existing road network, aims to improve traffic circulation along the whole coastline and to implement the environmental and public use of the line facing onto the sea. Considering the breadth and dimensions of the infrastructure, its impact on the city as a whole and on the coastal environment, the project introduces some exceptional solutions, designed according to a principle of consistency with the geography and the new landscape configuration.

The main goals of the project concern the geographical structure of the coast, the areas around the Gombey Customs, and the system of islands.

The Gombey Customs area divides the coastal landscape into three different typologies. To the north are the open seascapes: a sequence of urban fronts with medium and tall buildings, interspersed with coastal mountain spurs. As this is the coast with the most potential for creating more tourist and cultural attractions, new centers dedicated to these are envisioned.

Further to the north, it is envisioned to create a new part of the city by reclaiming land from the sea. The configuration is based on the principle of interspersing the areas to be built on with stretches of sea, which, approaching the land, will encounter green spaces, forming a lake and the new center of the science- and tech-oriented city between them.

To the south of Gombey, the canals of the first stretch bypass Macao and then pass between two areas that are to be urbanized. The landscape is characterized by mountain relief further from the coast and will be marked by three different positions. The first faces onto the oldest part of the city of Macao and extends into the second, where the new central business district will be built, which, spread out on both sides of the canal, will be located opposite the opening to the sea, level with the three bridges that currently link the two islands of Macao.

The third area is a stretch of canal in which the new commercial and productive constructions occupy land reclaimed from the sea from which rise small mountain reliefs. The analysis of the landscape highlights a rich morphology of numerous coastal islands.

These specific landscape conditions suggest orienting the project in the direction of specific morphological relationships:

1.
General view from the north

2.
General planimetry and study sketches

Following pages

3.
The road-park system: general planimetry and typical cross-sections

4.
The new archipelago in the Beaver Yeli Island District: planimetry and study sketches of the cultural center:

1–4: Arts center

5–6: Resort

7: Exhibition hall

8–9: Five-star hotel

10–12: Opera house

13–16: Haibin Beach

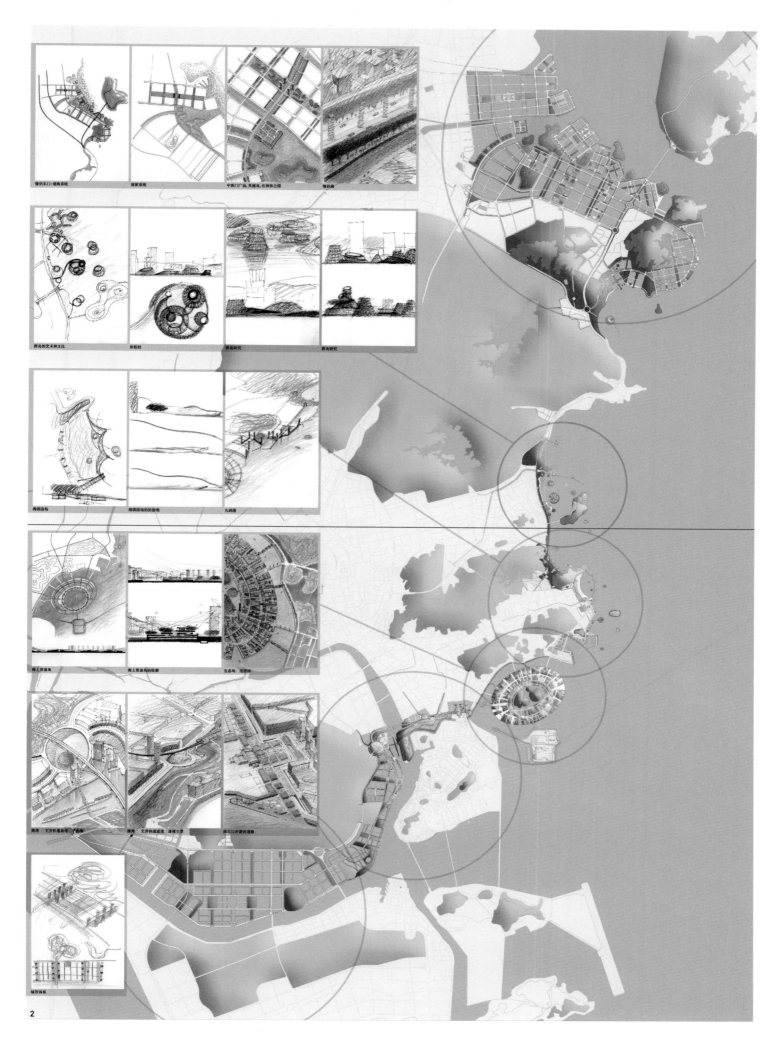

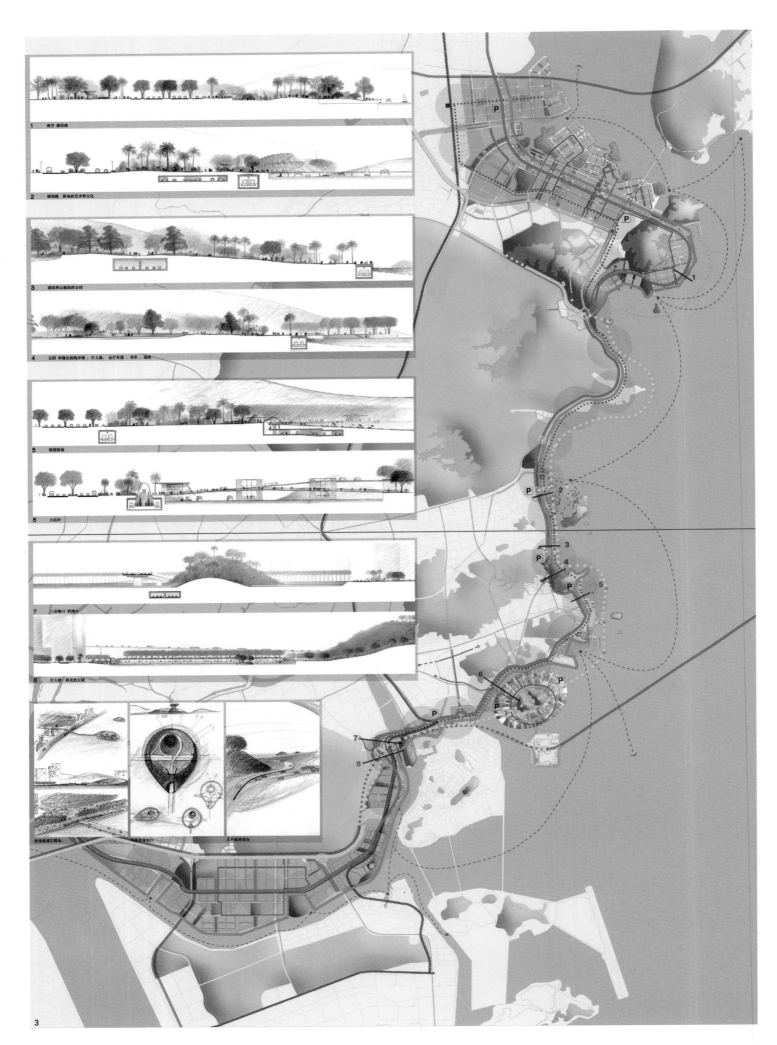

1 南方 镶切路

2 镶切路 群岛的艺术和文化

3 湖泊和山脉海的公园

4 公园 和漫长的海岸线：行人道，自行车道，冬季，地铁

5 海滩浴场

6 大运河

7 三岔路口 的纽带

8 行人桥 拱北的丘陵

快速通道在郊海。   海通道通出口   湾内都都自岛

3

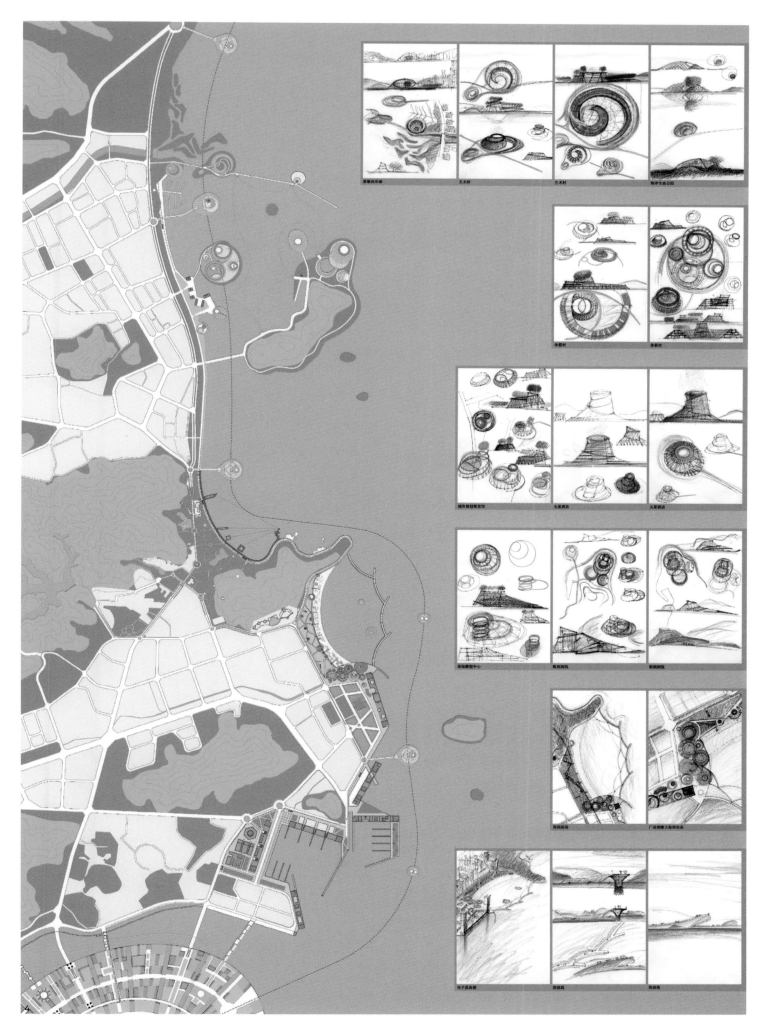

Urban—natural

The alternation between the built-up areas, the urban fronts on the coast, and the natural parts offers a rich and varied model suitable for new construction, thus guaranteeing variety, transparency, and reciprocal integration between the parts, which can already be appreciated in the current panoramas.

Mountain—sea

Today there is a very strong visual connection where the mountains meet the water. These territories should be preserved as fixed points in the landscape. The same relationship is proposed in the new construction, creating open visual channels through which to observe the geography, even in the areas occupied by the new functions.

Land—sea

Today there are many islands and reefs in the sea facing the coast, making up one of the most important geographical configurations and attractions, offering further opportunities for contact with the sea. This special condition suggests augmenting the system with new artificial islands, which can be created due to the shallowness of the sea, to build an archipelago in which the islands can also be partly buildings for tourist facilities, services, and new attractions. The archipelago thus offers the opportunity to double the extent of man-made geographical landscapes through the formation of inhabited islands, with houses, shops, and offices, where the city is reorganized on a human scale, thus distinguishing itself from the vast scale of road and transport infrastructures. Interpreting the existing geographical conditions, the new archipelago can develop the current urban structure to generate new morphologies, landscapes, and urban environments.

5 and 6.
The new mobility scenery in Wanchai.
Study sketch

7.
The large island: axonometric sketch

8.
The large island: the junctions with surrounding areas

9.
General view from the south

10.
The new archipelago in the Beaver Yeli Island District. View from the north.

EXHIBITION AND CONFERENCE CENTER DESIGN IN NEW SOUTH DOWNTOWN AREA, TONGZHOU DISTRICT
2005

Gregotti Associati International
(A. Cagnardi, V. Gregotti, M. Reginaldi)
Partner:
Tianhua Architecture Planning &
Engineering Limited (X. Huang)
Sistema Progetto S.p.A. (A. Vettese)
Solly Cohen & C. S.p.A. (S. Cohen)
With: I. Chiarel G. Donato,
G. Gramegna (Associates), R. Bonomi,
C. Castello, S. Costa, A. Cotti, J. Muzio,
M. Parravicini, P. Seria, S. Zauli

The competition project concerns the urban design to urbanize a zone of expansion that includes an area for fairs and conventions. The site is made up of a large free area situated in the far south of Tongzhou, crossed by a canal and bordered by a motorway slip road.

The subject has been tackled by proposing a new town made up of a settlement system formed from an archipelago of compact and variously oriented blocks by means of a common matrix in the form of an orthogonal grid. This framework guarantees at once cohesion and internal consistency, as well as the relative autonomy of individual structures, forming an open design that integrates extensive green areas into the open spaces among the urban fabric thanks to the reciprocal rotation of their foundational axes. The buildings themselves include various urban functions, such as services for the resident population, accommodation facilities, commerce, and special functions relating to culture and leisure time, and are in large part characterized by the presence of variable-density residences: medium density (max seven floors – ratio 1.5 GFA/m²); high density (max twenty floors – ratio 2.2 GFA/m²); special area (max thirty floors – ratio 3 GFA/m²).

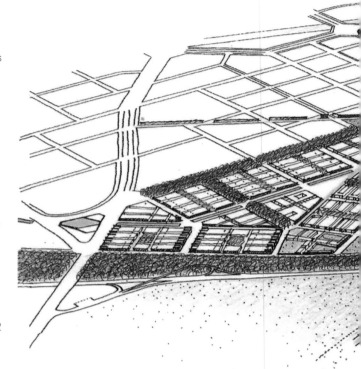

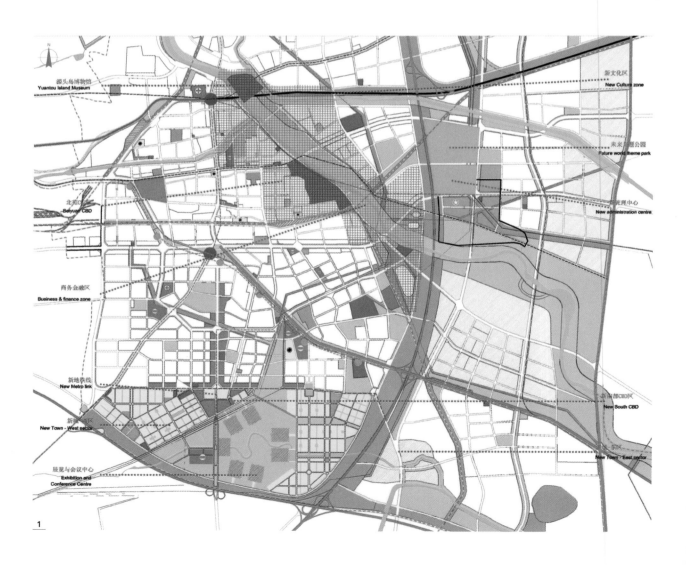

1.
Urban setting. From the current
master plan.

1

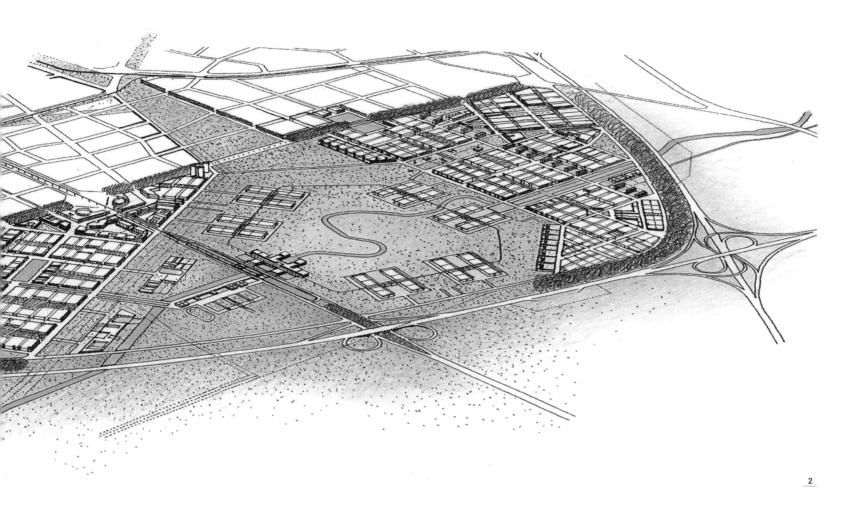

2.
Preparatory general axonometry of
the project proposal

The network structure of the new urban construction allows morphological exceptions, both in terms of a ground plan with public and private green spaces and canals/water plazas, and through the inclusion of buildings for different purposes, even for special uses. In particular, the project proposes to create a new urban structure with a high degree of coexistence of integrated uses and functions, in order to avoid the single-function quarters that nowadays characterize Chinese urban expansion.

The new town upon completion of the urban system is organized into two main sectors situated in the east and west of the central part of a large park. The new easterly sector contains more residential structures together with the relevant services: schools, shops, facilities, public services, culture. At the junction with the large north–south road is a special area of shops, entertainment, and culture and a high concentration of accommodation facilities to cater to trade fairs.

The westerly sector presents a higher degree of internal use, which, as well as housing, shops, and services for the local residents and those of southern Tongzhou, will also include an area destined for productive activities (Urban Ecological Industry). In this part of the new town there will also be rows of special housing known as SOHO: Small Offices, House Offices, multiservice apartments.

Between the two sectors of the new town will be a large hexagonal park, in which will be located the trade fair and conference zone, made up of six large satellites, each arranged in pavilions half hidden by the vegetation.

The conference center is positioned where the pavilion system joins the north–south arterial route linking the new town with the existing quarters in the north. The building is connected with the hall and the central pavilion, making it possible to use the two basic centers together, according to different purposes.

All the elements of the trade fair complex are linked together by a raised people mover.

The problem of the proximity of the motorway slip road that delimits the area to the south has been resolved by putting in a greenbelt, which is connected at various points to the large internal park. The halfway link between the area and the preexisting areas to the north offers a chance to include a system of blocks dedicated to the new south central business district.

Main access to the trade fair area is along the existing north–south road, which has been widened to enhance access. Thanks to the presence of the canal, it is characterized by water plazas and fountains. The main underground park-and-ride parking lot is also located in this area.

Each satellite includes four pavilions, two each of two different dimensions: the double structure of type A (168 × 76 m with a total footprint of 12,768 m² and an exhibition area of 6,384 m²) faces onto the park; the two smaller type B buildings (80 × 76 m with a total footprint of 4,560 m² and an exhibition space of 2,280 m²) are situated on the outer side of the transport line. A single satellite has a total footprint of 34,656 m² and 17,320 m² of exhibition space.

3

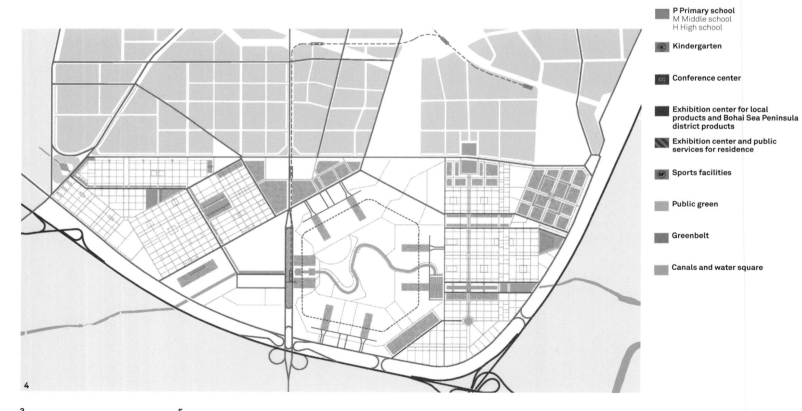

4

Residence: Medium density
max 7 floors
ratio 1.5 m² GFA/m²

Residence: High density
max 20 floors
ratio 2.2 m² GFA/m²

Residence: Special area
max 30 floors - ratio 3 m²
GFA/m²

Residences, office, and service
apartments
ratio 1.5 m² GFA/m²

Office, hotel, and commerce
ratio 2.0/2.5 m² GFA/m²

SOHO: Small Offices, House
Offices, multiservice apartments
ratio 3.0 m² GFA/m²

Office, hotel, and commerce
Special area
ratio 7 m² GFA/m²

Commerce
ratio 2.0 m² GFA/m²

Hotel and residence
ratio 2.5 m² GFA/m²

Facilities, public services, culture,
commerce, entertainment
ratio 2.5 m² GFA/m²

Facilities, public services, culture,
and park
ratio 1.0 m² GFA/m²

Urban Ecological Industry/UEI
ratio 1.5 m² GFA/m²

Entertainment and culture
ratio 1.0 m² GFA/m²

P Primary school
M Middle school
H High school

Ⓚ Kindergarten

CC Conference center

Exhibition center for local
products and Bohai Sea Peninsula
district products

Exhibition center and public
services for residence

SF Sports facilities

Public green

Greenbelt

Canals and water square

3.
Master Pplan: proposed functions

4.
Traffic network and underground
parking system

5.
Water and green spaces

6.
Urban structure

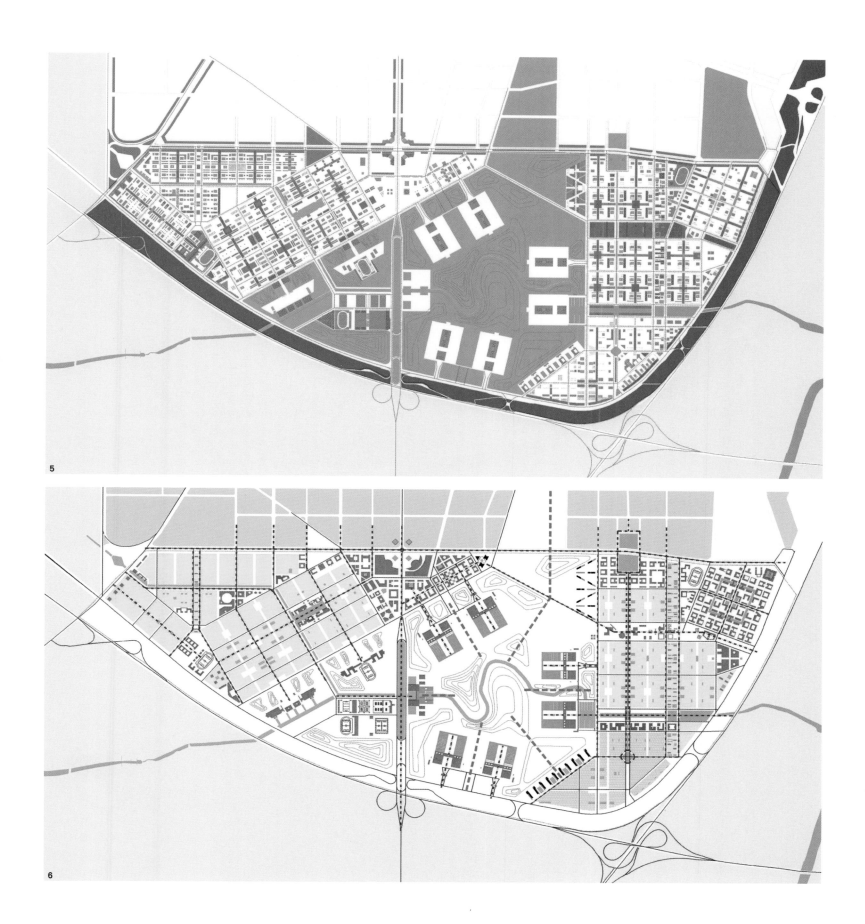

7.
General site plan

8.
The pedestrian and water system:
plan and study sketches of the
squares, avenues, public facilities,
buildings, and spaces

9.
Western business district: plan and
study sketches

10.
Exhibition district: plan and study
sketches

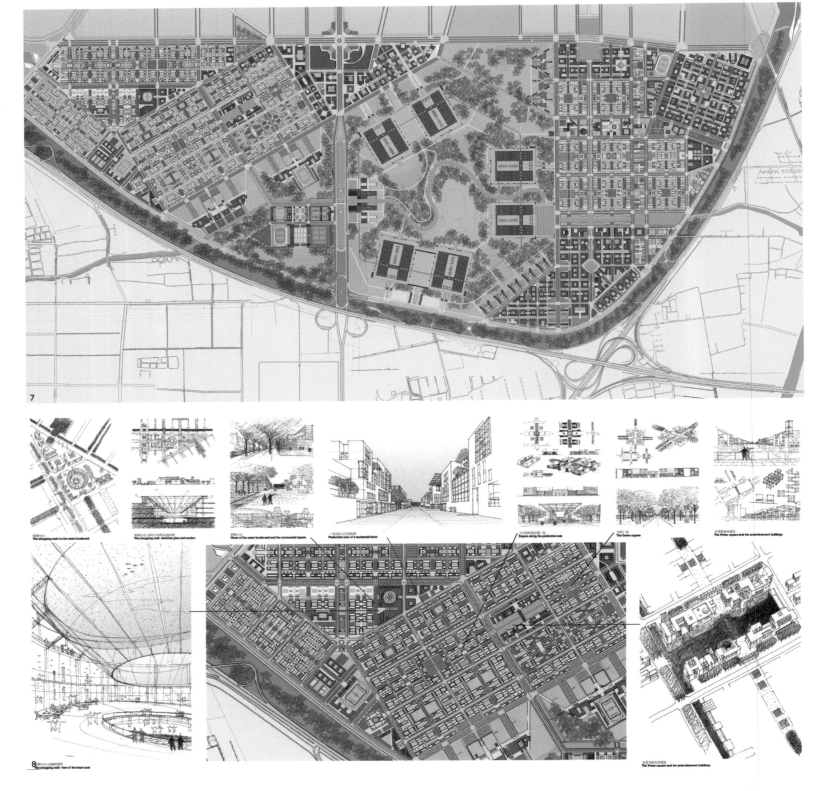

The six satellites together have a total footprint of 207,390 m² and a total of 103,920 m² of exhibition space. Since each pavilion is constructed on the principle of modular extension, they can easily be resized according to requirements, even in terms of different programs of realization based on the phasing of operations.

All pavilions are connected at ground level by a service ring road for trucks. The exhibition area is located on the ground floor. In the courtyard between pavilions, there will be services for the public and meeting rooms.

The smallest pavilions of the four satellites positioned on the eastern and western sides, facing the urban area,

as an alternative to permanent exhibitions, can be used for "urban-oriented" functions: shops, entertainment, cinema and theater, restaurants, and leisure-time activities.

The significant enlargement of the park also allows for outdoor use, such as temporary exhibitions, shows, concerts, and sporting events. The system made up of the pavilions and the park offers a great deal of flexibility in dimensions and use.

Parking for exhibitors is located along the external ring road connecting the satellites. It is also possible to build further underground parking lots for visitors between the pavilions.

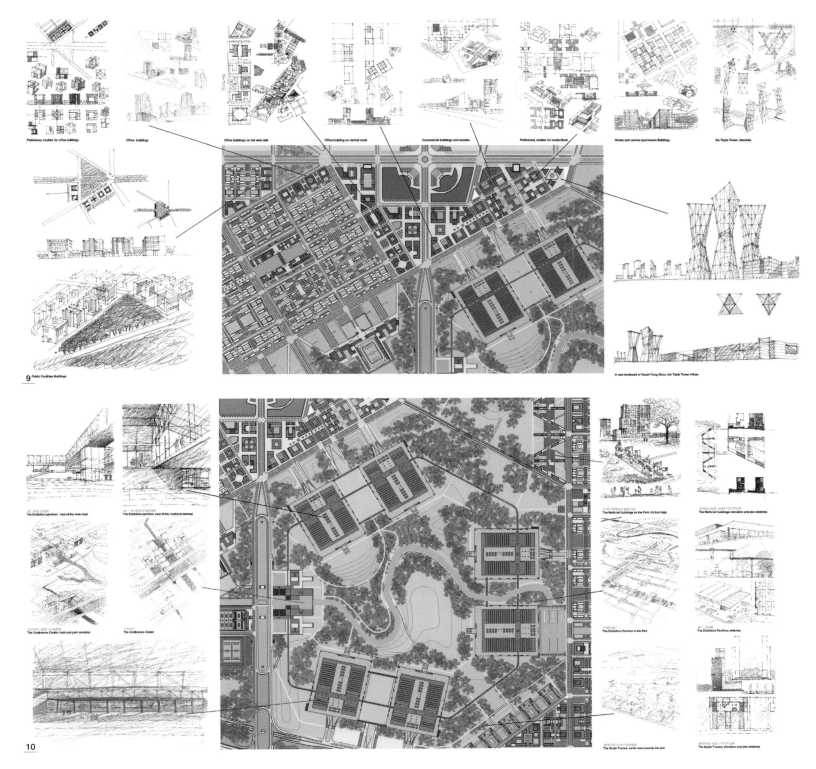

Gregotti Associati International
(A. Cagnardi, V. Gregotti, M. Reginaldi)
Partner:
Tianhua Architecture Planning &
Engineering Limited (X. Huang)
With: I. Chiarel, G. Donato,
G. Gramigna, T. Macchi Cassia,
M. Trovatelli (Associates),
A. Boccacci, C. Calabrese, C. Castello,
B. Medini, M. Parravicini, C. Scortecci,
P. Seria, S. Zauli

The study of the new proposal for the Central Belt is part of the development of the central zone of Pujiang, seven years since the beginning of the building of the city which has now reached an advanced stage.

During these years, the urban area surrounding the new city of Pujiang has been developed through large sections dedicated to highly advanced technological production and new residential quarters. Pujiang can thus be realistically considered the core of a nationwide extended urban-development sector.

The proposal to develop the greenbelt in the current phase allows the combining of those parts of the new city, which have already been built or which are in their final stages, and also the integration of the processes of overall urban development in the area. The goal is to orient the construction of the settlement of Pujiang in a broader perspective, considering the enlargement of the Shanghai catchment area, especially in terms of tertiary and specialist sectors.

The underground railway line that will be running in the short term, the touristic nature of the lake, the network of navigable canals enlarged to cover the whole city, and the existence of a nucleus of functions of excellence on a nationwide scale all strengthen Pujiang's role as an urban hub in the metropolitan area of the Minhang District. This role can be further consolidated when the greenbelt is extended to the banks of the Huangpu, thus opening up a port on the river to allow for a new system of water-based links between Pujiang and the whole Shanghai area.

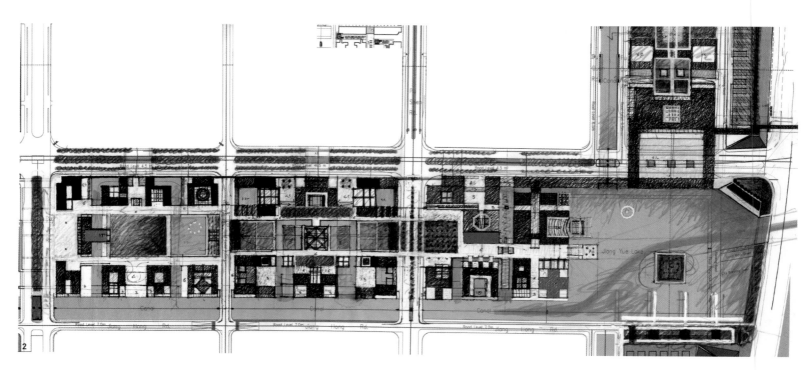

1.
Urban setting of the central
east-west route

2.
Planimetric study sketch of
the morphological layout of
the central axis

3.
Axonometric study sketch
of the plano-altimetric
organisation of the built area
and of the layout of the open
spaces in relation to the lake
and the lateral canals

4.
Study sketches of a public
building

5.
Axonometric study of the
central park area

6.
Study of the staging post on
the lake

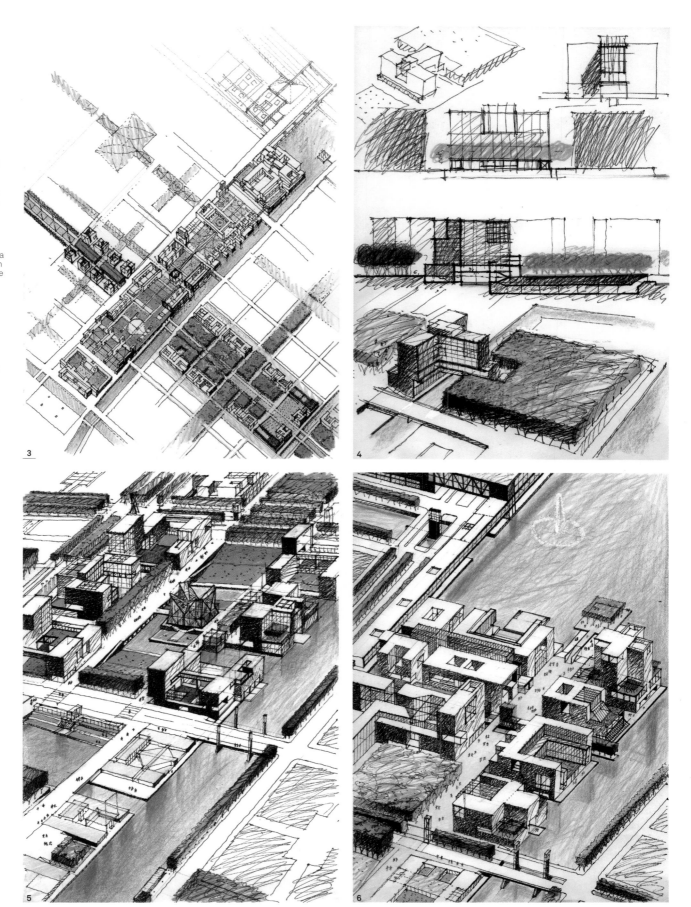

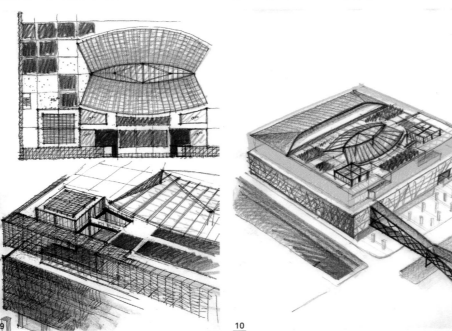

During the development of the general and implemental urban design instruments, increasing importance was given to the intersection of the two main directions: the east–west axis (greenbelt) and the north–south road axis which runs alongside the river, crossing the entire city and linking Pujiang with external areas outside the confines of the new city. This infrastructural intersection is a key element as the main public services, such as the city hall, the courthouse, and educational institutions, are aligned along the north–south route (N5) in the southern part of the greenbelt, up to the large square in the south.

The enlargement of the greenbelt toward the river, next to the service complex along the N5 axis, should be considered the backbone of the whole urban framework of Pujiang.

The new proposal for the Central Belt, involving the first westerly section between Puxing Road and the N5, confirms its general layout, the role already envisioned in the 2001 competition stage, i.e., the heart of functions of excellence for the new city.

In particular, the project for the central axis includes rare functions, such as the complex of buildings dedicated to cultural programs (museum, music, performing arts, exhibitions, etc.), and also the arts center with artists' studios, exhibition spaces, and areas dedicated to the open-air market.

Three different hotel and residence complexes are also envisioned to satisfy the needs of visitors requiring temporary lodgings. The hotels will also cover the needs of tourists attracted by the cultural functions and the environmental quality of the area, represented mainly by the system of waterways—the large lake and the east–west canal (40 m across) that flows into the Huangpu River—as well as the green areas culminating in a large, Italian-style garden. These specific environmental components are characteristic of the enlargement of the settlement with a particular view to the landscape, as well as geographical importance.

The settlement system is organized through a sequence of islands split between the two sides of the central belt: on the northbound side near the residential quarters and on the southbound side near the canal. The center, an area around 100 m long, will contain a park offering various alternatives and attractive elements. On the whole, it will be like a great garden, a meeting place for the entire city.

The buildings are conceived as blocks, open on all sides. This arrangement increases the external views from inside and allows water to be brought into the greenbelt. These internal canals strengthen the idea of "the city on water."

At the side of the Central Belt, a shopping center is being, built which will occupy an entire urban block. This structure will also serve as a spatial bridge and will be where roads leading to the underground station for Shanghai will be separated into pedestrian lanes and vehicle lanes. This can be seen on the western edge of the lake and in the construction being built on the north bank of the Central Belt itself.

7.
Nighttime prospective view of the shopping center from the southeast

8.
View from the southeast of the shopping center being built

9 and 10.
Study sketches of the shopping center

11.
Study sketches of the winter garden at the center of the public park

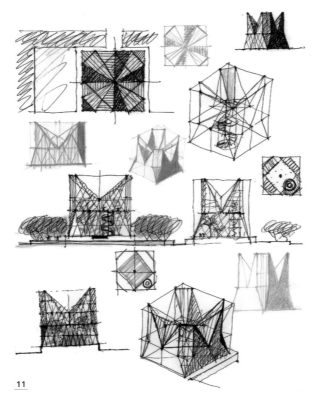

11

12.
Prospective view of the central road from the west

13.
Nighttime prospective view of the central road from the east

14.
Prospective view of the lake

15.
Nighttime prospective view from the southern canal

EUROPE
MODIFICATIONS, REVERSALS, AND SHIFTS

Ich habe den Geist Europas in mich genommen—
nun will ich den Gegenschlag thun!

Friedrich Nietzsche[1]

An "architectural plurality"[2] of projects and completed works distinguishes Gregotti & Associates' activities in Europe from 2008 to 2014. These projects are all linked by the idea of precisely piecing together the fragments that contemporaneity has dispersed across the "posturban horizon."[3] The multiplicity of reference conditions for the cases looked at represents a sample of the current physical characteristics of contexts and possibilities offered by the highly differentiated geocultures that make up the European archipelago: more a cultural identity in crisis than a single continent.

Corresponding to the dissipation of the ancient urban shape in infinite suburban sprawl is the disintegration of the town into spaces contending with geography and history, "virtual environmental bodies"[4] structurally lacking in typology and centrality. Proposing a methodology of urban landscape design based on an idea of recomposition, then, means rebuilding the reciprocal morphological and cultural connections between city and architecture, a dialogue through which to root operations within a sort of Husserlian common language. It is not, however, a "search for a perfect language in European culture,"[5] but rather a restoration of the conditions of a cultural unity through the modification by meaningful parts of the structures of the human-geographical space.

This is why the case studies presented here seem united by a sort of grammar of design thought that includes a component that demonstrates the value of urban and architectural design. Mostly the outcomes of competitions, these projects support the idea that the borders of the discipline of architecture can once again be reestablished in relation to the overall history of European settlement geography, characterized, due to its very origin, by a "plural culture."[6] As well as the general crisis and the uncontrollable phenomenon of globalization, there exists a crisis deriving from the European idea of modernity[7] the same idea that regards even architecture as a social practice—a modernity that was capable of generating modifications, reversals, and shifts, in which "the very will to break away could not be separated from the consideration of the past as the main interlocutor of the new."[8]

This legacy represents the basis for reconfiguring a design methodology that, by opposing the detachment from the context of architecture-turned-design, can reattach the architectural product to the overall urban system, "a connection nonetheless implemented within European culture."[9]

It is the design of open spaces that represents the main unifying feature in the various city-scale projects collected here. The ground, organizing public space, designing green areas, giving new meaning to residual and abandoned areas, and the design of open space are identification tools that define the supporting structure of every modification; they configure, each time, the relationship between architecture and place.

Whether it is defining a new residential settlement scenically situated on the ridge of an urban foothill (the Duranne), taking on a technical-functional theme in a bus station in the heart of Aix-en-Provence as an artificial reinterpretation of the hill of Mont Perrin, or transforming a former industrial area into an urban hub (Terminal Nord), the ground design coincides with a settlement principle. That seems obvious even in the case of the vast, high-altitude square of "Trento Nord," which, by introducing a new scale of relations, reorganizes the functional and landscape relationships between the railway area, the historical city, and the imposing relief.

An analogous significance is assumed by the Langhirano urban regeneration plan, an example of a more reduced but equally important scale in terms of the expression of a working method, as well as an idea of a city.

In the case of the competition project for the new capitol in Rome, the design of open space assumes the value of a mold for the settlement: a system of public spaces reorganizes the environmental morphology of the area in relation to the Roman archaeological stratum.

The Research Tower in Padua perhaps represents the borderline case of this approach. Being a point of reference for a vast, fragmented industrial area anchored only to the road infrastructure, it transforms the indifferent *terrain vague* into a supporting surface, a base fabric that anchors the tall building entrusted with measuring element between new urban expansion and the historic city center.

In tackling individual buildings, the design methodology rests upon the dialectic between distinction and commensurability. Each case establishes an architectural specificity that, without mimetic or "contextualist" deviations, identifies the places with a language of its own, interpreting the human-geographical traces and signs. Proportionality, therefore, acts through the new to confer identity and institutional value on the preexisting.

A particularly important case in this sense is the Pirelli Headquarters RE 2. The completion of the so-called "Pirelli enclosure" in the Bicocca urban hub in Milan is a chance to build a complex micro-landscape, which, through ground design and the organization of green areas on various levels, fixes the organic sediment of the new building and solidifies its external faces toward the regulatory layout of the city itself. The architecture distinguishes itself morphologically and, at the same time, redefines its relationship with revived structures (the old factories converted into a university), the fifteenth-century building of the Bicocca degli Arcimboldi and the cube of Pirelli Headquarters RE 1.

The archaeological approach of critical commensuration between new construction and the history of places, transcribed in the architectural forms of an urban bastion, can also be seen in the plans to convert the Florentine Fortezza da Basso as an exhibition and conference center, Milan's Ex Cavallerizza into a library, and ancient villas into the plaster cast gallery of Italian sculptures.

A third group of projects is represented by the plans for the area around Paris and the area to the east of Turin: a human geography based on cities, on plans broken up by suburban sprawl in the outskirts, but still considered persistent historical urban forms, cornerstones on which to anchor the new regulating designs of urban development and the capital functions introduced by the plans.

But the relationship between distinction and commensurability can also be developed in an interior architecture. The work carried out on the Sala degli Scarlioni in Milan's Sforza Castle is a theme of symbolic value, which adheres to an ideal cultural continuity with the BBPR studio, responsible for the shift in modern heritage in terms of its relationship with the "preexisting environment."[10] The reorganization project based on the interpretation of the historic outfitting of 1952 offers a chance to take stock: the last possible variation of the relationship between "project and destiny."[11]

1   I have taken into myself the spirito of Europe—now I shall make a counterattack!, Nietzsche, F., *Aurora e Frammenti postumi 1879–1881*,8 [77], Adelphi, Milan, 1964.
2   Rykwert, J., *Europe and its Mongrel Architecture*, in *Rassegna* 76, The European Archipelago-1998 p. 65–67.
3   Choay, F., *L'orizzonte del posturbano*, edited by D'Alfonso, E., Officina Edizioni, Rome, 1992 and Webber, M., *The Post-City Age*, in *Daedalus: The Journal of American Academy of Arts and Sciences*, vol. 97 no. 4, 1968, pp. 1091–1110.
4   Purini, F., *Virtual enviromental bodies*, in *Casabella* no. 597–598, January–February 1993, pp. 80–83 and 125.
5   Eco, U., *The Search for the Perfect Language (The Making of Europe)*, Blackwell Publishing, Oxford, 1997.
6   Diderot, D., *Encyclopédie*, 1750–1765.
7   See the well-known reasoning from Edmund Husserl's conference (1935), published in id. *Crisi e rinascita della cultura europea*, edited by Cristin R., Marsilio, Venice, 1999.
8   Gregotti, V., *L'identità dell'architettura europea e la sua crisi*, Einaudi, Turin, 1999.
9   Gregotti, V., op. cit.
10 Rogers, E.N., *Le preesistenze ambientali e i temi pratici contemporanei*, in *Casabella-Continuità*, no. 204, February–March 1954.
11 Argan, G.C, *Progetto e destino*, Il Saggiatore, Milan, 1965.

Bird's-eye view of the Research Tower, Padua. International competition, first prize (2008).

Gregotti Associati International
(A. Cagnardi, V. Gregotti, M. Reginaldi)
Partner:
Architecture: CFL
Landscape design:
Michel Corajoud and Yannick Salliot
Engineering: IOSIS
Sustainability project: ELIOTH
With: P. E. Colao, M. Trovatelli
(Associates), C. Castello, B. Colombo,
S. Grande, M. Parravicini, C. Scortecci

The settlement principle of the new urban center represents an alternative to the sprawl typical of the furthest outskirts of European cities in recent times. The two structural elements of the project are the plan of the ground and of the open space, in the double meaning of the new settlement's role in the landscape and the view over the landscape as a qualitative attribute of the settlement.

These two principles presuppose critical attention not only regarding the social and geographical context in its current condition, but also in relation to the history of the region's best settlements and, in general, of the different ways of being to be found in the dense network of small conurbations of Europe's town tradition and the life of its citizens. This includes the problem of reopening the new center, which is socially and functionally highly mixed and a fundamental element in urban life, as the example of Aix-en-Provence demonstrates. The overall image for those driving along the road linking it to the city will appear as a strongly unifying element even in the arrangement of the buildings making it up, as many ancient towns located in elevated positions do.

The ground plan and public space are integrated by the new access system, from the design of the internal and surrounding open spaces to the residential buildings, the parts laid out to connect with the existing built area, the constitution of the central place, the strategy for the location and choice of public services, and the design of the outside edges.

The most important part of the new settlement is made up of a double row of architectural elements of 44 × 44 m in a U shape. Laid out in different positions and aligned in a north–south direction, the buildings are located at a height of between 20 and 40 m above the existing access road. An elongated central space about 60 m wide is thus formed in two stretches of 380 m to the north and 280 m to the south, divided by a central hill (where the open-air theater is located), placed at the center of the east–west axis which extends to connect with a part of the existing settlement and to the east with a pedestrian street leading to a traffice circle located on the main access road (D543).

The central public space itself is organized on two levels: the first, lowered to the east, forms an internal road with shops and services on both sides; the second, 5 m above the first, forms an oblong square with overlooking housing.

The buildings that define the settlement to the east are detached from each other so that the landscape toward the city of Aix-en-Provence and the mountains can be seen from the square.

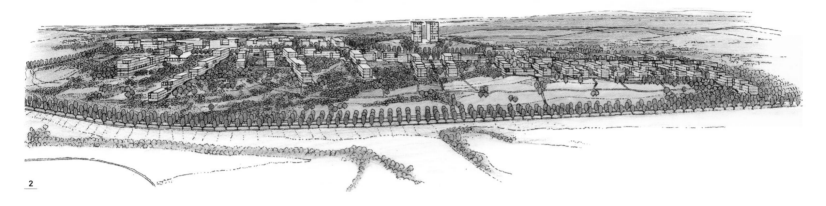

2

1.
Territorial setting. Top right, Aix-en-Provence old town.

2.
General view from the west

3.
General plan of the new settlement system

None of the planned buildings stand more than three stories above the level of the square, which falls away in the east and rises in the west following the lay of the land. They are envisioned with terraced roofing suitable for trellised arbors, with a considerable overhang to protect from the sun, while stairways and elevators are planned sloping down toward the south, supporting the buildings' solar panels.

To the south where the landscape is more open with greater relief, a series of three linear buildings will extend downhill. The last of these, a hotel, forms an alignment with a building to the west as a gateway for those arriving from the south to reach the large traffic circle.

Next to that, as a southern terminal element to the large elongated square, will be positioned the Duranne town hall. To the north, on the opposite side, there will be a small church and a large structure for public services, including a multifunctional hall, a library, exhibition halls, and other cultural resources of the area.

The center of the new Duranne also posed the problem of its connection with the existing city. While in the southwestern area of the new consolidated center, around

3

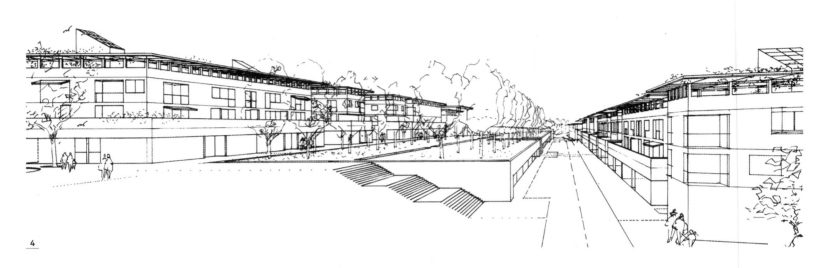

4

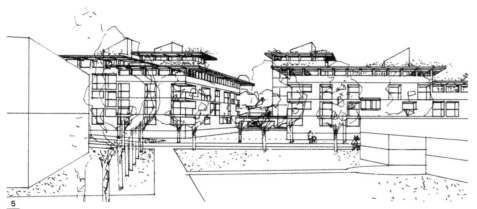

5

the school, will be a series of settlements that are directly connected to the existing built-up area right along the quarter's main east–west road, two green spaces to the east and in the middle connect the new and the existing cities.

Three pedestrian crossings will pass over or under the D543, providing a southern link for cyclists and pedestrians to the large park east of the central nucleus. They are delimited by the northeastern settlements and the green space in the southeast. Beyond that, a vast sports facility is planned, augmenting the existing ones. The central area of the thalweg has an analogous role of connecting the nuclei, which have already been built and those still to be completed with the new center.

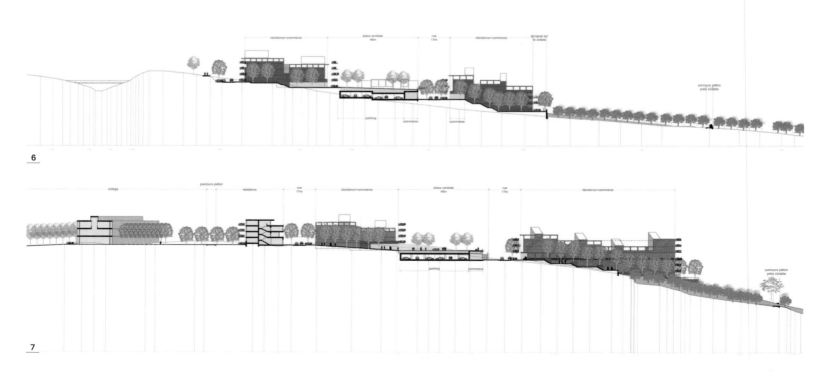

6

7

Gregotti Associati International
(A. Cagnardi, V. Gregotti, M. Reginaldi)
Partner:
Structural project and plant
engineering: ITE Partenaires,
Landscape design: Land srl
Transport and traffic: Centro Studi
Traffico (P. Gemini)
H.Q.E. Certification: Oasiis
With: P. E. Colao, M. Destefanis,
T. Macchi Cassia (Associates),
C. Castello, E. Lucchini-Gabriolo,
B. Medini

1.
Study sketch of the typical section of
the roof in relation to the hill
2.
Planovolumetry of integration into
the urban context
3 and 4.
Study sketches of the relationship
between the new building and the
city: the restaurant on Place Joret
and the offices on El Sadate Square

This project sees a technical-functional theme—a
bus station—as an opportunity for urban architecture.
In particular, even though it fulfills the technical requisites
of the competition, the building and the proposed external
arrangement are based on the idea of integration with the
other buildings and public, tertiary, cultural, exchange, and
infrastructural functions that characterize the city center,
including the railway station and parking lots.

The idea of reclaiming an important architectural
and urban benchmark role for this special infrastructure
is reinforced by the fact that it is located in a place
characterized by the presence of an important boulevard
linking the city center with the western suburbs and by a
hill that is an important landscape feature, penetrating the
otherwise solid urban fabric.

The proposed Gare Routière is indeed an element that
will fit into the existing system of urban public spaces
around it. In particular, the reestablishment of the southern
part of the hill as a screen of vegetation and an integral
part of the boulevard is expressed by the roof of the new
building, which includes an observation deck facing north
toward the housing. The elongated building has two ends,
important urban elements that redefine the place, today
characterized by heterogeneous elements (the heights
of buildings, different functions, differentiated roles
organized on the grid of the historical city), a specificity that
is reflected in the unitary but autonomous architecture,
one tertiary and the other connected with leisure
(restaurant). In the same way, the "hall of lost footsteps,"
which interprets the urban plan as a paved square, and
the system of pathways tracing the relationship between

distribution within the building and crossing the city (roads
and footpaths) are also elements that support the idea of
a station as a civic monument of the city, sensitive to the
identity of its particular built environment.

In consideration of the special relief characteristics
of the site—the green hill in the middle of the city—the
project idea is based on the principle of building an organic
relationship and a relationship of continuity with it, and this
forms the starting point of all the architectural and urban
settlement decisions. Considering the difference in altitude
between the hill and the level of the city, the actual function
of the exchange hub represented by the station is assigned
to the large roof, planned as an ideal extension of the hill
itself, the so-called Mont Perrin.

To the east the project proposal envisions a building
defined as the traffice circle El Sadate, destined for public
administration offices, which is in harmony with the heights
of the existing buildings around it. The construction is
formed from two sheets running one on top of the other
toward the north, which are developed as unitary but
autonomous elements and identify the system of great
access portals for vehicles coming into the station, as well
as the main access to the public offices and the pedestrian
entrance to the hall of lost footsteps.

To the west, the traffice circle Joret is redefined by the
presence of a second building for use as a restaurant, as
requested by the competition program. This building has
a largely free floor plan, with a height proportional to the
existing buildings around it, especially the nursery school,
the police station, and the Méjanes library, in a central
position along the visual axis of Avenue de l'Europe.

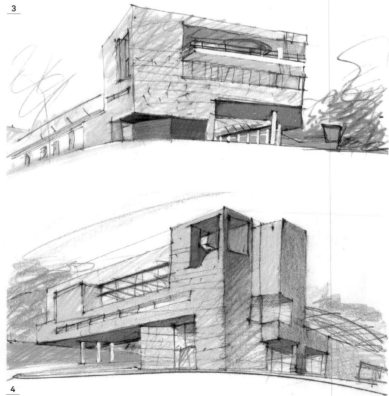

5

In this case, the building is made up of a sheet at right angles to the hill, which it is aligned, by means of a projection that integrates and leaves open to view the natural connecting movement between the hill itself and the city, thus distancing itself from the existing housing around it.

The base of the building is arranged from a cutting that emphasizes the main entrance and the public access route to the bus station. The use of broad glazed surfaces acts as a marker: a large loggia-patio situated on the top floor highlights the public-service value of the building.

The station roof is the morphological and connecting element between the two ends, as well as the link between the different heights of the site.

On the north side of the building, the relationship between the hill and the city is identified by means of the layout of the station's main public spaces: the hall of lost footsteps, the arcade linking the bus bays and the travelers' arcade.

The morphological structure of this side of the building redefines the urban value of Boulevard Coq, forming the station square with pedestrian and vehicle access routes.

In order to express the image of public urban architecture, the building will be entirely clad in stone with warm tones unifying the surfaces, tones typical of the building tradition of Aix-en-Provence. The sense of unity given by the material lends the building a certain natural monumentality, which is reiterated inside to underline its public value. The light, transparent roof, in continuity with the hill, represents an element of counterpoint. It is made up of a structural framework in iron and glass that had been integrated with a photovoltaic film, giving it the classic green color of stations, and also emphasizing its belonging to the hill and to the natural geography of the site in general.

5.
Northerly view

6.
View of the western end (public administration offices) overlooking traffic circle El Sadate

7.
View of the car hall

8.
The hall of lost footsteps with passenger services

Gregotti Associati International
(A. Cagnardi, V. Gregotti, M. Reginaldi)
With: P. E. Colao (Associate),
B. Colombo, C. Scortecci
Sociological analysis: G. Martinotti
Landscape design: M. Corajoud

In the context of the "ten projects for Paris" initiative promoted by Prime Minister Sarkozy in 2009, the Gregotti Associati studio was invited by the Minister of Ecology, Sustainable Development, and Energy to offer an eleventh proposal.

Paris, together with London, is one of the great European metropolises, but, unlike London, its relationship with the surrounding area of the Île-de-France (and even up to the North Sea for some) is rather more complex and interactive, even though the polycentric hypotheses of the last ten years have been hindered by the very history of the centrality of the city. Moreover, the *villes nouvelles* themselves today seem like a form of urban enlargement.

For all this, the development and strategic relationship of public transport, both aboveground and underground, as a structure essential to the life of the city, is inevitable.

The expansion envisions to the northwest along the Seine, toward Roissy Airport, the easterly expansion, now consolidated, of Marne-la-Vallée, and the future structuring of Saclay and at Orly Airport to the south only go toward consolidating the city's centrality.

As well as the considerations of the general proposals, eight projects have been selected as examples, and another eight in specific points where an in-depth study has been carried out.

The first is that at the center of the Arassey site and its vocation for research and the university; the second is that of Bourget-Roissy and its reconnection with the city; the third is the Défense and its relationship with Paris's two airports.

For the projects in the city of Paris there are, among others, the linear park of Saint-Denis, the densification of some Grands Ensembles, the proposals for the rationalization of some of the big railway termini, and the proposals for the tidying up of some big historical fortifications, such as Noisy.

The need to coordinate the presence of its six rivers in a system of settlement opportunities has also been emphasized.

1.
General setting: the greenbelt and the project area

2.
Project zone 3: Montesson–La Défense

3.
Setting of the ONIs (Operations of National Interest)

4.
Project zone 4 Paris: intramuros–première couronne

5.
Project zone 5 Paris: intramuros–première couronne

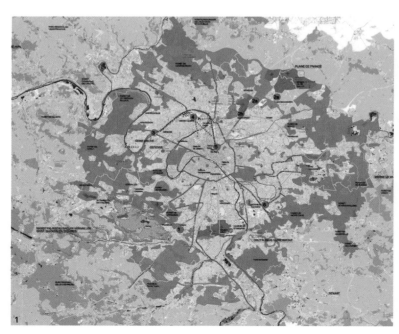

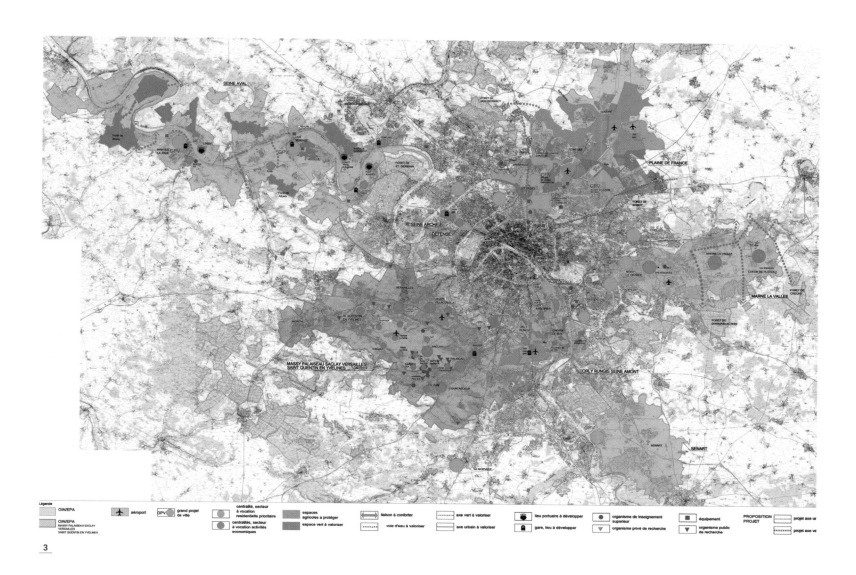

3

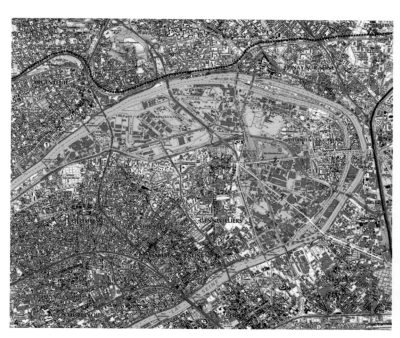

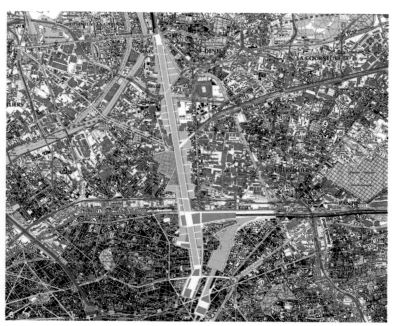

UDINE, ITALY
TERMINAL NORD BUSINESS PARK AND PLAN TO TRANSFORM THE FORMER BERTOLI STEELWORKS AREA
2008–2013

Gregotti Associati International
(A. Cagnardi, V. Gregotti)
With: C. Calligaris, I. Chiarel,
M. Destefanis, G. Gramegna,
T. Macchi Cassia, C. Pirola,
M. Trovatelli (Associates), R. Bonomi,
C. Castello, G. A. Giannoccari,
B. Medini, J. Muzio, P. Ronchi,
C. Scortecci, S. Wenzel
Structural project: ENCO Engineering
Consulting
Plant engineering and
technological network: P.En.T.A. srl,
S.T.I. Engineering srl,
Work management: L. Celè

The Terminal Nord business park is situated in the area once occupied by the Bertoli steelworks, located along Via Tricesimo, the main commercial route, heading northward from the center of Udine for 17 km, which over the past twenty years has modified the settlement situation of the city and the surrounding towns, attracting to the area the most extensive commercial presence in the Friuli region.

The transformation of this former industrial area represents an opportunity for modification of the territory in the sense of urban addition, a new center made up of services, offices, housing, recreational, and commercial activities.

The project to change the function of the area from industrial to executive-residential, for the characteristics of the program and the dimensions and morphological consistency of the new settlement, aims to repair the settlement situation of the existing urban fabric. The general planimetric configuration of the intervention has a simple design, organized into distinct and recognizable functional parts, connoted by a sequence of interconnected public spaces, marked by precise architectural references, in sequence along the network of pedestrian routes which guarantee access to the internal areas. In relation to its surroundings, mainly due to the extensive road network, the morphological and volumetric organization is reinforced at the edges according to a well-defined curtain, while the architectural image of large scale is underlined by an extensive curvilinear building that organizes the activities of the business park.

The recovery plan was composed for buildings able to strongly suggest the future development of the whole

1.
Urban setting

2.
General plan of the project.
The settlement principle is based on a system of public pedestrian spaces, which give structure to the new multifunctional urban fabric.

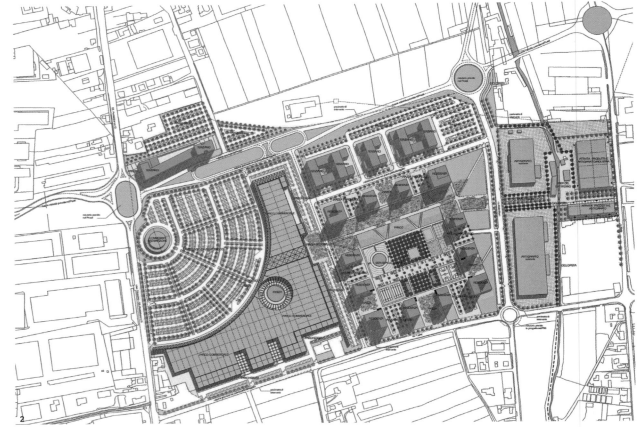

3.
General bird's-eye view. Foreground, the circular restaurant and the 33,000-m² shopping center with square and parking lots.

4.
General view from the east (rendering)

5.
View of the circular-arch bus shelter of the shopping center, which extends for 400 m. In the background, tertiary buildings.

6

7

8

6.
Partial view of the large square/
parking lot. On the left, tertiary
building. In the background, the
signage framework (site photo).

7.
Eastern end of the tertiary building
on the square/parking lot

8.
Study sketch of the signage
framework

9.
View of the bank headquarters
located at the northwest corner of
the business park

10.
View of the entrance area of the
shopping center's covered circular
square

11
View of the shopping center bus shelter

12 and 13.
Views of the covered circular square

14.
View of one of the distribution spaces inside the shopping center

surrounding area of the intervention. All these elements together, organized according to a principle of linear alignment oriented along the east–west road, envisions a circular restaurant building at the Via Tricesimo crossroads, surmounted by a metal structure for displaying luminous signs; a commercial complex delimiting the parking area; a circular central square; a park and the green pedestrian crossing route punctuated by four fifteen-story towers; the residential blocks around the edge of the park; the rows of buildings for offices and services along the north edge of the new road established by the plan; the paths and green routes joining the service areas in the former Battiferro area; and the craftworks next to the ditch on the eastern edge.

The Terminal Nord business park, the first realization of the general plan for the area, constitutes the entire northwest face of the area and determines its dominant architectural image due to its greater visibility in relation to the main access roads. With a 400-m diameter arch and the unusual cross section of its facade, the awning of the main commercial building creates an opening onto a geographical perception of a visual field that extends from the buildings toward the mountains in the background. In the urban context of Udine, this curvilinear morphological device describes a new figure, a topographically important place on the crossroads between the two main transport routes. This 33,000-m² mat building for commercial activities is organized according to a single cross section with a depth of 8 m around its whole 400-m semicircular extent. It is crossed in a single place to give access to the 40-m diameter circular square, covered by a funnel-shaped structure, which is glazed and has no central support, so as to seem suspended above water. The covered square is an explicit evocation of the loggias of the markets, which can be found in the historic center of many Italian cities.

The semicircular awning of the covered square, the shopping arcade, and the green square that the tree-lined path of the central park leads out from are strongly urban in character, thus avoiding the architectural indifference often encountered in many kinds of contemporary open-air commercial structures.

Gregotti Associati International
(A. Cagnardi, V. Gregotti)
With: T. Macchi Cassia, C. Pirola
(Associates), F. Campello, S. Ferrari,
B. Medini, J. Muzio, P. Ronchi
Structural project: S.C.E.
Electrical project: Studio tecnico
P.I.G. De Stefani
Mechanical project: DIGIERRE 3

The new headquarters of the Pirelli Group are located in a complex covering an area of 70,000 m² at the northern edge of the area of the Bicocca in Milan, once headquarters of the Pirelli firm. In this area, which also contains the fifteenth-century building of the Bicocca degli Arcimboldi, the Pirelli Tire Research Center, and the building for services and offices named 143, a planning consideration was developed on the theme of enclosures, since the area is destined to bring together various architectural presences linked with the industrial group.

For the headquarters of Pirelli Real Estate, which covers a total area of 26,000 m², a location between Via Bicocca degli Arcimboldi and Via Piero e Alberto Pirelli was chosen.

The building, named Headquarters 2, completes the first cubic block (with a footprint of 14,000 m²), built around the former cooling tower of the old industrial complex.

The planning and architectural decision to salvage and rebuild the entire zone and its buildings was made by identifying what exists and testifies to that continuity of

activity and production, which historically built this specific work environment in the area. According to this structuring, the project was developed to complete the headquarters of the Prelios company. The project preserves the existing road layout within the complex and develops the open spaces, increasing the presence of greenery.

Headquarters 2 consists morphologically of a building shaped like an upside-down L aligned with the building named 134 and next to the extension of the block with a garden that makes up the ground floor of the services of Headquarters 1. The new block, with an overall footprint of 12,000 m², thus describes the edge of Bicocca degli Arcimboldi park, which it redefines by enlarging it. The volumetric configuration of Headquarters 2 constitutes the completion of the basement on which the cubic form of Headquarters 1 rests, but without altering the latter's strong image.

The inverted L-shaped body is completely glazed in the direction of the park so as to guarantee a view from the offices. The northerly, easterly, and westerly faces, on the other hand, are covered with anthracite gray plates of grès, very similar to the first block.

The new building consists of two underground floors, a ground floor, and five floors aboveground. On the underground floors are located the central systems, parking lot (181 spaces for cars, including 4 disabled spaces, and 90 spaces for motorcycles), and storerooms, with no offices. The two parking-lot levels are subdivided into two fireproof compartments and are served by a two-way ramp with access from the private road within the complex; the parking lot can be reached on foot via stairways and elevators within the building.

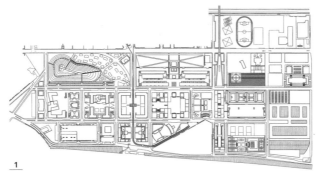

1

1.
Position of Bicocca area

2.
Plan of the ground floor.
Left, gray: Pirelli RE 1 Headquarters

3, 4, 5, and 6.
Planimetric sketches of the layout of the various levels, from the parking-lot level to the third floor, relative to Headquarters 1 and the park of the fifteenth-century villa Bicocca degli Arcimboldi

7.
View northward from Headquarters 1. On the right, the old Pirelli industries building reclaimed as seat of the university's faculty of humanities.

8.
View toward the south: in the background, Headquarters 1, and on the right, hidden by vegetation, the fifteenth-century villa

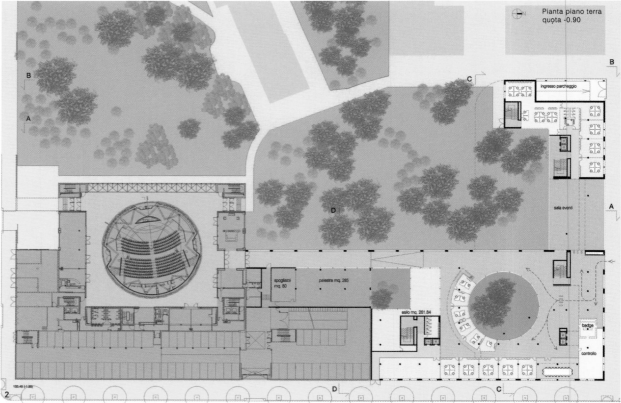

2

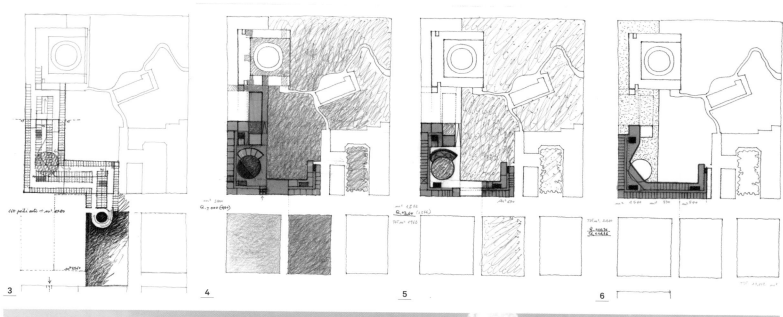

3

4

5

6

7

8

9

10

11

12

On the ground floor is located the double-height entrance hall, common to the two blocks. The hall is characterized by the presence of two large patios with plants: the first, round and glazed, lets light into the building near the elevators and the computer labs; the second, rectangular and similarly glazed on three sides, delimits the company crèche within the building and the connecting passage between the two parts of the headquarters complex.

The ground floor, with a public entrance at the same level as the ground outside, has a reception, a waiting room, bathrooms, computer labs, and a local storeroom. The ample triple-height waiting room is glazed on the north and south sides, thus creating a view of Arcimboldi Park from the overlooking street within the complex.

The five aboveground floors house computer labs, meeting rooms, waiting rooms, smoking rooms, break areas, terraces with greenery, toilets, and local storerooms.

The southern face of the aboveground floors is characterized by an interactive high-tech curtain wall facade, which faces onto Bicocca Park; the other faces, in continuity with the external finish of Headquarters 1, consist of windows alternating with insulated walls.

The flat roof, accessible from the technical area on the fifth floor, houses ventilation for the stairs and technical shafts.

9, 10, 11, and 12.
Study sketches: the northern face with main entrance and pond; general axonometric view of the Pirelli complex from the north and from the south

13.
Overall view from the southwest, inside the so-called "Pirelli enclosure"

14.
Bird's-eye views of the general model from the northeast and southeast

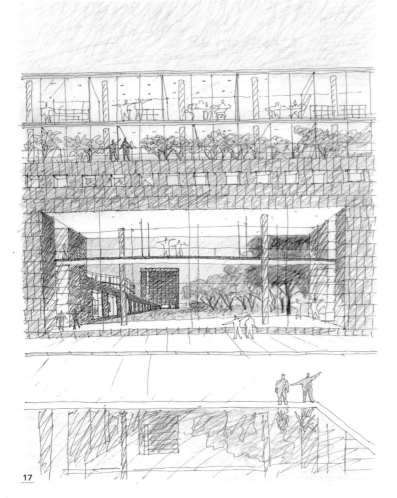

15.
View facing south from the
entrance hall. In the background,
Headquarters 1.

16.
The three-stcry waiting hall

17 and 18.
Study sketches of the entrance hall
and circular patio

19.
General view from the south. To the right, the faculty of humanities building of Bicocca University.

20.
General view from the northeast corner. In the background, to the left, the cubical form of Headquarters 1.

21.
View from the north. In the center the entrance hall glazed on the north and south faces. In the background, Headquarters 1. To the left, the humanities department of Bicocca University (reconverted industrial building).

22.
View of the entrance hall looking toward the circular patio

FEASIBILITY STUDY FOR THE REORGANIZATION OF THE FORTEZZA DA BASSO
2013

Gregotti Associati International
(A. Cagnardi, V. Gregotti)
With: G. Gramegna, G. Donato
(Associates), C. Scortecci,
M. Parravicini
Plant engineering: Manens-Tifs

The feasibility study for the reuse of the Fortezza da Basso, for fairs and conferences is based on the principle of reconstructing the density of the settlements, which, right from the beginning, has been a characteristic of the area within the city walls, according to a building practice based on an idea of measured densification. The project translates this principle into a series of new areas regulated by the geometry of the fortifications, as a form of completion consistent with the nature of the historic buildings around it. The structure of the building, being characterized by ordinary architecture, has managed over the centuries to interact with the monument that is the renaissance fort, built according to Antonio da Sangallo's design in the 1530s to discourage anti-Medici rebellions, a citadel that right from the start has always had multiple uses. Since the middle of the eighteenth century,

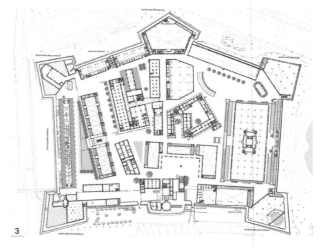

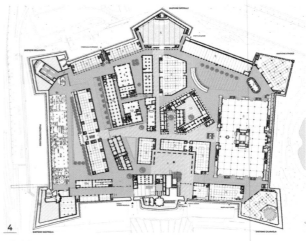

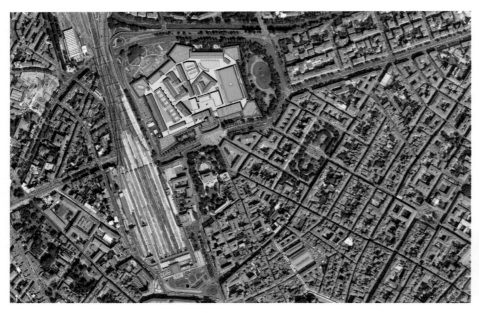

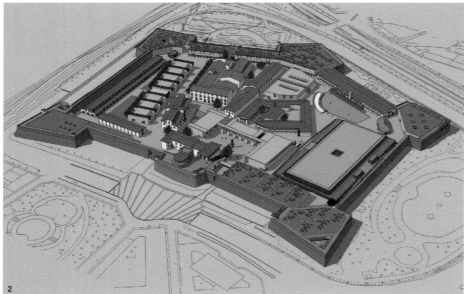

1.
Urban setting

2.
Aerial view of the salvage project from the southeast. The new pavilions are shown in gray.

3.
First-floor plan

4.
Ground-floor plan

5.
View of the entrance square

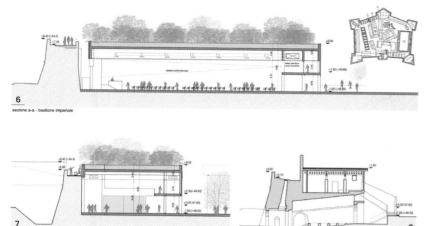

6
sezione a-a - bastione imperiale

7
sezione b-b

8
sezione c-c - edificio casamatta

9

6, 7, and 8.
Typical sections of the multifunctional space of the northern walls and central ravelin

9.
View of the eastwest axis

the fortress has been largely demilitarized and has been used for manufacturing, craftsmen's workshops, housing for poor families, and a correctional institution. In 1865, the building of Poggi's relief roads along the foundations of the demolished city walls introduced a system of connecting gardens around the fortress. Since 1967 it has been entrusted to the Mostra dell'Artigianato, which built a new pavilion in 1976, introducing a marked leap in scale from that of the existing buildings. Even today it represents a heteronomous presence difficult to relate to the fragmented set of buildings, which, though modified over time, represent a substratum of historical reference. The Strategic Environmental Assessment, which is the reference document that the feasibility study for the reorganization of the fortress was devised on the basis of, nonetheless holds the 1976 pavilion to be neither demolishable nor modifiable.

The plan for overall reorganization in three successive stages also includes the clearing up of the open spaces randomly situated within the walls, concentrating them in three large areas (about 1,500 m² each), suitable for fairs and outdoor events, one of which coincides with the area of the main entrance.

A covered passageway connecting the Arsenal-Basilica and orderly room group of buildings with the Lorraine Theater is envisioned within the walls.

This idea of reorganizing all the internal spaces of the fortress satisfies the need to increase the exhibition area within the framework of a more rational reorganization of the available space, which will thus increase from 50,000 m² to 74,000 m², including a large space for conferences or concerts with capacity for 2,000 people, also usable as exhibition space.

As for the processes of figuration of the new buildings, they must be built with particular care, so that the magnificence of Sangallo's architecture, the profile of ordinary building work of the existing historic buildings, and the need to lend the new fairs an image of clarity and solidity compared with the urban density of the finished whole are given adequate consideration.

This operational principle is completed by the individual and collective layout of the internal flooring (c. 33,000 m²), to be made from blocks of porphyry so as to contribute to the unity of the whole and an ordered use of the internal green spaces, as well as the extension, where possible, of the green areas on the roofs of the new buildings along the walls (green that can be walked on, or not, as the case may be), which in turn should respect the visibility of the internal part of the especially restored Renaissance walls.

The new buildings, which are to be faced with pietra serena, have first and foremost the function of reconstructing, where possible, an ordered interior facade to the fortification walls, both to the north and the south.

The three new central buildings proposed (with a total area of 24,000 m²) have various urban functions: completion to the north and definition to the south of a square forming the entrance to and delimiting the area designated for the fairs toward that of the so-called "semiprecious stone works" (workshops where works of art are restored and conserved), whose independence should be emphasized. In this latest new pavilion an underground floor is also envisioned with its own access ramp for goods. Staff will have their own entrance, separate from the rest, and their own reserved parking or maneuvring area, while external and service access will be together.

The main service entrance is located in the southwest area, near the outside parking area, on the west side. Inside, in the southwest corner, beneath the existing green area, will be parking for light goods vehicles and general warehouses, and the already existing management offices will be extended and reorganized (in the former town theater storeroom building, now partly a storeroom for the building to be restored).

Underneath the northwest corner will be located the general systems control unit. In both the northwest and southwest corners the overlying vegetation will be reconstructed.

The southeast gate has been chosen for entry by the public, also because of the future tram stop. Next to this the Cavaniglia Pavilion will be restored with the reorganization of the southeast corner and the archaeological remains found there. At the side of the pavilion next to the entrance will be located the entry services and the ticket office.

Among the general rules of the project, it has been decided not to exceed the height of the walls at the edges, to reconstruct the continuity of the walkway along the walls and to use a 4 × 4-m module for the new pavilions, a net internal height of 6.5 m and a net minimum height of 3.5 m. Every pavilion will have natural light, from above where possible.

To the left of the entrance there is also the possibility of a separate use for visiting the central pavilion; this could also allow tourists to walk the walls, independently or in connection with events.

BRERA NEWSPAPER LIBRARY AT EX CAVALLERIZZA
1998–2012

Gregotti Associati International
(A. Cagnardi, V. Gregotti)
Partner: F. Maffeis
With: A. Aschieri, N. Bignardi
Structural project: Bosi
Plant engineering:
Manens Intertecnica

The Newspaper Library project of the National Library of Brera, Milan, concerns the historical building known as Ex Cavallerizza situated in the Porta Vittoria area next to the city center. The main building of the project is a large building in an eclectic style, not of particular monumental value but with characteristic architectural features to be preserved externally and a vast space inside, which lends itself well to public use.

The first part of the work carried out consisted in the focused restoration and recovery of the structure and fixtures of the preexisting building to bring it in line with the needs of the new library.

Once the historic shell had been restored, the perception of the great internal space was kept unified, moving back the platforms from the plane surfaces and the perimeter windows. The new fixtures were also installed in accordance with the original structure,

thanks to their distribution under the floor and in the false ceiling.

The internal space was reorganized on four levels: two belowground for the archives and two aboveground for services, reading, and consultation.

The building also opens onto a courtyard partly occupied by a house that was in a bad state of repair. This will be used for the offices and has been radically modified and joined to the newspaper library by a glass structure, which also houses the main entrance. The reception area leads on to the various sections, including the large reading room on the upper floor. On the mezzanine is a conference hall with one hundred seats; it can be subdivided and has a separate entrance so that if necessary it can be used autonomously.

The overall floor area of the project is 4,820 m². The newspaper library boasts around 13,000 m of shelving.

1.
Transverse perspective section: the two preexisting buildings salvaged are linked by a central entrance and distribution block

2.
Longitudinal perspective section of the new area within the envelope of the Ex Cavallerizza

3.
View of the three-dimensional model: the envelope of the Ex Cavallerizza has been sectioned to give a view of the interior space

4.
View of the entrance area connecting the two salvaged buildings

5.
Internal view of the distribution space on the first floor

6, 7, 8, and 9.
General plan of the various levels, from the basement to the second floor

10.
Internal view of the reading room on the ground floor

11.
View of the new intermediary entrance and distribution building

12.
View of a multiheight work space

1

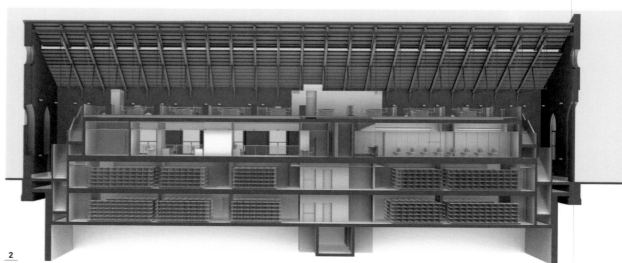

2

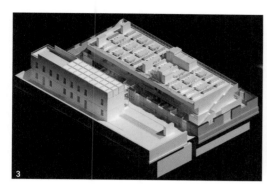

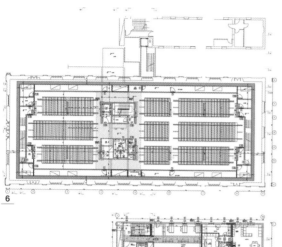

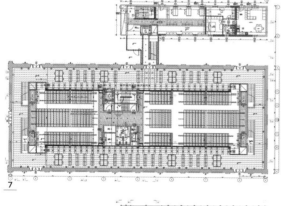

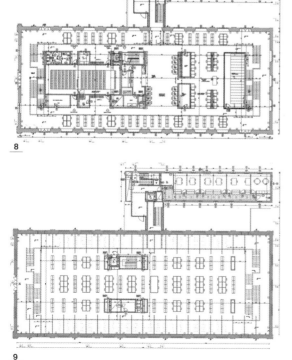

BERGAMO, ITALY
BLESSED VIRGIN MARY OF LORETO PAROCHIAL COMPLEX
2000–2008

Gregotti Associati International
(A. Cagnardi, V. Gregotti, M. Reginaldi)
With: I. Chiarel, S. Franzino,
G. Gramegna, M. Pavani (Associates),
J. Muzio, C. Scortecci, B. Medini,
G. Porta, P. Ronchi
Structural project:
SZ Sajni & Zambetti
Plant engineering:
Manens Intertecnica

This project, winner of a national competition, concerns an area of the western part of the lower city of Bergamo, characterized by the presence of a compact sixteenth-century building, which is important in the space of the ancient city, today compromised by the process of urban drift, which has modified the values and hierarchies of the place with large residential buildings.

The long, narrow plot that is the object of the competition to double the size of the church is crossed by a waterway that divides it into two parts (the waterway itself was recently covered so that the surface could be used as a parvis), while an avenue marks the entrance and lends perspective depth to the facade of the existing church.

The new church, with a larger hall to accommodate the larger population of the quarter, and the new spaces for the pastoral ministry and for the vicarage make up the necessary material to consolidate and reconstruct a new centrality for the parochial headquarters in the built environment of this part of the city.

It is in the definition of the relationships between the constituent parts of the whole parochial complex that the new project finds its logic and defines the new setting. The route of the central avenue and the watercourse,

at right angles to each other, define the field where each element is located in a precise relationship of proximity: a spatial unit with a symbolic value of center with respect to the whole surrounding urban settlement.

The parvis takes on a greater architectural value with the new buildings. The two churches, old and new, arranged in mirror image of each other, establish a relationship of reciprocal correspondence and architectural and dimensional cross-references.

The plan of the new church consists of a 30 × 30-m square. The building is arranged, in order to reinforce its morphological centrality, according to the geometrical relationship between two symbolic shapes: the circle inscribed in the square.

The circle, within the hall, is a ring of light on the ceiling. Tangential to the four sides of the square, it touches the ritual points: the baptismal font, the pulpit, the altar, the sacrament, and the penitentiary. To reinforce the idea of the participation of the faithful in the liturgy and reduce as much as possible the separation between the celebrant and the congregation, the building of a significant raised presbytery has been avoided: it is the altar, in line with the main entrance of the parvis, that constitutes the focal point of the whole organization of the ritual space.

1.
Planovolumetry of setting. On the right, the seventeenth-century church

2.
The relationship between the new building and the preexisting church

3.
Typical transverse section

4.
Easterly view of the new church and transverse section of the parish building

5.
Plan of the ground floor

6.
Plan of the first floor

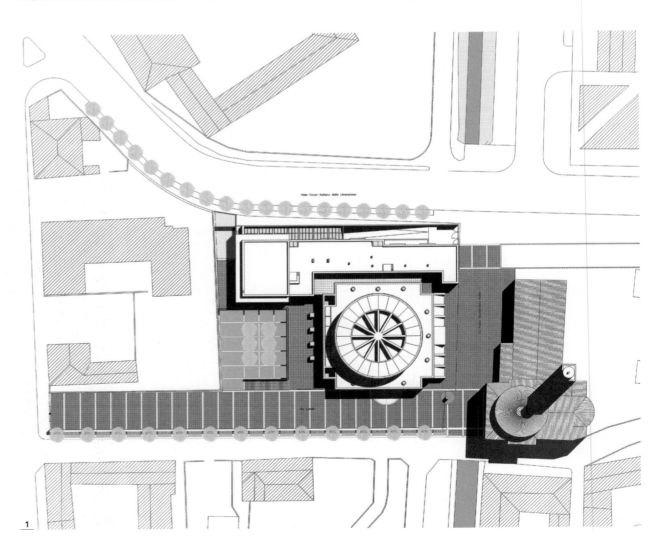

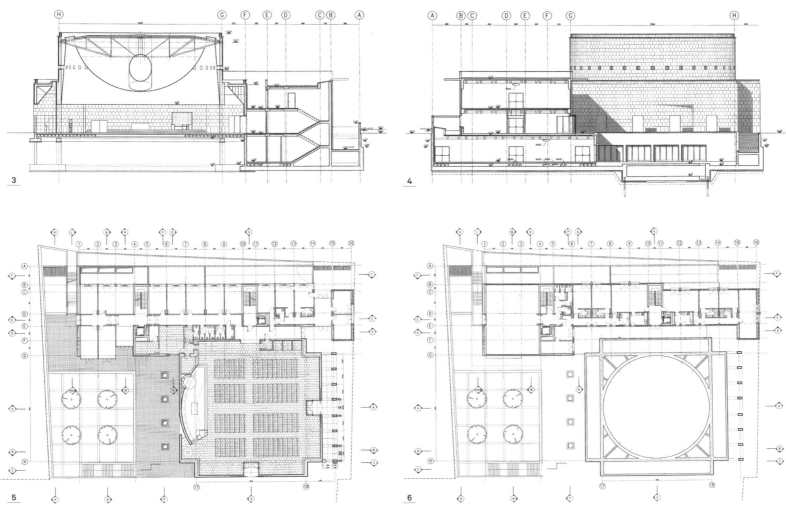

7.
View of the eastern face with entrance porch

8.
South entrance

Outside, the building is clad in stone and is characterized morphologically by a foundation surmounted by a truncated conical form. In the constructive section it is made up of two concentric sloping planes in reinforced concrete forming the ring-shaped skylight of the congregation hall. This form can be seen from the upper city and the surrounding buildings as a sort of crater, evocative of a special place.

The ring of light is created by a circular cut, 2.5 m wide, on the flat ceiling of the hall, guaranteeing overhead light directed so as to be able to control the brightness during the day. The lighting is further characterized by the application within the skylight of a series of windows of graded colors on the Goethe scale, which shine individually according to the time of day and the direction of the sun's rays. More lighting is realized around the whole perimeter of the square hall, contained within the built depth of the wall so that a specific light intensity can underline the relationship between the two main figures, which define the internal space of the congregation hall.

Some wooden seats are located around the perimeter between the structures of the wall to highlight the square figure at floor level. The central seats are simple free-standing seats that can be easily gathered up and at the same time allow increased flexibility in setting up for the ceremonies.

Two windows looking out onto the garden define the depth of the apsidal wall where the altar, the pulpit, the see, and the sacrament are. The floor of the hall is made of wood, while the stone inlay highlights the places where the rituals are carried out.

The organization of the open spaces connecting the buildings is fundamental to constructing the spatial and architectural unity between the existing buildings and those of the new project.

A building independent from, but linked with, the new church is the front of the parochial complex that faces onto Via Corpo Italiano di Liberazione and acts as parochial house and space for the pastoral ministry. Arranged on three floors, including one underground, which opens onto a sunken garden (accessible via a ramp from the central avenue), the building reflects the architecture of the built environment of the city in its dimensions and construction material and emphasizes the church building by the contrast.

The central avenue, paved and bordered on the western side by a 1.6-m-high wall where the stations of the cross are depicted, adds architectural value to the entrance and to the procession area. The sunken garden increases the volume of the new church and is configured as a defined and protected space for open-air recreation.

A vertical element between the parvis and the avenue is the only reference point in the perception of the perspective of the two places and lets one see their contiguity.

Considering the presence of a ditch below the parvis, a water jet similar to a geyser symbolically brings back this element, which has marked the character and development of the whole urban area.

9.
Detail of the top part of the new building (northeast corner)

10 and 11.
Setting of the square from the entrance

12.
View of the square from the porticoed main entrance

13, 14, and 15.
View of the altar area

16 and 17.
View of the pulpit

18.
View of the upturned calotte vault
with central lumen and peripheral
skylight

19.
Baptismal font

Gregotti Associati International
(A. Cagnardi, V. Gregotti)
With: I. Chiarel, M. Destefanis,
G. Gramegna, G. Morpurgo
(Associates), F. Battisti, C. Castello,
E. Lucchini-Gabriolo, J. Muzio,
S. Zauli

1.
Study sketches of the settlement
principle and the general
morphological arrangement
in relation to the relevant
characteristics of the urban
context: the urban structure of the
project area, the railway yard of
Ostia station, and the strip of open
space delimited to the north by the
Aventine Hill and ancient walls and
sixteenth-century Ardeatine bastion.
The drawing below left shows the
base as an element of connection
and interaction between the various
buildings.

The general aim of the competition project for the new
headquarters of the capitol is the realization of an
integrated administrative hub able to contain the demand
for infrastructure services determined by the spread
of offices and services all over the city in facilities that
are unsuitable in terms of accessibility, flexibility, and
environmental comfort conditions. Indeed, the dispersion
of the offices of the Rome's city hall, which nowadays
lie partly in the historic city center, incurs considerable
environmental costs, especially in terms of the urban
ecosystem rather than the individual impact caused by the
isolated system of buildings or connected infrastructure.
The decision to gather the administrative functions of the
city hall together in a single compartment is thus in itself
a factor in overall improvement in terms of environmental
burden, quality of the resources, and the manageability
and environmental sustainability of the city.

The area concerned was created by the demolition
of the former tobacco factory (whose chimney has been
maintained as a historical reminder) in its connection with
the strip of spaces facing onto the large yard of the railway
of Ostiense station. Themes linked with the geographical
and cultural quality of the setting emerge—in other words,
the urban complexity that the new construction must deal
with: the degree of artificiality present in these areas,
the morphological characteristics, the specifics of the
architecture, the density of the archaeological substrate,
which comes up as a special reference horizon, as well
as the transformations currently underway with an eye to
the future of the city, which are being realized especially
along the Ostiense road.

It is in this perspective that the project highlights
the public nature of the new structure of Capitol Two,
a relocation and coordination of the services essential to
the city of Rome. An essential role has been assigned to
the coincidence between architecture and urban design,

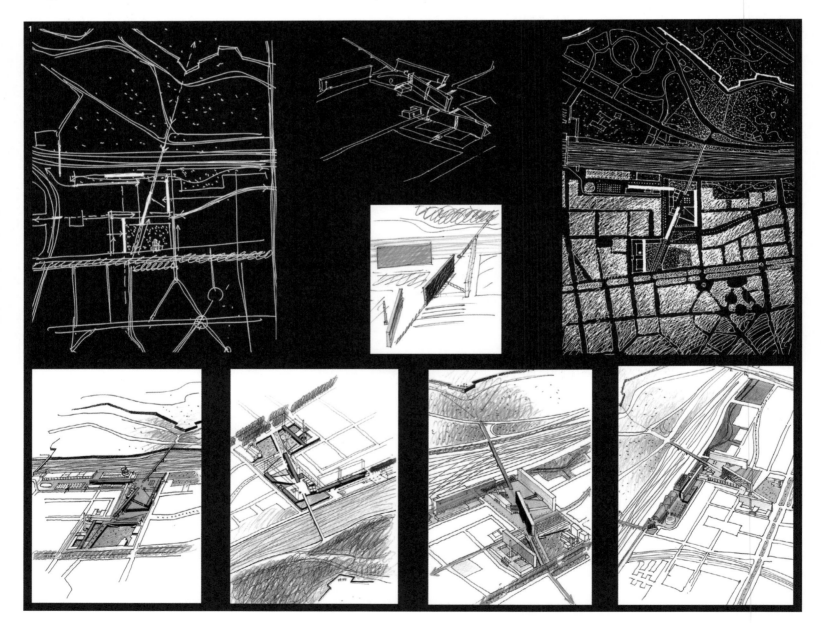

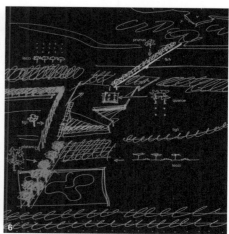

which represents at the same time a divergence from any position that reduces it to an aesthetic or technical object in the style of big company offices (but not falling short of the commitment to efficiency and flexibility of use) and an affirmation of the public nature of the project and of the fact that it is an open system, like a design that attributes meaning to the space between the built objects and its habitability.

The morphology of the new urban system is based on two essential elements: the system of four thin blocks 40 m high, 150 m long and 10 m deep, formally and functionally interconnected, and a large raised square looking beyond the open space of the railway, toward the Aventine Hill with the Caracalla baths on its slopes, toward the Appian Way and the Bastione Ardeatino, redesigned during the Renaissance by Antonio da Sangallo the Younger, and toward the center of Ancient Rome. A tree-lined pedestrian road connects the raised square and the foot of the

Aventine above the railway station, heading in the direction of the Caracalla baths.

The "block" buildings, made even thinner to the eye by the articulation of their overhanging ends, define a large open pedestrian space for public-private exchanges, in contrast to the surrounding density and chaos. The transparent facades, the big windows of the narrow blocks, look out onto this space. Three of these facades protect the open space from the different urban character of the outside with fronts made from various materials: brick, veined marble, travertine—the same ones used for centuries in the city of Rome.

The fourth block, parallel to the railway, whose full face is toward the south, is to be built from Cor-Ten steel, and is enlivened by a system of double windows and the jutting-out elements of the solar collectors arranged over the facade.

Each face has its own way of sitting on the ground, of being crossed, of recalling the material of its own opposite

2.
General view of the model of the new capitol from the Aventine Hill (north). In the foreground, the footbridge above the railway yard.

3.
View of the model from the south

4.
General view of the model from the west

5.
View of the central area of the project from the southwest

6.
Study sketch of the system of greenery, which ideally leads (thanks to the footbridge) toward the green area next to the ancient walls

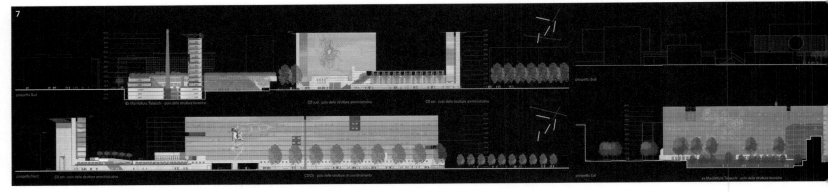

7.
Typical general longitudinal views/
sections

8.
Bird's-eye view from the west

9.
General planovolumetry in the urban
context

face, of highlighting the places of free assembly for the
office staff with double height.

The vast pedestrianized zone envisioned also allows
the building of progressive levels of access with different
arrangements of trees on the large square to the south,
each connected with the wide green space leading into the
whole system from the Ostia bypass.

The raised 27.4-m high square recalls the historical square
of the capitol: the access ramp to the south, the large
sculpture acting as a point of connection toward the center
of Rome symbolically indicated by the walkway over the
railway, the constitution of a special protected space open
to the public, with some special functions, such as the
library, the multifunctional halls, the fitness center, and
an exhibition hall. In addition, there are the central glazed
lobby and four monumental trees, the great triangle of
the fountain, which marks the entrance from the east and
the portico to the south leading onto the middle green
floor (23.6 m high), which protects the restaurant inside.
On the large windows of the block buildings are stamped
images of the archaeological remains of the city and a plan
of the area of greater Rome. The new square is intended
to represent a place of synergy between citizen and
administration: symbols of such synergy are the four great
trees and the monument at reception located on the axis
that ideally connects south and north, the historical center
and consolidated outskirts of the city.

The tree-lined pedestrian street that joins the
raised central square with Viale Marco Polo and the foot
of the Aventine Hill, characterized by the presence of
the fortifications of Sangallo and the Caracalla baths,
represents not only a necessary visual pointer toward the
city center, but also, thanks to the railway yard, the only
direct northerly connection, whose section leaves a tree-
lined route at a height reached by a short ramp crossing
diagonally from the raised square (27.4 m).

The base on which the three blocks containing the
offices of the Rome municipality sit, as well as being the
functional and morphological link between the various
elements and those where the archives are accessed,
also plays a role in reducing the monumental scale of
the large slabs relative to life on the square. While to the
south the green floor 23.6 m up acts as the open space
of the restaurant inside and intermediate level to the
campaign floor on the northern edge, the additional
space planted with trees toward the railway, at a height
of 23.6 m, functions as a covering for the space containing
the entrance to the entire system's centralized
installations, as well as access to the parking lot.

One of the main entrances to the system is from the
south, from the Ostiense ring road, which will take on a
new importance once the planned Rome–Ostia bypass is
built. The proposal envisions integrating the ring road's
existing system of trees with the trees planted along the
pedestrianized street of Santa Gallia. The project also
structures the new green space in the area of the former

tobacco factory, the existing garden around the church to
the east, and the tree-lined Giovanni da Verrazzano Square
in a single system, thus forming a vast green area where
one enters the square of the new complex, screening it off
from the existing buildings to the south.

The accessibility of the new capitol is also based on
the proposal of a system of local public transport, which
will connect it with Ostiense railway station and the
underground. The stops in the project area are situated in
front of the entrances to the new buildings. Staff arriving at
the new capitol by car can reach the internal parking lots of
each of the three sections (C3, C5, and the former tobacco
factory). The car park is connected to the lobby of each
individual building, a checkpoint both for staff and the public.

The parking system consists of three elements
(P9, P7, P13). The main one (P9), as well as being an
element serving the commercial areas, is also an
important morphological mediation with the outside
area to the northeast of the new administrative system.
For this reason, the space is open and protected by metal
grilles facing the railway and closed with a travertine
facade facing to the south, thus underlining, with different
material, its function as intermediary with the railway
yard. Furthermore, the open space between parking lot P9
and block C3/C5 constitutes the pedestrian connection
with the green terrace of the new capitol, the green areas
to the east and Via Cristoforo Colombo. Parking lot P7,
on three underground levels, defines the new 12 Ottobre
1492 Square. With its own paved and treed roof, available
for the transfer of temporary market activities, it becomes
an intermediary element with the municipal headquarters
and the commercial buildings.

Parking lot P13, also on three underground levels,
serves the whole surrounding zone and also compensates
for the removal of the parking spaces planned along Via
Camperio. The roof at the surface forms the new Giovanni
da Verrazzano Square, which will contain green areas
and trees.

The characteristic architectural elements are the
double facade of the blocks that distribute the office
spaces; the common foundation, representing the
connecting element between the blocks; the public spaces
and the existing context; the crowning, which integrates the
photovoltaic solar collectors; the four materials used for the
facades (bare bricks for the building that takes the place of
the former tobacco factory, Cor-Ten steel for block C3, black
marble for block C5 south, travertine for block C5 east);
and the four glazed facades. The latter are characterized
by large prints. The first ones represent the relationship
to the past, making reference to the history of the city of
Rome: two fragments of the marble plan of the city in the
days of Septimius Severus (193–211 AD) and a fragment of
the Pianta del Monte Capitolino (Giovanni Battisti Piranesi,
Le Antichità Romane, 1756). Reference to the present is
provided by the plan showing the geographical extent of the
territory of the municipality of greater Rome. The print on
the western face of building C3/C5 is a fragment of Marcel

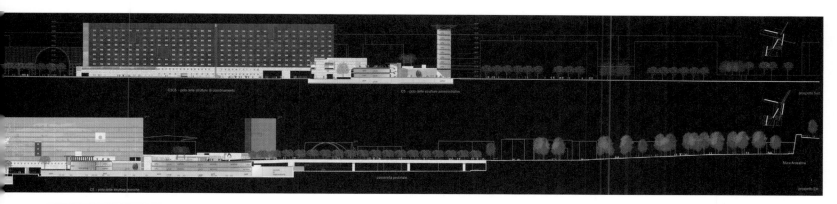

Duchamp's *The Large Glass* (1915–1923). This inexplicable work of art, a metaphor for the knowledge at the root of modernity, is a reference to the future as an interrogative: the project is open toward the future through the symbolic burden of modern art and toward critical internationalism, with the city of Rome interrogating itself on its own function and identity.

The criteria adopted for arranging the open spaces and the green areas are based on the idea that Capitol Two represents a special field in expectations regarding the spatial relationship between interior and exterior and with the urban backdrop—Capitol Square as a physical and symbolic microcosm of the city. In particular, the project organizes a system of external spaces with a basic and rigorous structure in which the green component represents a consistent element able to contribute to the identity and recognisability of the place.

As with the architecture of the buildings, the materials used in the public spaces and green areas also assume a decisive character, not just for their form, but also for the very identity of the site. The organizational choices for the outdoor spaces were directed toward identifying the state of greatest balance between the representational needs of the place and continuity with the surroundings.

In particular, while maintaining the necessary arrangement of the directional section in parts, all the elements of continuity of the various external surfaces were highlighted, even when they were located at different heights, through connections and links allowing the physical and formal integration of the various parts of the complex and avoiding the risk of being characterized as residual spaces or belonging strictly to individual buildings.

The use of vegetation confirms the existing nature of the reference area. The prevalence of mineral external surfaces, partly to be built on the floor, has necessarily limited the use of trees, favoring those species whose roots are not too invasive, interspersed with ornamental shrubs and lawns. The roofs of the buildings are a further element of structural integration between vegetation and the built environment, for controlling microclimatic variation and purifying air and rainwater.

The system of green areas is mostly of a structured and decorative nature for the public spaces and the spaces enclosed in the built sections. The proposal envisions an arrangement thatt—starting from a pedestrianized internal connecting ridge, with composite flooring and green elements—opens up into spaces, which differ in terms of the nature and characteristics of their organization.

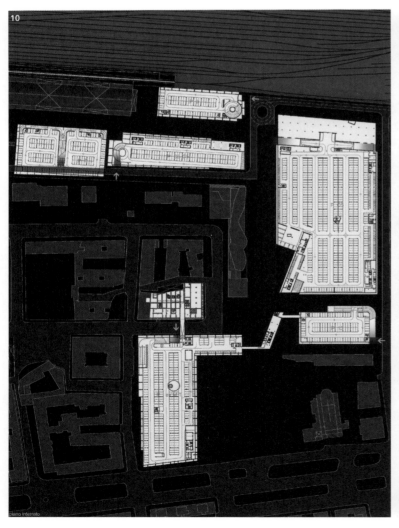

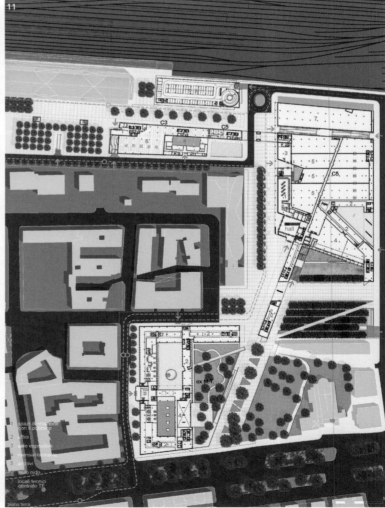

12.
View of the raised square from the south

13.
View of the square of the new capitol from the north. Foreground, the footbridge to Rome city center.

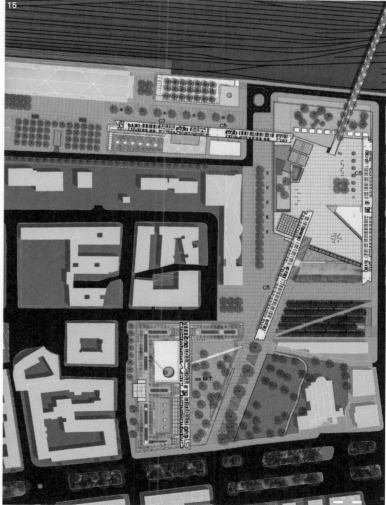

CASALBELTRAME (NOVARA), ITALY
PLASTER CAST GALLERY OF ITALIAN SCULPTURE
2002–2013

Gregotti Associati International
(A. Cagnardi, V. Gregotti, M. Reginaldi)
With: G. Gramegna (Associate),
C. Castello, B. Medini
Structural project: BCV Progetti
Plant engineering:
Manens Intertecnica
Lighting: P. Castiglioni

Casalbeltrame is one of the few places in the Piedmont area of the Po plain to have maintained intact its own settlement principle. With this in mind, the new project, winner of the competition for the plaster cast collection of twentieth-century Italian sculpture, tries to maintain the necessary continuity.

The project area includes an eighteenth-century villa and all the buildings around it, according to the ancient constitutional basis of the agricultural courts. It is with reference to this urban structure that an idea of contiguity has been proposed, albeit with functional independence of its parts, both the large courtyard and the new pavilion of the plaster cast gallery. It has also been proposed to continue the existing porticoes, making them turn onto the face of the new pavilion, thus ensuring continuity between the various parts.

The new building has a square floor plan and is built entirely of exposed Piedmont bricks, both inside and out, on a 7 × 7-m module, with a cross section over two different heights: one series of open, peripheral zones with a net internal height of 5 m, laid out around a single central space of 780 m², with a net internal height of 9 m. This space can be divided up according to the given organization by light screens (curtains) hung from crossed metal roofing beams or with freestanding wooden shelves, which function

1.
Detail of one of the masonry bays (7 × 7 m), which form the perimeter (site photo)

2.
Perspective section of the central area

3.
Plan

4 and 5.
Typical sections

6.
View of the central space being built

7.
Study perspective of the entrance area

8.
Perspective view of a detail from the central space

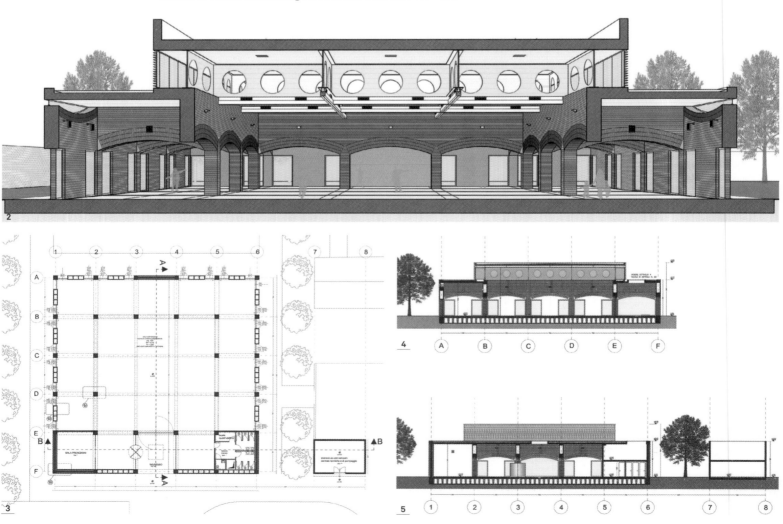

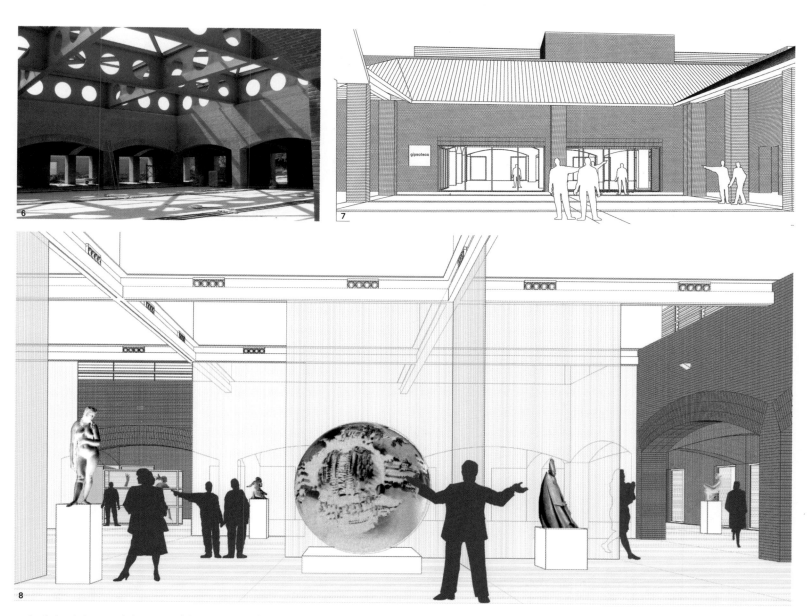

as both backdrop and showcase (closed or open) for small and particularly delicate sculptures. The shelves come in modules of 2 × 3 m high, and so with two elements a continuous backdrop can be formed for the entire span. They can be put away inside the first module to the left of the entrance area.

Sculptures can be flexibly arranged with defined spaces, placed side by side with each other in a single continuous space of 1,300 m², or flexibly subdivided according to necessity. The floor is made from enriched and polished cement.

Natural lighting is ensured by a pair of glass doors fixed at the sides (the glass can be covered by external curtains to the south and west), while a continuous window on all four walls, protected by an adjustable brise-soleil, ensures lighting for the central space in the highest part. Artificial lighting is generated by two different systems: in the peripheral part with adjustable wall fittings (designed by Piero Castiglioni), located on the upper part of the walls, thus also compensating for the backlighting effect of the glass doors; while in the central part a series of spotlights attached to the lower surface of the metal beams provide lighting.

This system is supplemented by diffuse lighting, which is obtained by reflection from the walls toward the ceiling, leaving the spotlights to provide 70 percent of the requirement and thus reducing possible overdramatic effects on the sculptures.

The first entrance module contains an information counter (and a possible ticket office), the necessary bathrooms, and, above them, a small office/storeroom.

An important role is played by the open space, defined by the walls, pergolas, and rows of trees at its edges, which thus delimit three other open spaces of various sizes, with a lawn, which can be used for temporary or permanent open-air sculpture exhibitions. These open spaces are thus also linked with the existing structures and in continuity with regard to their settlement principles.

Following the competition indications, a service entrance was envisioned from Via Umberto I, giving access to a space (separated from the exhibition spaces by a wall) in which large articulated trucks can maneuver to load and unload sculptures, to manage the systems (located in a separate structure), and for other general maintenance services.

RESTORATION OF SALA DEGLI SCARLIONI IN SFORZA CASTLE
2013

Gregotti Associati International
(A. Cagnardi, V. Gregotti)
With: G. Gramegna (Associate)
Museum fitting: G. Agosti, J. Stoppa

The renovation project for the Sala degli Scarlioni stems from the decision by the Commune of Milan to transfer Michelangelo's *Rondanini Pietà* to the Spanish Hospital located in the first courtyard of Sforza Castle.

The Sala degli Scarlioni, arranged by the BBPR studio in 1952 (the year the statue was bought, when their project for the entire castle museum was already finished), was reorganized to house the new display, which brings together Milanese sculpture from the early sixteenth century, to which only the first part of the hall was originally dedicated.

The guiding principles of the new organization were to tackle the completion of the Sala and include other pieces of early sixteenth-century Milanese sculpture, some of which were already located in various parts of the museum, maintaining maximum respect for the arrangement of the Sala and its ceiling on several levels, and to see to it that there is an overall spatial unity, dismantling the upper part

of the stone screen offered by BBPR in 1952 to separate Bambaia's works from the *Rondanini Pietà*, since they belonged to two different Italian cultures.

Therefore the Bagarotti monument is to be moved into the second part of the Sala so that, with its considerable height, it can still validate the lowering of the floor introduced during the original exhibition. The arrangement of the pieces was reorganized in order to dedicate the first part of the Sala to Bambaia's works and the second part to some of his contemporaries.

It is planned that an elevator will be installed in an existing opening in the wall dividing the Sala degli Scarlioni from the Sala delle Armi to allow for disabled access to the lower part of the Sala degli Scarlioni.

To maintain continuity with the general atmosphere of the BBPR arrangement, the various pieces have been placed according to the details of the original museum layout, already present in the castle's other halls.

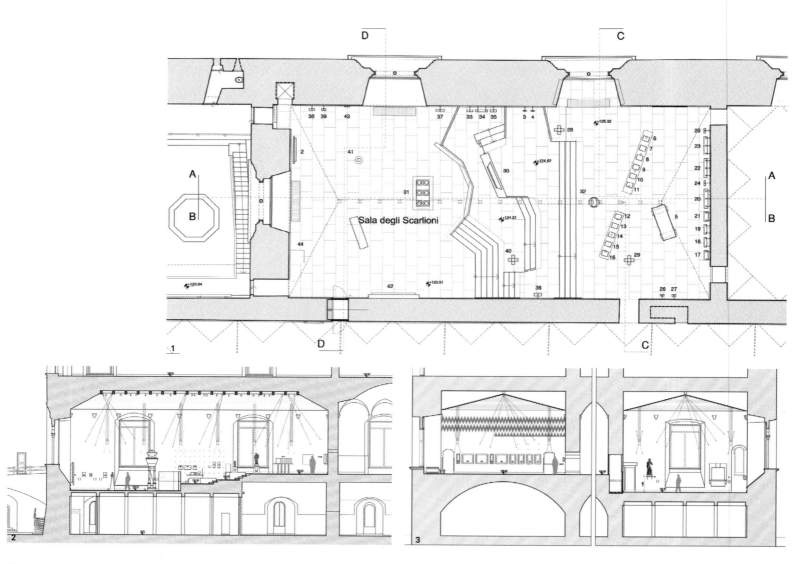

1.
Plan of the reorganization project

2 and 3.
Longitudinal and transverse sections

4 and 5.
Views of the hall reorganized according to a new overall spatial unity, in ideal continuity with the former layout of the BBPR study

TURIN, ITALY
DETAILED PLAN FOR CORSO MARCHE
2006–2014

Gregotti Associati International
(A. Cagnardi, V. Gregotti)
Partner: SITI Istituto Superiore sui
Sistemi Territoriali per l'Innovazione
With: S. Butti, I. Chiarel,
M. Destefanis, T. Macchi Cassia,
M. Trovatelli (Associates),
C. Castello, C. Calabrese,
B. Colombo, F. Ciafrè, D. Cornago,
D. Ferrari, E. Lucchini-Gabriolo,
G. A. Giannoccari, B. Medini, M. Pani

The proposal consists of reforming the urban territorial structure of the eastern Turin area, which centers around Corso Marche, the main road traversing this urban territorial complex from north to south.

Just as generally happens in big Italian cities and the conurbations formed over recent decades, the outskirts of the city of Turin are also made up of areas once connected in relationships of dependence and now strongly interrelated. Each Commune has organized its own territory into central and peripheral zones, defending itself from interference by large schemes promoted by outside needs. The contrast between settlement needs and environmental defense has left an ambiguous territory made up of different kinds of suburbs. Assuming the marginality, the unevenness of the current arrangement as a condition, and the residual space as a resource, the proposal promotes the regeneration of these parts of the city, no longer in the sense of spare areas for further individual projects, but as a new contextual condition in which to relaunch the recuperation and the promotion of Turin's future. The historical city has a characteristic settlement structure, based on a plan that makes history and geography interact, the historical Roman nucleus with the multipolar system of strongholds (Stupinigi, Venaria Reale, Certosa di Collegno, and other monumental presences), through a system of relationship plans of great morphological value, still valid as a general system of reference.

In the area of Corso Marche, it can be seen how the push to settle Turin created a continuous urbanized stretch all the way to Rivoli (east) and a more industrial and tertiary projection beyond Mirafiori (disused FIAT industrial area) toward Orbassano and Rivalta (southeast). Between these two built-up stretches, there is mostly agricultural land, although the isolated industrial sites have laid the basis for future transformations. The curve of the ring road has become the preferred site for services. The Sangone and Dora valleys show recognizable territorial continuity. In this context of high complexity and interferences between urban, infrastructural, and territorial characteristics, the main themes are the building of important infrastructure, (railway, motorway, urban avenue), which modify the city's level of accessibility; the recuperation of the industrial outskirts; and the construction of a future organization.

The proposal directs the choices to achieve a result comparable to the center of an extended Turin, which includes the territories of several communes, through the new organization of the mobility infrastructure:

- the railway (a section of the Turin–Lyons TAV) will be underground;
- it is planned that the motorway that crosses the ring road will also be underground and usable by urban traffic. The new route functions as a high-speed urban road beneath Corso Marche with five surface connections;
- the surface road, Corso Marche, will become a tree-lined urban avenue with the valley of the river Dora at the north end and Piazza Mirafiori at the south. Two "roots" stretch out from these ends, smaller vehicular and pedestrian roads that through Dora Park to the north and Sangone Park to the south, reach all the way to Venaria and Stupinigi parks. The whole system extends for 15 km, crossing the route of the ring road.

This infrastructural combination becomes the foundation for the development of a real urban revolution. The guaranteed high level of accessibility to Corso Marche and the presence of territorial-level special functions can, if well integrated with the existing city, relaunch the urban whole as a system, recentering the great Turin as a whole. The sequence of new urban functions of the recuperated territory, which is able to integrate into the dimension of the great city (starting in the south), includes:

- Piazza Mirafiori, where the new avenue meets up with the existing road network;
- Agricultural/historical park next to the avenue without any buildings on the park side;
- City of health and science in the areas along Corso Allamano;
- Capitol, a new center above the railway crossings;
- University city and sports field in the Grugliasco area;
- Reform of the facades on the avenue on the stretch leading to Corso Francia;
- Reform of the Alenia industrial area with planned aerospace museum;
- Campo Volo Park and airport;
- Viewpoint over Dora Park.

In this way, a unique urban form will be created, which, pivoting on "capital functions," reassembles the built urban territory and completes it with the new avenue, forming large open spaces, a necessary complement for new public uses.

1.
General view of the territory of Corso Marche looking northward

2.
The relationships created by the new Corso Marche: general plan of the project areas and their infrastructural connections

3 and 4.
Studies on the settlement morphology of some new centers, located at the junctions of the route of Corso Marche between the peripheral districts of the eastern Turin area

5.
Bird's-eye view of the so-called "capitol", an urban center where special national functions are concentrated

6.
Study sketch of the typical section of the project for the infrastructural axis, which envisions an underground motorway and high-speed railway line

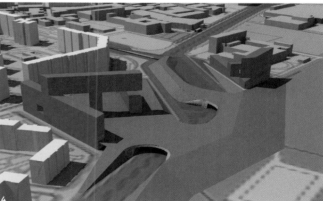

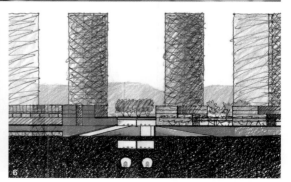

Gregotti Associati International
(A. Cagnardi, V. Gregotti)
With: M. Destefanis, T. Macchi Cassia,
G. Morpurgo (Associates), C. Castello,
C. Scortecci, E. Lucchini-Gabriolo,
B. Medini, F. Campello, S. Ferrari,
P. Ronchi, S. Zauli
Structural project: BCV Progetti
Plant engineering:
Amman Progetti srl
Engineering: Sc Sembenelli
Consulting srl

The international competition concerned a large rectangular plot within Padua's industrial estate, located to the east of the historic city center and separated from it by the large green area of Roncajette, which will become the Veneto city's applied science park. The area is densely built up, with plots overflowing with warehouses, some of them very large, and the ring road passes through the middle of it, alongside the plot that is the object of this competition.

The winning proposal is based on the decision to arrange the building in an L-shaped plan, which offers a series of different possibilities that are more flexible than the historically and typologically traditional central plan. The limited 14.2-m depth of the building also allows better lighting, diffused over the whole surface of the ground plan, and offers observation points that are differently lit during day according to various orientations and points of view, which means that the overall vision of the structure is made more complex.

It is a consistent multiplication of the building's appearance, a variety intentionally highlighted by the decision to arrange the tower in an L shape height-wise, to punctuate the continuity of the faces with a series of exceptions—which also correspond to special functions like meeting halls, rest areas, and double-height spaces for free interdisciplinary exchange—and to vertically cut the eight-story height so as to highlight its planimetric and volumetric complexity.

The building covers thirty-six floors, the highest part reaching 137 m, with a total surface area of 50,000 m².

The L shape of the tower, together with the mat buildings next to it, also makes it an urban landmark, through the relation between its different parts, in terms of the sequence from the access point on the public road (Corso Stati Uniti).

The tower is separated from the access road by a large treed area, which opens onto the squares, joining the parts dedicated to services along the north–south route, which crosses the whole area to be transformed.

To preserve as far as possible the current condition of an area characterized by a lot of greenery, even by transferring some of it onto the roofs of the mat buildings, is one of the aims the project is striving for. It defines a clear relationship with the environment, with a view to the reordering of the whole area according to the future scenarios envisioned by the plan for Roncajette Park and the future doubling of the industrial estate, with its relative landscape and ecological suggestions.

The project thus revolves around the possible redesign of the urban landscape with a view to rebuilding an ideal reference to the urban nature of Padua's historic city center, highlighting a particularly meaningful approach within an industrial district where the recognizability of the parts is considered a secondary quality.

These are the settlement decisions from which the whole plan of the building developed, both in terms of the system of functional needs of the various parts and their relation to each other, and in terms of the hypotheses of future enlargement foreseen by the announcement.

From the point of view of spatial and typological organization, the L-shaped tower is directly connected to two different mat buildings. The first, to the east, satisfies the need for 6,000 m² of surface area for chemical research and is connected to the main entrance and the first two floors of the tower, which provide 2,700 m² of space for related research.

With a height of 6 m, the chemical research block is organized on a structural grid of 12.8 × 12.8 m, with twenty spaces with overhead lighting—divided into four research rooms each or some free combination of these—reached by a network of corridors with a prevalence of resting and meeting places that determine their direction.

1.
View from the south

2.
Nighttime view from the northeast

3.
General planovolumetry of the project in the urban context of Padua's industrial area

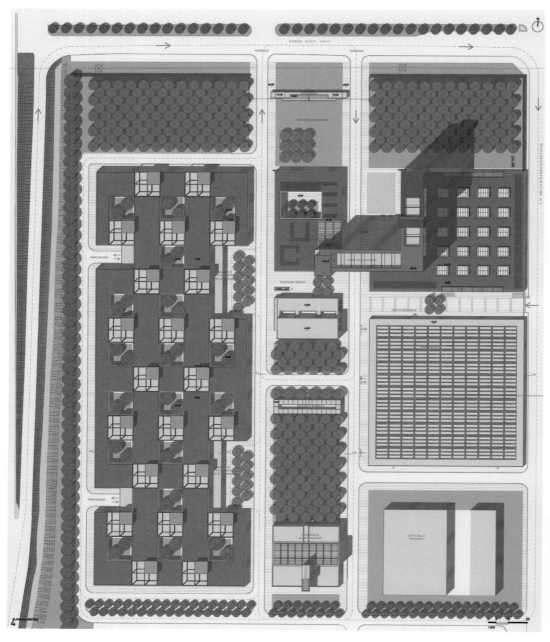

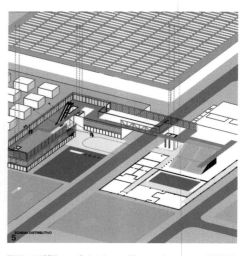

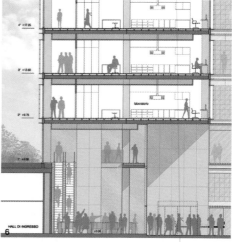

4.
General planovolumetry

5.
Distributive layout of the entrances

6.
Transverse section of the entrance hall

7.
Entrance area to the tower

8.
Plan of the first floor

9.
Plan of the ground floor

10.
Plan at +36.00 and +39.76 m

11.
Plan at +51.00, +54.75, +58.50, +62.25, +66.00, +69.75 m

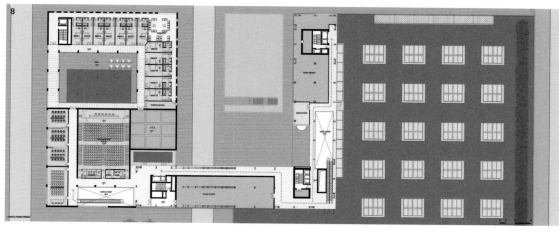

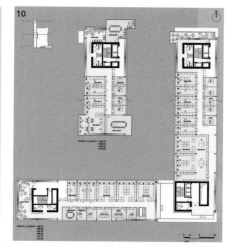

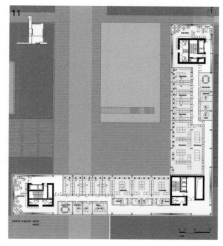

The spaces for research are externally delimited by a ring of individual studios and meeting spaces, organized on a basic module of 19 m² and relative combinations.

To the sides of the skylights sticking out of the roof (which is covered in greenery on a 35-cm layer of lightened earth) are the tubes of the extraction hoods of the laboratories.

The studios around the edge have a net height of 2.7 m: on the upper floors up to a height of 6 m are located the independent substations.

The second mat building, located to the west of the tower, contains general services and common areas on two levels. On the ground floor, as well as in the lobby and the foyer, are coordination and reception services, while an escalator leads to the first floor 6 m up, where the entrance to the 300-seat conference hall and four meeting halls can be found.

On the ground floor of this block, toward the north and east, are a restaurant, café, and shops. On the first floor is the guest area with twelve rooms overlooking the patio within the restaurant.

The main access to the service block for cars is from the north–south entrance route, which also provides access

to the tower a few meters before that on the opposite side. A second entrance is envisioned in the south, from the pedestrian square that connects the west block with the existing service building, which is to be preserved.

The main entrance and exit for the whole complex has been kept on Corso Stati Uniti, a route already consolidated for the connection with urban traffic.

The tower and the service blocks are set back from the entrance by 70 m, and have a lawn and some woodland made up of a regular layout of local species of tree, which underlines the monumental aspect, as an urban signal, of the image of the new complex.

The entrance to the tower is located to the east of the access road, as the backdrop to a 1,250-m² square with a large ground-level pond separating it from the woodland.

From the entrance lobby, which has the necessary reception and surveillance and service spaces, there is access to the central group of elevators to the north and to the chemical research block. Access to the three groups of stairways and elevators is on the first floor (+6 m). Passage between the tower and the research block can be found on the second floor, in the form of a bridge crossing over the main access road, which connects the two parts.

12.
Nighttime view from the north

13.
Northerly view and typical transverse section

14.
Westerly view and transverse section of the lower block of the public services (conference hall)

12

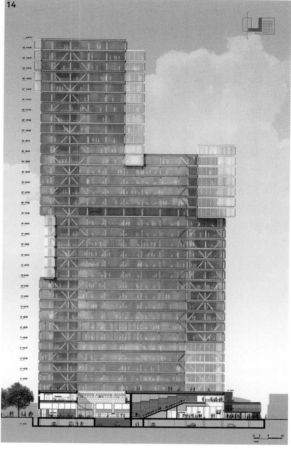

Below the whole system of the L-shaped tower and the mat buildings is located, on a single story, part of the required parking lot (10,000 m² with 380 spaces). Below the tower are the required 300 m² of storage space for chemical research, the general stores and access to material for service elevators, as well as the storeroom for polluting substances.

The free area behind that to the south, 10,000 m², is reserved for parking, with a single level underground and two aboveground, which, together with the area below the new structure, satisfies the requirement of 40,000 m² of parking lot. On the metal roof of the parking lots are located photovoltaic panels.

The central strip (42 m wide + 10 m of footpath) is occupied to the south of a deep green space of 4,600 m² by the cylinder storage area from where special gas lines are supplied and by the technical area, which serves the whole system.

The future enlargement (40,000 m²) is foreseen to the west of the new mat building and L-shaped tower complex will be made up of a two-story mat building with some elements with three storeys and with green 16 × 16-m patios with parking underneath. This will also facilitate building later on. The future expansion served by a perimeter road will be a functional and morphological continuation consistent with the settlement principles proposed for the competition phase of the project.

The body of the L-shaped tower, with a cross section of 14.2 m, is based on a regular 6.4 × 6.4-m grid, a 3.75 m interfloor distance, slab floors with a 15-cm floating floor and with a 50-cm space in the ceiling for the technical systems either with or without a false ceiling according to necessity and with a free height from floor to false ceiling of 2.7 m (according to the competition requirements). The vertical metal structure is formed from 500 mm HE outlines of constant size and variable cross section, fireproofed, with diagonal struts, exposed on the inside in the strategic position indicated by the structural plan.

The external walls are made up of concrete-framed transparent glass panels with an internal surface of sealed double glazing. The airspace between the two walls (20 cm) is opened floor by floor for vertical ventilation during the summer and closed during the winter. In the upper part of each floor is a continuous emergency opening 50 cm high.

The choice of materials reinforces the image of the building as a "new generation factory." The interiors, destined for technical and scientific research by various bodies (the National Research Center and other laboratories belonging to universities or associated with private companies and businesses), offer a layout with a wide range of possibilities and are flexible to accommodate needs that will likely change over time. There is also the possibility of using an equipped roof for outdoor experiments.

TRANSFORMATION OF THE FORMER INDUSTRIAL AREAS OF TRENTO NORD

Gregotti Associati International
(A. Cagnardi, V. Gregotti)
With: G. Donato (Associate),
A. Boccacci, B. Colombo, C. Castello,
D. Cornago, M. Parravicini, P. Seria,
S. Zauli
Transport and traffic: Centro Studi
Traffico (P. Gelmini)

1.
Urban setting

2.
Bird's-eye view from the southeast

3.
View of the model. In the foreground, the artificial hill at the northwest corner of the area.

The detailed plan for the transformation of the former SLOI and Carbochimica industrial areas, situated in the northern part of Trento, is a unitary study prefiguring a variant to the General Regulatory Plan, necessary to direct the urban regeneration of the area.

The areas are spread over 142,000 m², crossed by the Brenner Railway. Disused for over twenty years, this vast border zone is an extensive, discontinuous urban void whose morphological weight is very important in the overall balance of the outskirts of the provincial capital of Trentino; it is an abandoned place, which is slowing down the development and regeneration of the edge of the city along the railway, a technical presence of great territorial value for the whole northern strip of the city. The reclamation project promoted by the municipal administration also requires complex preliminary work to resolve the serious problem of land polluted by the chemical works that took place there.

The design directions of the detailed plan prefigure a transformation based on the idea of giving the area back to the city on the basis of an overall idea of public space. The project is structured on a multifunctional model, which promotes the urban integration of disused areas, thanks especially to the interaction between commercial areas, tertiary sector buildings, and wide public green spaces, to which housing will also be added to complete the existing neighborhood.

The project envisions the creation of an extensive complex with the function of uniting the two sides of the city by passing over the railway yard, thus creating a new raised urban ground, characterized by the presence of four tall buildings with a triangular ground plan. These play the role of visual reference elements, which give a sense of proportion to the large public urban space, marking its limits and defining a scale intermediate between the settlement structure of the city's outskirts, the noteworthy historic city center and the historical-geographical horizon represented by the Alps and the Doss, the hill that, together with Dosso di San Rocco and Dosso di Sant'Agata, made up the triad of hills of the ancient city. The ideal reference to the settlement principle of the Roman Tridentum lends the urban design the foundational air of a new center, able to represent the horizon of an overall renewal of the city in the area of greater infrastructural crossing that is destined to become the new gateway to Trento.

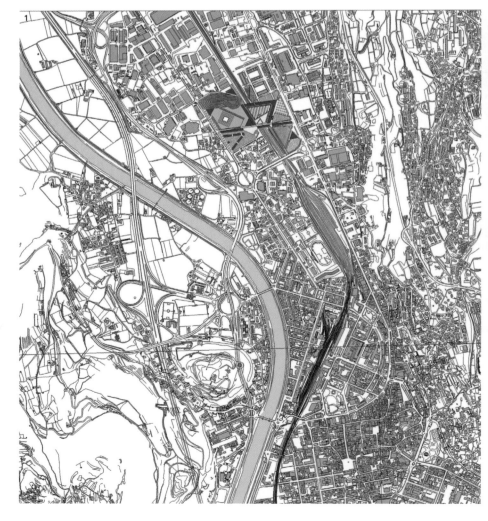

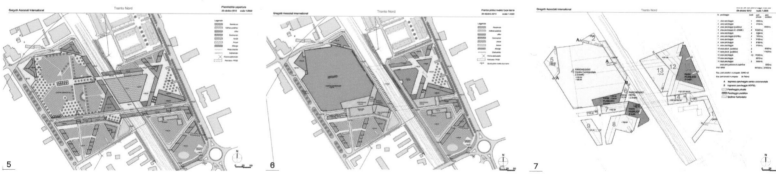

4.
General aerial view from the southeast

5, 6, and 7.
Plan of the functional and distributive program of the various levels

8.
View of the urban space of the large square above the railway that unites the two sides of the city

141

Santa Bona Senior Citizens' Residences
Gregotti Associati International
(A. Cagnardi, V. Gregotti)
Partner: E. Casagrande
With: L. Araldi
Structural project and plant engineering: POOL Engineering S.p.A.

Senior Citizens' Services Center
Gregotti Associati International
(A. Cagnardi, V. Gregotti)
Partner: AT&T Associati
(E. Casagrande)
Structural project, plant engineering, and work management:
POOL Engineering S.p.A
With: L. Araldi

1.
Planovolumetric of the urban setting of the Residenze Sanitarie Assistenziali S. Bona
2.
View of the model from the south-west
3.
Southerly view
4.
Northerly view
5.
Westerly view
6.
Easterly view

The settlement principle of the project is part of the peri-urban context as a limitation element. The project assigns to the base of the building system the role of reconnecting buildings and green spaces with no road access in a measured plan and at the same time relating in a structured way with the surroundings, partly rearticulated by the new road layout. To be built in concrete, ennobled by sand treatment, on one hand the building system redesigns the urban morphology of the context on a territorial scale; on the other, next to the buildings, it participates in the geometric composition of the facade itself, becoming its "natural" support. Marking the break between this surface and the overlying one in straw-colored plaster will be an insert of white stone.

The regular nature of this large area becomes more complex along the stretch overlooking the main road: here it is patterned with more structured elements marking on the outside the presence of the courtyards connecting the residential blocks. On the other side, near the corner nodes, this same element structures the final front of the church and technical services buildings. Both of these elements act as final fronts, both of the linear structure of the administrative and general services and of the iteration of the residential structures with an internal courtyard.

The second issue faced by the project concerned the characterization of the functional differences in volume and distinct relationships. The concentration of services for guests and staff (closely related to access and the parking area) was related to the internal vehicle system and structured on the model of the urban front. The matching structure of the actual residential modules, arranged around internal courtyards and connecting

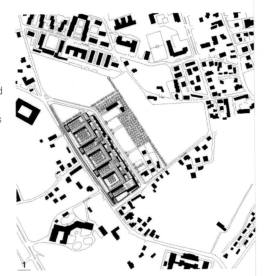

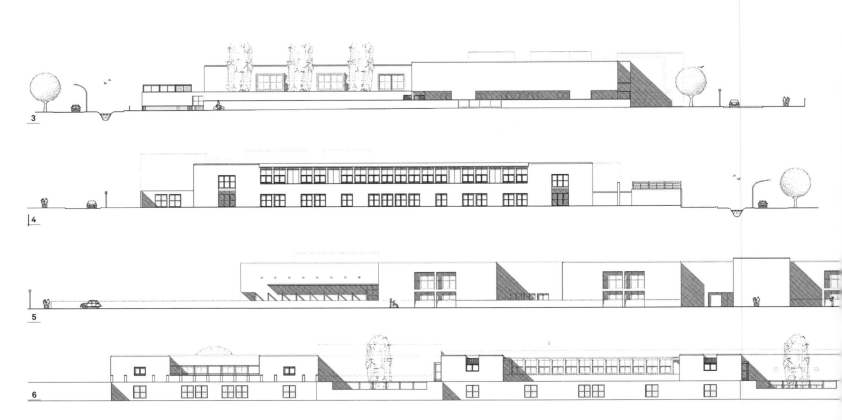

gardens with a deep arcaded loggia on the upper floor, in their geometrical relationships and colors mirror the same compositional elements of the adjacent farmhouses so typical of the Veneto plains. The slight difference in height between the two systems is limited to the two aboveground floors, although it emphasizes on the one hand this planovolumetric layout, on the other hand it eases and spreads the entire complex over a vast portion of land, camouflaging its overall impact. The materials used also reflect this functional differentiation: the starkness of the general services building, negatively articulated by volumetric excavations, is contrasted with the more familiar arrangement of the residential courtyards, where the ground floor's plastered walls with regular openings support the impetus of the white cement pillars and thin, prefabricated roof above.

7.
Residenze Sanitarie Assistenziali
S. Bona

8 and 9.
Partial views of a courtyard and an entrance to a module in the finishing stages

10.
General plan of the ground floor

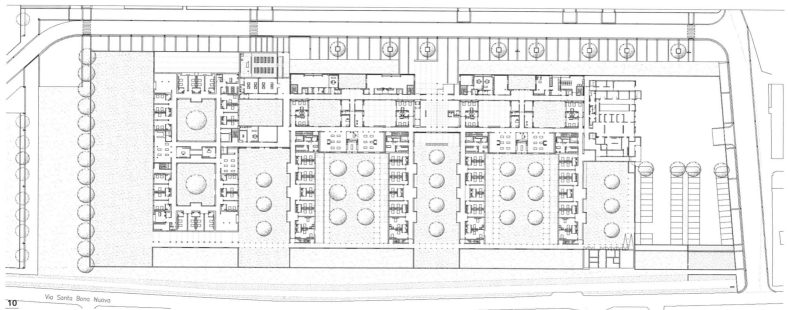

Via Santa Bona Nuova

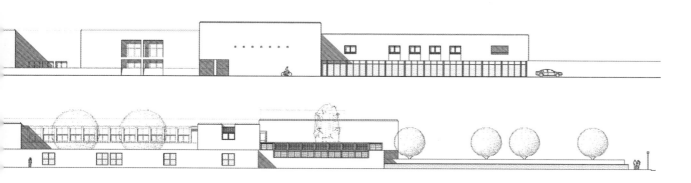

A connective fabric of buildings and internal minicourtyards serves to connect and regroup the double morphology of this project. These are buildings destined to perform a dual function: they house the module services in a central position relative to the residential structures and contain the most important spaces of the entire structure (the entrance hall, the conference center, the covered square, the hydrotherapy room, etc.) next to the connecting areas of the residential modules. This particular compositional function is highlighted in the treatment adopted for the external finishings, already present though not prevalent in the other buildings: a modular sequence of panels in smooth white cement.

The trees translate this functional program into a natural morphology: they are spread throughout the residential courtyards while they are organized vertically in the connecting courtyards in a sort of symbolic reinterpretation of the surrounding space.

The housing capacity of the project has been organized according to the criterion of functional units and modules, with three modules with three and a half units, providing 240 beds, as well as a day center.

Each module has its own open space facing outward, at once protected but open toward the surroundings.

Two further open-air areas share between them the three different modules and mark the aspects of the main elements of the general services. A series of internal patios provides a pattern for the spaces dedicated to common services, giving them a dimension of intimacy in their relationship with the external spaces and modulating the use of natural light for the internal spaces, which also extend to the small open environments on the first-floor level.

11, 12, and 13.
Residenza Sanitaria Assistenziale Istituto Rosa Zalivani: detail from garden, plan of the ground floor and main face

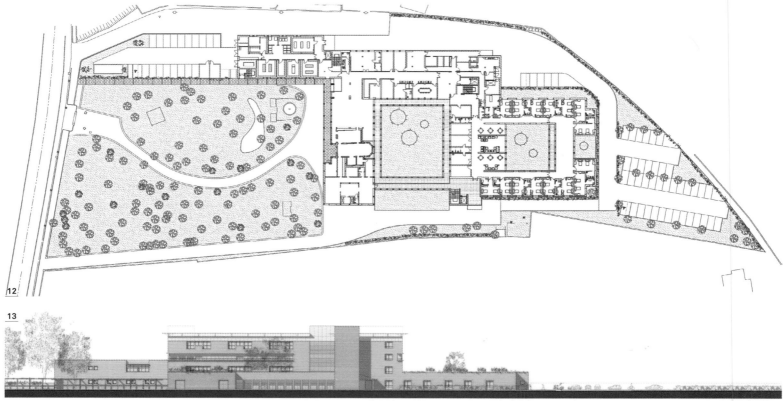

A 2.4 × 2.4-m grid regulates the geometry of the planimetric development of this whole that is very complex in its parts, but which, in its rigorous and ordered geometric alignments, in the simplicity of the buildings and the materials used, seeks to offer an image of social solidarity and community togetherness.

The modular typology envisioned by the project, which groups buildings together, develops the theme of the internal garden. Avoiding the distributive system of corridors typical of hotels and hospitals to which groups of rooms are attached, the connecting fabric has been developed according to the criterion of functional and operational islands. Special attention has been paid to service routes for staff and to access routes for visitors.

14.
View of the entrance area

15 and 16.
Views of the courtyard and patio

17.
View of the garden

Gregotti Associati International
(A. Cagnardi, V. Gregotti)
With: G. Gramegna (Associate)

Reorganization proposal A:

1.
Territorial setting

2.
Urban setting

3.
Planovolumetry of the new urban center

4.
Detail of the main courtyard opening onto the bridge

5.
Bird's-eye view of the new urban center

This project for urban regeneration concerns a set of spaces covering an overall area of about 80,000 m², coinciding with the southern edge of the settlement, delimited longitudinally by the presence of the wide Parma River. The original nucleus of Langhirano, with the current town hall at the center, is a slightly raised zone. The historic town center is crossed by an ancient east–west road, which, coming down from the hill, arrives at the river where once there was an ancient crossing point to the south of the present-day bridge.

The main orbital road to the east of the old center, now Via Roma, has recently become the axis of urbanization in the direction of the river and the line of demarcation between the residential zone and the area occupied by new productive activities.

The strip along the river is mainly occupied by structures for the seasoning of cured meat products, whose position is determined by the airflow along the valley bottom. They are long, narrow plots with tall buildings at right angles to the river. It is a built-up area with its own very regular morphology, representing a clear separation between the ancient town and the river, served by roads laid at right angles. Of these, the main one is Viale Vittorio Veneto, which, crossing the bridge, forms the only link between the two banks and is the only route for traffic going to and from a parallel industrial area on the other side of the river.

Within the ancient nucleus are consolidated the main public services: the town hall, elementary schools, and a group of small shops around the square.

In the industrial part, especially to the east of the historic center, buildings have begun to be reused, and the older industrial establishments have been replaced. There is also a museum and the house of culture. The whole area is therefore ready to be reorganized together.

The regeneration project envisions a quota of new buildings limited to two to three stories, with an area of 40,000 m², which conforms with the existing housing and avoids excess concentration of buildings, as well as conditions of strong attraction and concentration of traffic.

The proposed new urban center will be improved together with the old one, with three new pedestrian squares and a network of cycle lanes planned for the whole area.

This urban improvement makes it necessary to move vehicular transport from Viale Vittorio Veneto and reduce or eliminate heavy traffic from the center of the area. The dimensions of the existing roads are in fact rather

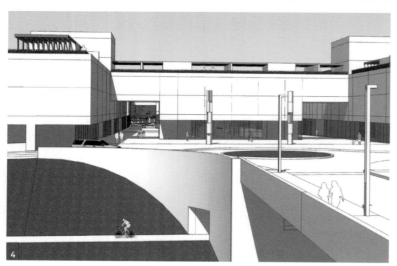

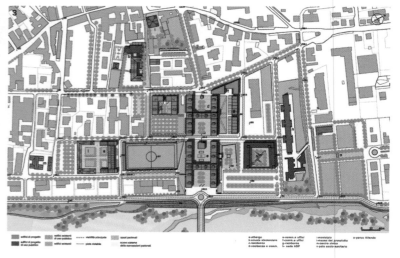

modest, and traffic is made even worse by the trees, which are to be preserved.

Current plans for a second bridge downstream from the existing one could deviate the heavy traffic from the north heading to the other side of the river, keeping it out of the center.

The feasibility study takes into account different opportunities of combining residential and service areas. The main functions proposed include a primary school, sheltered housing for the elderly (a hotel home), a hotel, public surface parking lots, green areas, a reorganization of the sports facilities, distributed shops, and the possibility to have a food research center or a shopping center.

The feasibility study is organized into two different tidying-up proposals, with fixed parts and variable parts. Overall, it is characterized by a new residential zone, which will have three pedestrianized squares along the line of Viale Vittorio Veneto between Via Roma and the river. In this way, the old center enjoys continuity of urban spaces with the riverine environment area. Along the orthogonal axis, parallel with the river, the new services together with the existing ones such as the civic center, the museum, the sports field, and, further north, the research center (or supermarket) and the sheltered housing form a whole, which, in continuity with the older nucleus, identifies the new center of the community. The pedestrian street between the town hall and the sports field, connected with the system of three squares, also pedestrianized, further accentuates the community-based nature of the whole project.

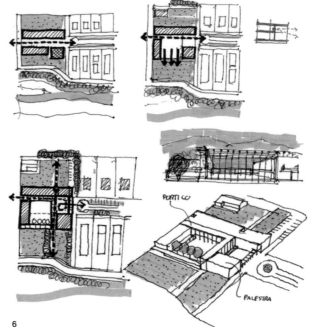

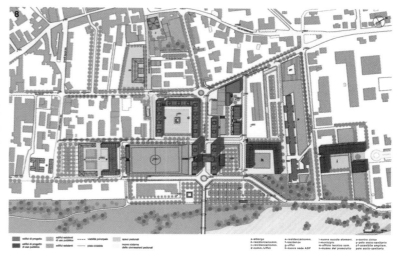

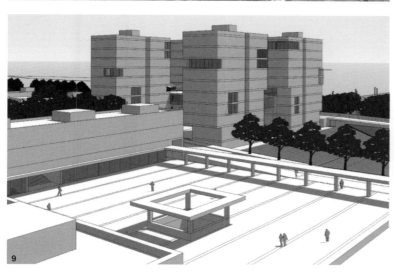

Reorganization proposal B:

6.
Study sketches of the school nucleus

7.
Territorial setting

8.
Urban setting

9.
View of the square with residential towers

10.
View of the nucleus

147

ANTHROPOGEOGRAPHY AND PLANNING
1953–2014

Franco Purini

Throughout Vittorio Gregotti's sixty years of activity in theory, critique, education, and planning, he has demonstrated a lively duality. Both at home and on the world stage, this has indeed been one of the clearest and most convincing testimonies as to how one can act in continuity with the problems posed by the best modern architectural culture derived from the cutting edge, which is the most conscious of the number and complexity of issues raised by territory and city at the beginning of the last century following the Industrial Revolution and the birth of mass society. Such issues have only increased over the century, making planning ever more of a challenge. Nonetheless, Gregottian continuity has not broken down into a mechanically deductive development of what, for the sake of simplicity, could be defined as the Bauhaus course, which is marked by the call for individual responsibility in a collective process of defining objectives and the means to attain them; and in tune with the real prospects of working in that territory or city. Gregotti never saw such prospects as absolute conditions; on the contrary, he saw them as a context of decision-making methods and realization processes, which could and should be surpassed by a planning action inspired by a principle of the utopia of reality formulated by Ernesto Nathan Rogers, his mentor. The continuity with the modern theories demonstrated by the auteur of La Bicocca has for this reason always been posed in terms that are creatively dialectical with alterations in mentality, changes in the productive system of architecture, the emergence of new expectations as regards living in a place. The duality mentioned thus amounts to the coexistence of a basically linear evolution in modern thought and the necessary reexamination of the motivations that sustained this very thought at the beginning of the twentieth century and continue to nurture it even today. Thus we have a self-conflicting continuity in which the fact of belonging to one cultural faction does not impede one from taking note of the evolution and conflicts that the development of that faction encounters over time.

In Gregottian architecture, two polarities are derived from the dialectical tension briefly mentioned above. The first is an orientation toward a theoretical and operational strategy compliant with certain founding principles of modernity, such as an awareness of the social implications of architecture, analytical rigor, the centrality of the process as opposed to any formal prejudice with the consequent rejection of linguistic self-referentiality, the development of internal planning solutions to a field of common interest with other arts and disciplines, attention to new techniques, without their effects ever being overstated but always attributed to the totality of the architectural phenomenon, the need for every intervention to be integrated as accurately as possible into the graduated articulation system of architecture as a spatial representation of territorial and urban hierarchies. The second is identified with a

continual adaptation, enhanced by critical distance, of such principles according to the various circumstances architecture has been through over the past six decades. Negative occurrences such as the media becoming ever more imposing after the birth of relative aesthetics, the consumerist logic that incessantly accelerates and burns out all architectural expression in an anxious quest for the latest novelty, the growing confusion between the arts, ever more dubiously interchangeable, the progressive disappearance of the differences constituting town and country and the parallel rampant spread of urban sprawl, the decline of the urban plan in favor of interventions lacking the necessary structural relationship with the layout and urban fabric, the abandonment of all typo-morphological parameters, Vittorio Gregotti has opposed all of these, not only from a theoretical point of view, but also, and above all, in his projects and buildings. The highly innovative proposal of the concept of architecture material, extended to the sphere of the contents that directly or indirectly draw on the substance of the discipline; the idea of territory as a new space for discourse, which can renew the project categories; the settlement principle as a logical precondition and at the same time as a primary instrument for any operation on the city, now justly considered as a system that has achieved a more or less definitive dimension, a vision surpassed in favor of the recomposition of the various parts of the urban organism, especially starting from disused areas, make up the most important contributions that Gregotti's work has made to the architectural debate from the 1950s to the present. It should be pointed out that the discontinuous continuity, which characterized his long and varied research was a choice that allowed him not to design and build modern architecture in the orthodox sense, that is, ritually conventional, but to bring to the contradictory world of rationalist architecture those ferments, even oppositive, which often arise from within this same architecture. On the other hand, such discontinuity in continuity, because continuity itself can also be interpreted inversely, has at the same time hindered Gregotti from not being influenced by historicist and performative postmodernism, a questionable consequence of the autonomist theories of architecture originating in the 1960s. Not entirely shared by Gregotti, these theories were, nonetheless, present in his disciplinary conception, but in the form of the conviction that architecture possesses its own dimension, made up of cognitive devices and consolidated operational statutes.

Phenomenology, structuralism, the Frankfurt school and its outcomes in recent decades, the école du regard, the Gruppo '63, of which he was an authoritative representative, Harold Rosenberg's "Tradition of the New," Tafurian criticism, all these created a theoretical landscape that Gregotti inhabited with intensity and originality, giving it memorable interpretations in prestigious journals which he edited, such as *Edilizia*

Moderna, *Casabella*, and *Rassegna*, and in numerous books. Let us not forget his interest in art, which found its highest expression during the 1976 Venice Biennale when, as director of the visual arts section, he came up with events that anticipated the global dimension that would come about years later, in 1989, after the fall of the Berlin Wall. In parallel with his writings, Gregotti has also produced architecture in which control of form, which for him is always, as already mentioned, the result of a process, never an apriority, is so accentuated as to lend it an air of holding back, of introversion, as well as, if it is not a paradox, an extremely clear and precise character. In his early works, one can detect echoes of Art Nouveau, Ridolfian hints, references to Perretian tectonic classicism and Peter Behrens' volumetric severity, but these were mere formative adventures; after a brief interest in technology and the Kahnian world, as in the houses on Via Palmanova in Milan, he arrived at and refined his own autonomous linguistic system. This system could not only be articulated on various scales, but above all it could also participate in the planning process as a set of diagrammatical signs able to connote spaces and volumes. Halfway between grammar and syntax, the architectural writing that derives from these signs amounts to the place of a conceptualism in which the rejection of all smug subjectivism becomes mental discipline, an inclination for an inspired exclusivity. All this is combined with the search for a truth of building as an effect of its authentic and lasting necessity. Finally, in Gregotti's work, understood as an artistic practice, which keeps redefining living by putting it into the broadest context of human awareness and expectations, the city and architecture are not separate entities, rather they participate in each other. In an ideal tension, which it has been written derives from the lesson of Edoardo Persico, whose modernity only increases with time, Gregotti has created parts of cities whose structure precedes and informs the architecture, just as the building is able to reveal its belonging to an order above and beyond its undoubted uniqueness.

During his long career, punctuated by key moments for the disciplinary debate, Gregotti was not alone. He shared the first phase of his activities with his peers Lodovico Meneghetti and Giotto Stoppino, with whom he planned and built buildings which brought their studio a certain fame, based on a careful critical-planning investigation on the themes prevalent at the time. Once this partnership wore thin at the end of the 1960s, there began a season for Gregotti that is still ongoing and in continual evolution, a season that has seen him select interlocutors for succeeding generations, thus creating a dialogue between visions of architecture, which are inevitably diverse, but perhaps for that very reason able to find a common ground dense with new cognitive and creative resources. After the initial phase, in which Gregotti participated, with Hiromichi Matsui, Emilio Battisti, Salvatore Bisogni, writers, and other architects, in the most important competitions of the 1970s, he founded Gregotti Associati around the middle of that decade. It is not entirely accurate to think of this organization as a studio, since from the very beginning it has been more of a situation, which saw various streams of knowledge converge in an experimental dimension unifying the many different thematic and scalar articulations of living in a place. Augusto Cagnardi, Pierluigi Cerri, Hiromichi Matsui, Pierluigi Nicolin, Bruno Viganò, and Spartaco Azzola were, together with Gregotti, the leading names in a season extremely rich in opportunities, allowing this veritable *factory* to express itself in the fields of graphics, exhibitions, design, urban architecture, and planning buildings. Gregotti Associati has been through various phases in forty years, characterized by the prevalence of certain themes over others. Some of its members have undertaken independent activities. Some passed away prematurely, while others, like Michele Reginaldi, joined the organization when it was already on the go for some time. Together with Gregotti, the architects of this organization's well-earned success in Europe and the world, assisted by a vast number of collaborators, proposed not so much a style, which they nonetheless fully achieved, as an advanced, precisely oriented, and receptive way of reforming the theoretical and operational project of architectural modernity in light of new paradigms that have emerged over recent decades, without, however, institutionalizing the planning procedure adopted into a method, but considering each problem as a field of hypotheses, each time different, to be verified in a patient game of thematic overlaps, contextual intersections, correspondences of discourse. In this way, Gregotti's lively duality has also left its mark on the organization he founded, since the recognizability of the architecture borne from it has constituted, as in the theater in Aix-en-Provence to mention but one of his works, something to be overcome each time in order to reaffirm the meaning and value of a creative itinerary that can only be accomplished by continually starting again on its confirmation, like Paul Valery's sea.

Born in Isola del Liri in 1941, architect Franco Purini studied under Maurizio Sacripanti and Ludovico Quaroni. He taught architectural and urban composition at the IUAV University in Venice and at the Faculty of Architecture in Rome. He is a member of the Accademia delle Arti del Disegno in Florence and the Accademia Nazionale di San Luca. In 2013, the president of Italy awarded him the Gold Medal in the Italian Order of Merit for School, Culture, and Art. One of his recent works is the Eurosky Tower in Rome. Amongst his latest publications is La misura italiana dell'architettura, *Editori Laterza, Rome-Bari, 2008.*

 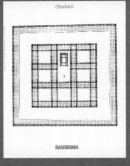   

 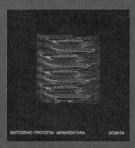   

    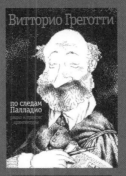 

   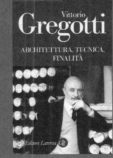 

 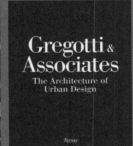    

BOOKS AND MAGAZINES EDITED BY MEMBERS OF GREGOTTI ASSOCIATI STUDIO 1960–2013

The complementary relationship between project, realization, and literature permeates all of Gregotti & Associates' work.

The specific activity of writing is an essential and unavoidable part of the studio's whole project and represents its methodological and cultural foundation.

Testifying to the permanent use of theoretical inquiry into architecture as a discipline with its own foundations, principles, and methods, and critical meditation on the project activity carried out, the two preceding pages display a collection of the covers of the main volumes produced and edited at the studio by partners and associates, specialist journals edited by Vittorio Gregotti and Augusto Cagnardi, special issues of architecture journals edited by Vittorio Gregotti, as well as the main monographs and published catalogs of various authors, historians, critics, and architects, on the work of Gregotti & Associates.

The architecture journals edited by Vittorio Gregotti, *Edilizia Moderna*, *Casabella*, and *Rassegna*, represented the privileged ground on which a considerable part of the international disciplinary debate was developed and continue to serve as an important instrument of critical confrontation. Vittorio Gregotti's books are a constant reference both in the study of architecture as culture and as a specific artistic practice, and in understanding contemporary urban phenomena in terms of their importance for design and their cultural and anthropological significance; for this reason, they have been translated into numerous different languages and can be found in all the main architecture libraries of universities around the world.

Casabella-Continuità, no. 240, June 1960 (issue edited by Vittorio Gregotti).

Casabella-Continuità, no. 254, August 1961 (issue edited by Vittorio Gregotti).

"España," *Zodiac*, no. 15, December 1965 (issue edited by Vittorio Gregotti).

Gregotti, V., *Elementi di Architettura*, Faculty of Architecture of Milan Polytechnic University (handout), Milan, 1966.

"La forma del territorio," *Edilizia Moderna*, no. 87–88, 1966 (editor, Vittorio Gregotti).

Gregotti, V., *Il territorio dell'architettura*, Feltrinelli, Milan, 1966.

Gregotti, V., *Il territorio dell'architettura*, Japanese edition, n.d.

Gregotti, V. (ed.), *L'arte moderna. Vol. XI. Architettura, urbanistica e disegno industriale*, Fabbri, Milan, 1967.

Gregotti, V., *New Direction in Italian Architecture*, George Braziller, New York, 1968.

Gregotti, V., *El territorio de la arquitectura*, Gustavo Gili, Barcelona, 1972.

Cerri, P., Nicolin P. (ed.), *Le Corbusier, Verso un'architettura*, Longanesi, Milan, 1973.

Gregotti, V., *Territorio da arquitectura*, Perspectiva, São Paulo, 1975.

Cagnardi, A., Fabbri M. (ed.), *INU. La riconversione urbanistica*, Dedalo, Bari, 1976.

"Recinti," *Rassegna*, no. 1, 1979 (editor, Vittorio Gregotti).

Tafuri, M. (ed. by Rota I.), *Il progetto dell'Università delle Calabrie e altre architetture di Vittorio Gregotti*, Electa, Milan, 1979.

Cagnardi, A., *Belice 1980: Luoghi, problemi, progetti, dodici anni dopo il terremoto*, Marsilio Editori, Venice, 1981.

Gregotti, V. (ed.), *Il disegno del prodotto industriale: Italia 1860–1960*, Electa, Milan, 1982.

Gregotti, V., *Le territoire de l'architecture*, L'Equerre, Paris, 1982.

Tafuri, M., *Vittorio Gregotti, progetti e architetture*, Electa, Milan, 1982.

Casabella (1982–1996 editor, Vittorio Gregotti).

Cagnardi, A. (ed.), *Strade, piazze, spazi collettivi e scena urbana*, Franco Angeli, Milan, 1983.

Cagnardi, A. (ed.), *Piano e progetto*, Franco Angeli, Milan, 1984.

Gregotti, V. (ed. by Vragnaz G.), *Questioni di architettura: Editoriali di Casabella*, Einaudi, Turin, 1986.

Crotti, S. (ed.), *Vittorio Gregotti*, Zanichelli, Bologna, 1986.

Terra. Rivista di scienze ambientali e territoriali (1987–1990, editor Augusto Cagnardi).

"*Vittorio Gregotti: Architetture*," Duom Gallery, Moscow, 1988.

VV.AA., (ed. by Colao P., Vragnaz G.), *Gregotti Associati: 1973–1988*, Electa, Milan, 1990.

Gregotti, V. (ed.), *Cinque dialoghi necessari*, Electa, Milan, 1990.

Gregotti, V., *Mio nonno esploratore*, Scheiwiller, Milan, 1993.

Gregotti, V., *La città visibile: Frammenti di disegno della città ordinati e catalogati secondo i principî dell'architettura della modificazione contestuale*, Einaudi, Turin, 1993.

Gregotti, V., *Le scarpe di Van Gogh: Modificazioni nell'architettura*, Einaudi, Turin, 1994.

Rykwert, J., (ed. by Borasio M., Colao P., Hansen H.), *Gregotti Associati*, Rizzoli, Milan, 1995.

Cagnardi, A., *Un senso nuovo del piano: Piani regolatori Gregotti Associati*, Etas, Milan, 1995.

Gregotti, V., *Recinto di fabbrica*, Bollati Boringhieri, Turin, 1996.

Gregotti, V., *Inside Architecture*, MIT Press, Boston, 1996.

Casabella, 630–631, January–February 1996 (last issue edited by Vittorio Gregotti).

Gregotti, V., *Racconti di architettura*, Skira, Milan, 1998.

Gregotti, V., *Venezia città della nuova modernità*, Consorzio Venezia Nuova, Venice, 1998.

Gregotti, V., *Identità a crisi dell'architettura europea*, Einaudi, Turin, 1999.

VV.AA., *Progetto Bicocca: I quaderni della Bicocca 01*, Skira, Milan, 1999.

Gregotti, V., *Sulle orme di Palladio*, Laterza, Moscow, 2002 (original Italian edition: Laterza, Roma–Bari, 2000).

Gregotti, V., *Diciassette lettere sull'architettura*, Laterza, Roma–Bari, 2000.

Ceribelli, E., Morpurgo G. (ed.), *Frammenti di costruzioni*, Skira, Milan, 2001.

VV.AA., *Progetto Bicocca: Quaderni della Bicocca 02*, Skira, Milan, 2001.

Pedretti, B. (ed.), *Officina morfologica: Le costruzioni di Michele Reginaldi*, Bolis Edizioni, Azzano San Paolo, 2001.

Pedretti, B. (ed.), *Gregotti Associati: La costruzione dello spazio pubblico*, Alinea, Florence, 2002.

Gregotti, V., *Architettura, tecnica, finalità*, Laterza, Roma–Bari, 2002.

VV.AA., *Progetto Bicocca: Il Teatro degli Arcimboldi*, Skira, Milan, 2003.

Morpurgo, G., *Gregotti Associati 1953–2003*, Rizzoli-Skira, Milan, 2004.

Gregotti, V., *L'architettura del realismo critico*, Laterza, Roma–Bari, 2004.

Morpurgo, G. (ed.), *Progetto Bicocca: Headquarters Pirelli RE*, Skira, Milan, 2005.

Gregotti, V., *Autobiografia del XX secolo*, Skira, Milan, 2005.

Pedretti, B. (ed.), *Quaderni senza parole. Il disegno di Michele reginaldi*, Bolis Edizioni, Azzano San Paolo, 2005.

Pedretti, B. (ed.), *Michele Reginaldi: Disegni e costruzioni*, Azzano San Paolo, 2005.

Gregotti, V., *L'architettura nell'epoca dell'incessante*, Laterza, Roma–Bari, 2006.

"Vittorio Gregotti: Ventiquattro disegni," *Antonia Jannone. Disegni di Architettura - Milano*, Grafiche Milani, Segrate-Milan, 2007.

Morpurgo, G. (ed.), *Festschrift per gli ottant'anni di Vittorio Gregotti*, Skira, Milan, 2007.

Morpurgo, G. (ed.) *Un ordine comprensibile/ An Intelligible Order: Gregotti Associati Banca Lombarda New Headquarters*, Skira, Milan, 2007.

VV.AA., *Gregotti Associati: La fabbrica del Corriere della Sera*, Skira, Milan, 2007.

Cagnardi, A., *Ritorni da Shanghai: Cronache di un architetto italiano in Cina*, Allemandi, Turin, 2008.

Morpurgo, G., *Gregotti & Associati: L'architettura del disegno urbano*, RCS, Milan 2008.

Morpurgo, G., *Gregotti & Associates: The Architecture of Urban Design*, Rizzoli, New York, 2008.

Gregotti, V., *Contro la fine dell'architettura*, Einaudi, Turin, 2008.

VV.AA., *Tra Torino e le Alpi: Il progetto "Corso Marche" per la periferia di Torino*, Allemandi, Turin, 200.

Gregotti, V., *Una lezione di architettura: Rappresentazione, globalizzazione, interdisciplinarità*, Firenze University Press, Florence, 2009.

Gregotti, V., *L'ultimo Hutong*, Skira, Milan, 2009.

Gregotti, V., *Tre forme di architettura mancata*, Einaudi, Turin, 2010.

Gregotti, V., *Architecture, Means, Ends*, University of Chicago Press, Chicago, 2010.

Gregotti, V., *L'architettura di Cézanne*, Skira, Milan, 2011.

Gregotti, V., *Incertezze e simulazioni*, Skira, Milan, 2011.

Gregotti, V., *Architettura e Postmetropoli*, Einaudi, Turin, 2011.

Gregotti, V., *Il sublime al tempo del contemporaneo*, Einaudi, Turin, 2013.

VITTORIO GREGOTTI
ERNESTO N. ROGERS
GIOTTO STOPPINO

1951 Milan
Fitting and organization of the "Misura e grandezza e dell'uomo" hall for the 9th Triennale
(accomplished)

1953–1969
ARCHITETTI ASSOCIATI
VITTORIO GREGOTTI
LODOVICO MENEGHETTI
GIOTTO STOPPINO

1953 Novara
Pavilion for the trade fair
(accomplished)

1953 Stradella (Pavia)
Sforza House
(accomplished)

1953 Novara
Transformable cinema (project)

1953–1959
Plywood armchair designed for the 9th Triennale

1954 Milan
Typical furnishing for an INA-Casa dwelling at the 10th Triennale
(accomplished)

1954 Cameri (Novara)
Residential hub for workers at the Bossi textile industry
(accomplished)

1955 Novara
Mixed-use tower building

1955 Novara
Tadini e Lambertenghi shop
(accomplished)

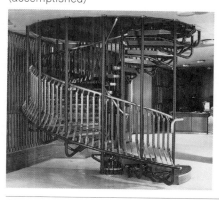

1955 Novara
L.G. apartment furnishing

1955 Novara
Casa Fontana
(accomplished)

1955 Novara
Tower blocks for housing, offices, and hotel
(project)

1956 Novara
Residential building in Via S. Adalgiso
(accomplished)

1956 Novara
Detailed study for the historic town center

1957 Novara
V.F.G. residential complex
(accomplished)

1957–1958 Gardone Valtrompia (Brescia)
Group of three INA-Casa buildings
(accomplished)

1957–1960 Milan
Building model for ten-story housing at the "Quartiere Feltre"
(accomplished)

1957–1961 Solcio di Lesa (Novara)
Holiday homes
(accomplished)

1958–1959 Cameri (Novara)
Four-story housing
(accomplished)

1958–1960 Novara
Residential building for a twelve-member cooperative
(accomplished)

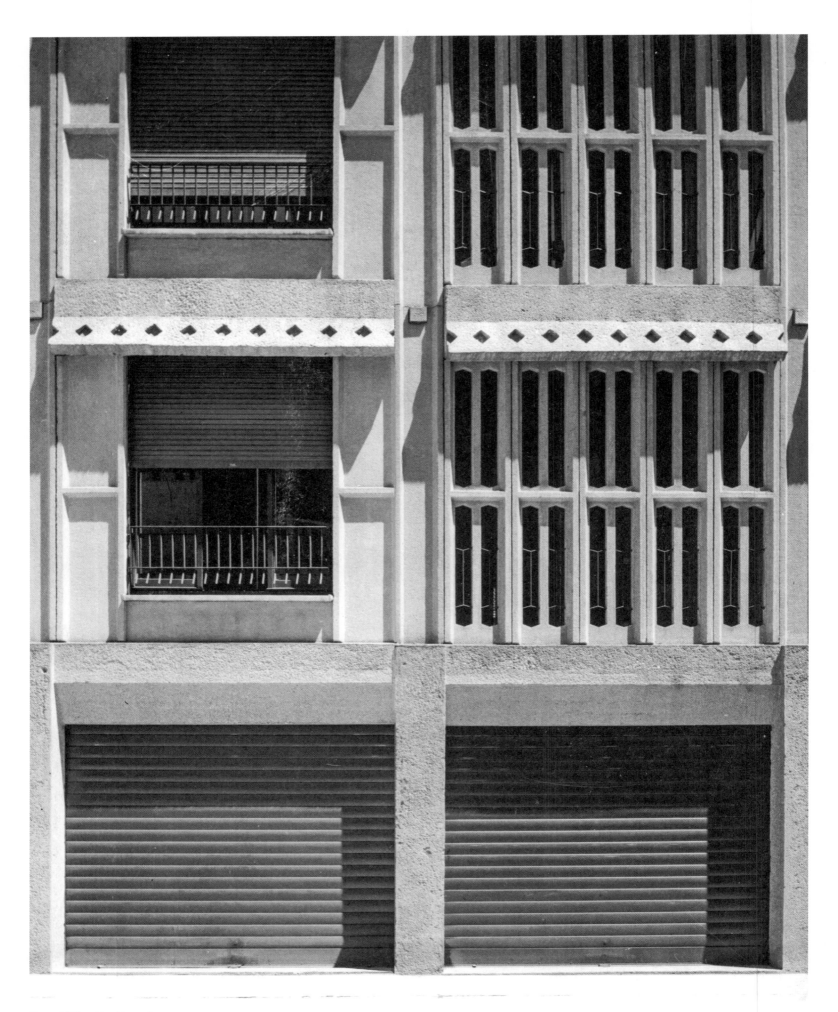

Novara, V.F.G. residential complex

1959 Alessandria
Municipal theater
Competition

1960 Verbania (Verbano-Cusio-Ossola)
Building to house the new courthouse
(competition)

1960 Romegnano Sesia (Novara)
House for the Mira brothers
(accomplished)

1960–1962 Borgomanero (Novara)
IACP residential building
(accomplished)

1960–1963 Bra (Cuneo)
Headquarters of the Banca Popolare di Novara
(accomplished)

1960–1961 Novara
Office building
(accomplished)

1961 Novara
New headquarters of the Civico Orfanotrofio Dominioni
(competition – second place)

1961 Milan
Rural dwelling at the 12th Triennale

1961 Casale Monferrato (Alessandria)
Tadini e Lambertenghi shop
(accomplished)

1961 Romegnano Sesia (Novara)
House of the people: cinematographer and cooperative dwellings (project)

1961–1962 Varese
Casa Poretti (project)

1961–1962 Portofino (Genoa)
House (project)

1961–1964 Omegna (Verbano-Cusio-Ossola)
Work on the town hall
(accomplished)

1961–1964 Cameri (Novara)
Four-story house for workers in the Bossi textile factory
(accomplished)

1962 Carimate (Como)
Duplex house (project)

1962–1964 Milan
Housing cooperative in Via Palmanova, Via Montegani, Via D. Da Settignano
(accomplished)

1963 Milan
13th Triennale. International Introductory Section
Partners: P. Brivio, U. Eco, M. Vignelli
(accomplished)

1963 Novara
General Regulatory Plan

1963 Novara
Plan for cheap housing

1963 Novara
Detailed plan for the area of the former Perrone Barracks

1964 Novara
U.C. Apartment
(accomplished)

1964 Milan
Introductory section on the theme of free time at the 13th Triennale
With: L. Berio, P. Brivio, U. Eco, M. Vignelli
(accomplished)

1964 Novara
Detailed plan "Alcarotti" of the area of the old stadium (project)

1964 Novara
Fitting out of the exhibition "Giovan Battista Crespi detto il Cerano" at the Broletto
With: A. Brizio and M. Rosci (ordinators)
(accomplished)

1965 Florence
Fitting out of the exhibition "La casa abitata"
(accomplished)

1965 Milan
Italsider pavilion at the Trade Fair
(accomplished)

1967 Portorotondo (Sassari)
Square and church

1968 Cameri (Novara)
New spinning mill for the Bossi textile factory
(accomplished)

1969–1974
VITTORIO GREGOTTI

1969 Palermo
La Rinascente department store (project)
Partner: F. Purini

1969 Turin
La Rinascente department store (project)
Partners: P. Brivio, F. Purini

1969 Milan
SMA Group supermarket La Rinascente
Partners: P. Parmiani, B. Paulis
(accomplished)

1969 Vigevano (Pavia)
SMA Group supermarket La Rinascente
(accomplished)

1969 Lucca
Shared housing

1969–1973 Palermo
ZEN residential district for 20,000 inhabitants
First prize in competition
Partners. F. Amoroso, S. Bisogni, H. Matsui,
F. Purini
(partially accomplished)

1969–1990 Palermo
New university science department
Partner: G. Pollini
(accomplished)

1970 Vienna, Austria
Plan for expansion of the city
International competition
Partners: E. Battisti, P. Calza, S. Bisogni, H. Matsui

1970–1972 Mortara (Pavia)
Office for the Bossi company (project)

1970–1973 Genoa, Milan, Trieste, Udine
Fitting out and restructuring of COIN department store (project)

1970 Milan
Carter administrative and trade center (project)

1970 Milan
Apartment on Via Circo
(accomplished)

1970
Signs for COIN department store

1971 Florence
University building
Partners. E. Barbagli, E. Battisti, P. Calza,
G.F. Dall'Erba, E. Detti, G.F. di Pietro, G. Fanelli,
T. Gobbo, R. Innocenti, M. Massa, H. Matsui,
M. Mocchi, F. Neves, F. Purini, P. Sica, B. Viganò,
M. Zoppi
First prize in international competition

1971 Gibellina (Trapani)
Plan for the new urban center
Partners: A. Samonà, G. Samonà, F. Pirrone

1971 Milan
Marco information supermarket
(accomplished)

1972 Rovellasca (Como)
Gabel textile factory and offices
Partner: B. Viganò
(accomplished)

1972 Cantù (Como)
Private homes (project)

1972 Milan
P. apartment restructuring
(accomplished)

1972 Milan
Restructuring of Schaoum site (project)

1973 Varazze (Savona)
Holiday camp (project)

1973 Milan
Ricordi sales outlet
Partners: R. Cecchi, P. Cerri
(accomplished)

1973 Milan
A. apartment furnishing
(accomplished)

1973–1979 Cosenza
Headquarters of Calabria University
Partners: E. Battisti, H. Matsui, P. Nicolin, F. Purini,
C. Rusconi Clerici, B. Viganò
First prize in international competition
(partially accomplished)

1974–1981 Milan
Fondazione Giangiacomo Feltrinelli (project)

1974 Malaga, Spain
Holiday camp for 14,000 people (project)
Partners: J. Martorell, O. Bohigas, D. Mackay

1974 Milan
Marco bookshop
Partner: P. Cerri
(accomplished)

1974 Setubal, Portugal
Residential district for 12,000 inhabitants
(project)

1974–1981
GREGOTTI ASSOCIATI
PIERLUIGI CERRI
VITTORIO GREGOTTI
HIROMICHI MATSUI
PIERLUIGI NICOLIN (LEFT THE STUDIO IN 1978)
BRUNO VIGANÒ (LEFT THE STUDIO IN 1976)

1974 Milan
Gregotti Associati studio, Via M. Bandello
(accomplished)

1974–1976 Adda
Project for the integrated development of the Adda
Partners: Cepro, Laris

1975 Milan
Apartment on Via S. Simpliciano
(accomplished)

1975–1982
Series for the publisher Bompiani
(accomplished)

1976 Laghouat, Algeria
Public administration center (project)

1976 Rovellasca (Como)
New Gabel dyeing and printing works
(accomplished)

1976–1979 Cefalù (Palermo)
Detailed plan for cheap buildings

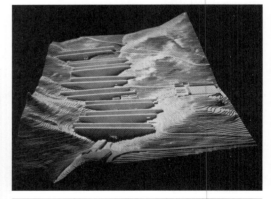

1976–1993
Graphic coordinated image for publisher Electa

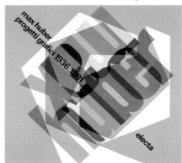

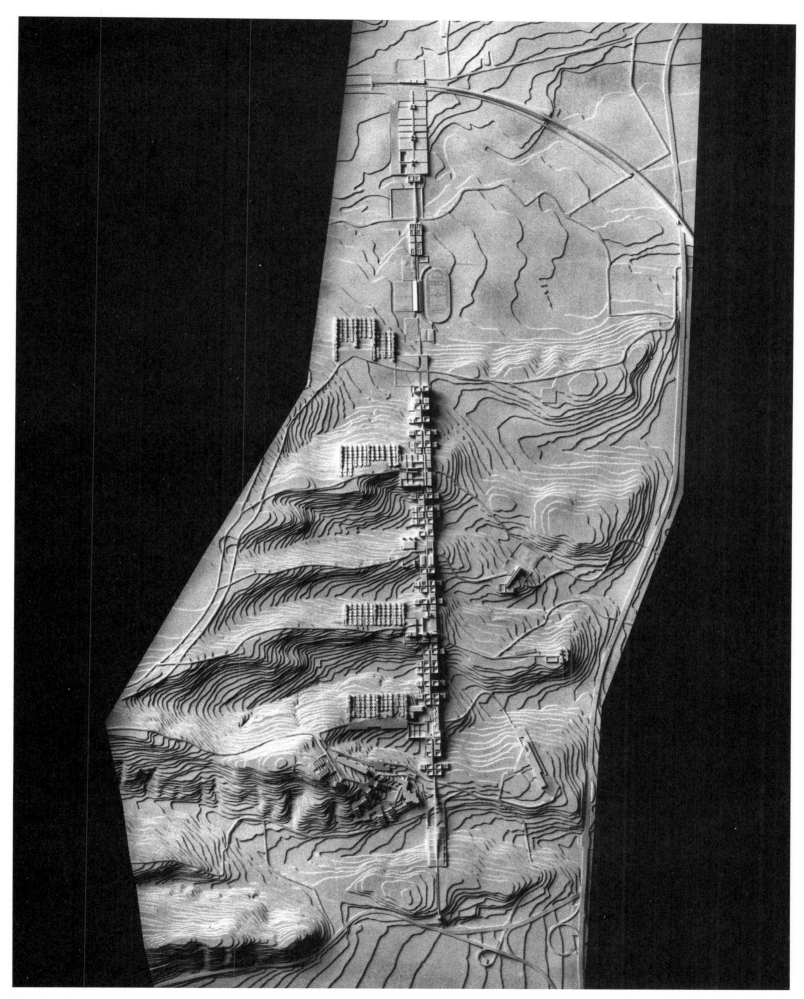

University of Calabria Rende (Cosenza), 1973–1979. Zenithal view of the model

1977 Milan
Missoni boutique
(accomplished)

1977 Novara
Single-family house

1977 Paris, France
Fitting out of the exhibition "Arnaldo Pomodoro" at the Musée d'Art Contemporain
(accomplished)

1977 Turin
Fitting out and visual communication for the exhibition "La carrozzeria italiana" at the Promotrice delle Belle Arti
(accomplished)

1977 Milan
Fusital doorknobs
(accomplished)

1977–1983 Oleggio (Novara)
Beldì house
(accomplished)

1978 Berlin, Germany
Fitting out of the exhibition "Peter Behrens und die AEG" at the Industrial Design Center
(accomplished)

1978 Milan
Marisa shop
(accomplished)

1978 Milan
General Market supermarket
(accomplished)

1978–1979 Turin, Rome
Fitting out of the exhibition "La carrozzeria italiana"
(accomplished)

1978–1986 Portici (Naples)
ENEA 1 photovoltaic research center
(accomplished)

1978–1980 Jeddah, Saudi Arabia
Women's education center
(accomplished)

1978–1999
Graphics for the magazine *Rassegna*
(accomplished)

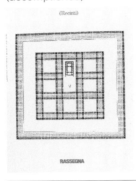

1979 Milan
Consultation for management center
Partner: Laris

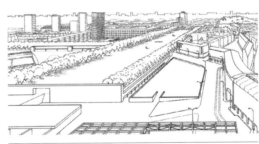

1979 Paris, France
Missoni boutique
(accomplished)

1979 Venice
Fitting out of the exhibition "Venezia 79: La fotografia" at the Magazzini del Sale
Partners: D. Ferretti, N. Valle
(accomplished)

1979 Geneva, Switzerland
Shopping center (project)

1979–1980 Abbiategrasso (Milan)
Work on Fossa Viscontea park (project)

1979–1981 Milan
Librex sales outlet
(accomplished)

1979–1990
Fusital doorknobs
(accomplished)

1979–1982
Lamps for Fontana Arte
(accomplished)

1980 Tokyo, Japan
Headquarters of the Italian Institute of Culture
(project)

1980 Paris, France
Ermenegildo Zegna sales outlet
(accomplished)

1980
Trademark for the book series Hokuspokus
Emme edizioni
(accomplished)

1980 Cameri (Novara)
Offices for the Bossi textile factory
(accomplished)

1980 Milan
Furnishing C. apartment
(accomplished)

1980 Milan
Fitting out of exhibition "Il project per l'Università delle Calabrie e altre architetture di Vittorio Gregotti," Studio Marconi
(accomplished)

1980 Mondovì (Cuneo)
Refurbishment and furnishing single-family house M.
(accomplished)

1980 Cervinia (Aosta)
Furnishing private house M.
(accomplished)

1980 Orta San Giulio (Novara)
Single-family house S. (project)

1980–1981 Paris, France
Fitting out of exhibition "Identité Italienne," Center Pompidou
(accomplished)

1980–1982 Venice
New ACTV shipyard at the Giudecca (project)

1980–1982 Berlin, Germany
Work on the Lützowplatz area-IBA
First prize in international competition
(partially accomplished)

1981–1988
GREGOTTI ASSOCIATI
AUGUSTO CAGNARDI
PIERLUIGI CERRI
VITTORIO GREGOTTI
HIROMICHI MATSUI (LEFT THE
STUDIO IN 1982)

1981
Laboratorio Politico series for Einaudi
publishers
(accomplished)

1981
Trademark for the Società Tessile di Como

1981–1982 Bulgarograsso (Como)
Accommodation and sports facilities
Monticello Ranch (project)

1981 Como
Spina Verde park (project)

1981 Cosenza
Fitting out of the exhibition "Il project per
l'Università delle Calabrie e altre architetture
di Vittorio Gregotti"
(accomplished)

1981 Rome
Poster for the exhibition "Roland Barthes:
Carte, segni" at Palazzo Pallavicini
(accomplished)

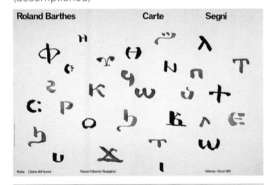

1981 Muggiò (Como)
Sports center (project)

1981 Monate (Varese)
Zoning modification of General Regulatory Plan
(La Motta)

1981–1982 San Marino
Tourist terminal and restructuring of road
layout (project)
Partners: C. Magnani, F. Messina

1981–1982 Milan
Neglia shop
(accomplished)

1981–1983 Sassuolo (Modena)
Educational center with park

1981–1982 Quattordio (Alessandria)
Chemical research center IVI
(partially accomplished)

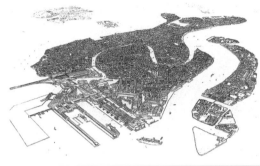

1981–1983 Venice
**Reorganisation of the port area of the historic
city center** (project)

1981–1983 Venice
Detailed plan for the Isola del Tronchetto
Partners: C. Magnani, L. Claut, U. Saccardo,
P.A. Val

1981–1983 Milan
Gabel exhibition system
(accomplished)

1981–1988
Coordinated image for Ubulibri
(accomplished)

1981–1988
Coordinated image for B&B ITALIA, Italy
(accomplished)

1981–2001 Venice
Residential area in Cannaregio
Partners: S. Azzola, E. Casagrande, C. Magnani,
F. Messina, P.A. Val
(accomplished)

1982
Trademark for textile company O'Tool
(accomplished)

1982
Series for publisher Costa & Nolan
(accomplished)

1982
Exhibition system for IBM
(accomplished)

1982 Milan
**Residential and craft settlement on Via Pietro
Custodi** (project)

1982 Milan
Tower for offices and public services at QT8
(project)

1982 Riccione (Forlì)
Center for tourist services (project)
Partners: G. Franchini, M. Federico

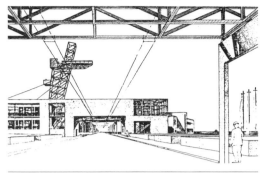

1982 Rome
Fitting out of the exhibition "Hic sunt leones"
(accomplished)

1982 Turin
IVECO regional center (project)

1982 Trieste
Scientific and technological research center
International competition by invitation

1982 Meina (Novara)
**Residential settlement, former Cascami Seta
property** (project)

1982 Luvinate (Varese)
Restructuring of Club il Poggio (project)

1982 Kontrijk, Belgium
B&B ITALIA stand at the Interieur '82 fair
(accomplished)

1982 Venice
Fitting out of the exhibition "Venice verde"
(accomplished)

1982 Naples-Ponticelli
Proposals for the creation of urban parks
(consultancy for the Earthquake Commissioner)

1982 Paris, France
**Fitting out of the exhibition "Vittorio Gregotti:
L'Architecture et le Territoire," Institut Français
d'Architecture**
(accomplished)

1982 Harvard University, Cambridge, MA
**Fitting out of the anthological exhibition
"Vittorio Gregotti"**
(accomplished)

1982–1983 Milan
B&B ITALIA stand at SMAU (Trade fair)
(accomplished)

1982–1983 Milan
**Castelli stand at the Salone del Mobile
(trade fair) and fitting out at the showroom**
(accomplished)

1982–1983 Milan
Industrial restructuring of Verona paper mill
(project)

1982–1983 Coldrerio, Switzerland
Single-family house (project)

1982–1983 Paris, France
Tête le da Défense
Recommended project at the international
competition by invitation

1982–1983 Paris, France
Universal Exposition 1989 (project)

1982–1984 Naples
Consultancy for Earthquake Commission

1982–1986
Graphic image for Unifor
(accomplished)

1982–1986 Scandicci (Florence)
General Regulatory Plan

1982–1995
Graphic image for *Casabella* magazine
(accomplished)

1983 Cologne, Germany
B&B ITALIA stand at the Salone del Mobile
(accomplished)

1983 Milan
IBM sales outlet

1983 Milan
Studio of sculptor Arnaldo Pomodoro
(accomplished)

1983 Stuttgart, Germany
Fitting out of the exhibition "Mobel aus Italie" at the Design Zentrum
(accomplished)

1983 Tokyo, Japan
Fitting out of the exhibition "Design Forniture from Italy" at the Sogetsu Kaikan
(accomplished)

1983 Turin
Twenty projects for the future of the Lingotto
International consultation by invitation

1983 Turin
Image for the exhibition "Venti progetti for the futuro del Lingotto"
(accomplished)

1983 Turin
Graphic image for the exhibition "Alexander Calder" at the Palazzo Vela
(accomplished)

1983 Florence and Paris, France
GFT fitting out at Pitti Uomo
(accomplished)

1983 Bologna and Rome
Poltrona Frau sales outlets
(accomplished)

1983 Barcelona, Spain
Master plan for the 1992 Olympic Games area
(competition)

1983–1984 Cameri (Novara)
Extension of the spinning mill of Bossi textile factory
(accomplished)

1983–1985 Ghedi (Brescia)
Residential buildings
Partner: F. Maffeis
(accomplished)

1983–1989 Modena
Detailed plan of the Corassori area

1983–2001 Milan
Restructuring of the Brera Art Galery
Partner: A. Citterio
(accomplished)

1984 Arezzo
Gardens of Arezzo (project)

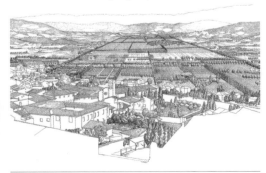

1984 Berlin, Germany
Fitting out of the exhibition "Das Abenteuer der Ideen" at IDZ
(accomplished)

1984 Courmayeur (Aosta)
Sergio Tacchini sales outlet

1984 Bologna
Castelli showroom
(accomplished)

1984
Graphic image for the 17th Triennale
(competition)

1984 Novara
Il Duomo Shop (project)

1984 San Leucio (Caserta)
Organization of the project workshop for the salvaging of the historic settlement

1984
Graphic image for the traveling exhibition "Achille Castiglioni"
(accomplished)

1984 Barcelona, Spain
Olympic sports facility
Partners: F. Correa, A. Milà, S. Zorzi
International competition by invitation - first prize

1984 Ceciliano (Arezzo)
General Regulatory Plan

1984 Como
Terminal for Northern Railways, Milan (project)
Partner: Studio Quaglia

1984 Florence
Museum of contemporary art (project)

1984 Florence
Fitting out of the exhibition "Arnaldo Pomodoro" at the Forte di Belvedere
(accomplished)

1984 Los Angeles, CA
Graphical applications for Knoll International
(accomplished)

1984 Milan
Participation in the Transport Project for the CNR

1984 Milan
Graphic image for RAI stand
(accomplished)

1984 Milan
Ungaro GFT showroom (project)

1984 Bologna
Fitting out of the exhibition "Detailed plan for the zona Corassori" at SAIE
(accomplished)

1984 Naples
Trademark for the Naples Foundation '99
(accomplished)

Achille Castiglioni   Designer

Rauminstallationen, Objekte und Industrial Design 1950-1984

Wien 1, Stubenring 5 (Eingang Weisskirchnerstrasse)   Dienstag - Sonntag, 10-18 Uhr   Eintritt frei

Image design for the traveling exhibition "Achille Castiglioni," 1984

1984 Rome
IBM sales outlet

1984 Rome
Archaeological park at the Imperial Fora
(project)
Partner: L. Benevolo

1984–1985 Brescia
Urban park at San Polo (project)

1984–1985 Fano (Ancona)
Work on the west beach (project)

1984–1985 Milan
Work on the Cadorna area (project)
Partners: G14 Progettazione, Studio GPI, A. Calvesi

1984–1985 New York, NY
Restructuring of a private house in Manhattan
(accomplished)

1984–1985 Venice
Logotype for Palazzo Grassi
(accomplished)

1984–1985 Livorno
La Scopara district for 7,500 inhabitants
(project)

1984–1985 San Marino
Building for offices and public-interest activities Molino
(accomplished)

1984–1986 Berlin, Germany
Houses on Lützowstrasse
(accomplished)

1984–1987 Arezzo
General Regulatory Plan

1984–1988
Coordinated image for Padua
(accomplished)

1984–1988 Arezzo
Extension of the town hall
(accomplished)

1984–1995 Cadoneghe (Treviso)
Building for housing and offices

1984–2006 Menfi (Agrigento)
Piazza Madrice, extension of the town hall, Federiciana Tower and Mother-Church
(accomplished)

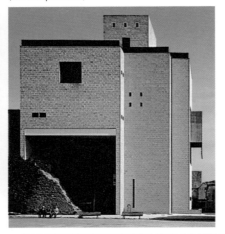

1985
Silver coffee set for Cleto Munari
(accomplished)

1985
Coordinated image for Molteni
(accomplished)

1985
Studio for the weekly *L'Espresso*
(accomplished)

1985 Lodi
Headquarters of the Banca Popolare di Lodi
International competition by invitation

1985 Marseilles, France
Institut Méditerranéen de Technologie
International competition by invitation

1985 Milan
B&B ITALIA stand at the Salone del Mobile
(Trade Fair)
(accomplished)

1985 Milan
Trademark of the 17th Triennale
Competition by invitation

1985 Milan
Marzotto showroom
(accomplished)

1985 Milan
SITEX stand at the Trade Fair
(accomplished)

1985 Milan
Castelli stand at the Salone del Mobile
(Trade Fair)
(accomplished)

1985 Milan
Unifor stand at the Salone del Mobile
(Trade Fair)
(accomplished)

1985 Novara
Open space planning

1985 Morciano di Romegna (Forlì)
Work on Piazza Boccioni
(accomplished)

1985 Palermo
Furnishings of the biology department of the university
(accomplished)

1985 Toronto, Canada
Participation in the exhibition "The European Iceberg: Creativity in Germany and Italy Today,"
Art Gallery of Ontario (AGO)

1985 Cambridge, United Kingdom
Fitting out of the exhibition "Vittorio Gregotti"
(accomplished)

1985 Spotorno (Savona)
Work on Via Aurelia and tourist facilities
(project)

1985 Venice
Poster and graphics for the performance "Il corso del coltello"
(accomplished)

1985 Milan
Restructuring of private house R. (project)

1985 Milan
Work on Piazza Meda
(accomplished)

1985–1986 Cologne, Germany
B&B ITALIA stand at the Salone del Mobile
(accomplished)

1985–1986 Cinisello Balsamo (Milan)
Headquarters of the Abet Laminati company
(accomplished)

1985–1986 Como
Sports facilities in the Lazzago plain

1985–1986 Foligno (Perugia)
Exhibition center (project)

1985–1986 Milan
Bardelli shop on Via Madonnina
(accomplished)

1985–1986 Milan
Restructuring apartment M.
(accomplished)

1985–1986 Salemi (Trapani)
Urban park
First prize in the international competition by
invitation

1985–1986 Cinisello Balsamo (Milan)
**Restructuring canteen and exhibition halls at
Magneti Marelli** (project)

1985–1986
Exhibition structure for Tacchini Sandy's corner
(accomplished)

1985–1988 Milan
**Plan for the transformation of the Pirelli area
at Bicocca**
First and second stage of the competition
First prize in the international competition by
invitation
(accomplished)

1985–1988 Rome
ENEA research center at la Casaccia
(accomplished)

1985–1990 Parma
**Headquarters of the Azienda Municipalizzata
Pubblici Servizi**
Partners: F. Mascellani, M. Felisatti
(accomplished)

1986
Series for the publisher Archinto
(accomplished)

1986
Valli and Colombo doorknobs
(accomplished)

1986 Frankfurt, Germany
Gym near Südbahnhof
International competition by invitation

1986 Ghemme (Novara)
Offices for Ponti factory

1986 Lugano, Switzerland
**Fitting out of the exhibition "I tesori
dell'Ermitage"**
(accomplished)

1986 Milan
**Graphic image for the RAI pavilion at the Trade
Fair**
(accomplished)

1986 Milan
Furnshing of apartment M.

1986 Milan
Restructuring of apartment C. in Piazza Castello
(accomplished)

1986 Milan
**Fitting out of the sale of futurist objects at
Centro Domus**
(accomplished)

1986 Naples
Redevelopment of the eastern districts
International consultation by invitation

1986 Paris, France
**Signs at the headquarters of IBM Europe at La
Défense**
(accomplished)

1986 Rome
**Graphics for the Quadriennale Internazionale
d'Arte**
(accomplished)

1986 Rome
Interchange terminal on Via Cristoforo Colombo
(project)

1986 Seville, Spain
Universal Exposition 1992
First prize in the international competition of
ideas

1986 Venice
**Catalog and graphics for the exhibition
"Futurismo e Futurismi" at Palazzo Grassi**
(accomplished)

1986 Vicenza
Work on Piazza Matteotti area
First prize in the competition of ideas

1986 Yanbu, Saudi Arabia
Harbor Island Park (project)

1986 Salzburg, Austria
Diakonisches Zentrum Salzburg-Aigen (project)

1986 Milan
**B&B ITALIA stand at the Salone del Mobile
(Trade Fair)**
(accomplished)

1986 London, United Kingdom
**Fitting out of Poltrona Frau stand at Harrod's
department store**
(accomplished)

1986 Frankfurt, Germany
Extension of Frankfurt University Bio-Center
(competition)

1986
**Graphic project of the book for the anniversary
of B-Ticino**

1986
Graphics projects for:
· book *El cuchillio barco*
· Fontana Arte – insert for *Abitare* February
· book for AEM *5 fotografi per l'energia*
· AMSA (SCS) – greetings cards and 1987
  calendar
· book *The Course of the Knife*, Electa
  Publishers
· *De Padova News*

1986 Milan
Feasibility study for a design museum

1986
Furnishing and accessories projects:
· Poltrona Frau sofa
· Molteni sofa
· Fusital trays
· marble objects for Ultima edizione
(accomplished)

1986–1988 Geneva, Switzerland
Alfa Romeo stand at the Motor Show
(accomplished)

1986–1987 Nîmes, France
Football and rugby stadium
First prize in the international competition
by invitation
Partners: M. Chausse, Beterem
(accomplished)

1986–1987 Rome
IBM technological center at Santa Palombo
(project)

1986–1988 Barcelona, Spain
Olympic stadium
Partners: F. Correa, A. Milà, Inco (S. Zorzi,
A. Fornari, F. Cortina), C. Buxadè, J. Margarit
(accomplished)

1986–1989 Genoa-Marassi
Luigi Ferraris stadium
(accomplished)

1986–1989 Rovellasca (Como)
Extension of the Gabel factory
(accomplished)

1986–2001 Arezzo
Educational center
With Mauro Galantino
(accomplished)

1987
Series for the publisher Bollati Boringhieri
(accomplished)

1987
**Coordinated image for the urban spaces
of Italia 90**
(accomplished)

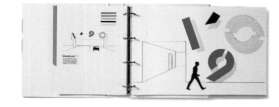

1987
Graphic image for "P.R.G. Turin"

1987
**Salvaging of the former ATB industrial area,
Brescia 2** (project)

1987
**Offshore multifuel power station
for ENEL-Ansaldo** (project)
Partner: Ismes

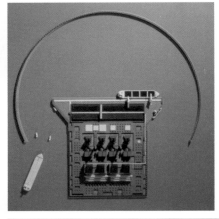

1987 Brescia
**Transformation of the Azienda Tubi industrial
area, Brescia** (project)
Partner: G. Lombardi

1987 Ferrara
Proposal for parking areas in the urban belt
Partner: N. Ventura

1987 Ferrara
**Proposal for the areas along the new Via
Bologna**

1987 Florence
Salvaging of the Murate
Partner: F. Landini
First prize in the international competition
by invitation

1987 Genoa
**Consultation for the General Regulatory Plan
of the port**

1987 Istanbul, Turkey
Project for work on Üsküdar's squares
Partner: B. Ciagà
Recommended project in the international
competition by invitation

1987 Madrid, Spain
**Fitting out of the exhibition "FIAT Las Formas
de la Industria"**
(accomplished)

1987 Milan
**Fitting out of the exhibition "I Maggiolini"
at the Salone del Mobile**
(accomplished)

1987 San Donato Milanese (MI)
Fifth SNAM office block (project)

1987 Mira (Venice)
Redevelopment of public spaces (project)

1987 Neuchâtel, Switzerland
Archaeological museum
International competition by invitation

1987 New York, NY
B&B ITALIA showroom
(accomplished)

1987 Paris, France
**Fitting out of the exhibition "Le Corbusier"
at the Center Georges Pompidou**
(accomplished)

1987 Rome
Rome City Stadium (project)
Partners: Reconsult, A. Bernardi

1987
**Graphic project for the book *Bruce Naumann*,
Rizzoli International Publications**
(accomplished)

1987
Furnishing elements for Fontana Arte
(accomplished)

1987
Folding seat of light alloy for B&B ITALIA

1987 Geneva, Switzerland
**Graphics for Alfa Romeo stand
at the Motor Show**
(accomplished)

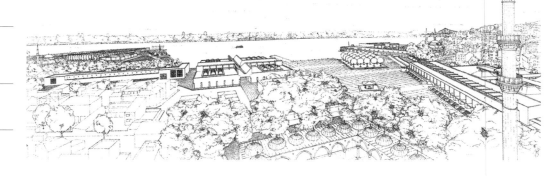

1987 Zurich, Switzerland
**Exhibition of Vittorio Gregotti projects – ETHZ
(Eidgenössische Technische Hochschule
Zürich)**

1987 Bergamo
Salvaging of the former Camozzi barracks
(project)

1987 Milan
**Fitting out of the exhibition of the
reorganization project of Brera Art Gallery**
(accomplished)

1987 Frankfurt, Germany
Alfa Romeo stand at the Motor Show
(accomplished)

1987
Scenography, commercials, and writing for RAI 3
(accomplished)

1987 Tokyo, Japan
Fitting out of the exhibition of Vittorio Gregotti projects at the MA Gallery
(accomplished)

1987 Milan
Fitting out of the exhibition "Forum del Design"

1987 Cameri (Novara)
Work on square and entrance to Via Martiri Partigiani (project)

1987 Ferrara
Fitting out of the exhibition "Arnaldo Pomodoro" at the Palazzo dei Diamanti
(accomplished)

1987 Arezzo
Restructuring of the old hospital (project)

1987 Arezzo
Salvaging for le Mura (project)

1987 Milan
Restructuring Bardelli shops
(accomplished)

1987 Venice
Graphic project and catalog for the exhibition "Jean Tinguely" at Palazzo Grassi
(accomplished)

1987
Graphics for:
· Alliance Graphique International conference
· advertisement for Abet Laminati in *Rassegna*
· books on Carol Rama and Beppe Novello for Archinto Edizioni
· book on Gabriel Bella for Fabbri editori
· conference on energy for AEM
· Italia '90 Championships

1987 Marseilles, France
Sergio Tacchini showroom

1987 Arezzo
Parking localization study

1987 Milan
B&B ITALIA stand at the Salone del Mobile (Trade Fair)
(accomplished)

1987 Milan
Fitting out of the exhibition "Arte in Lombardia Gotico-Rinascimento" at the Brera Art Gallery
(accomplished)

1987 Scandicci (Florence)
Project study for Scandicci center

1987 Stockholm, Sweden
Alfa Romeo stand at the airport
(accomplished)

1987 Milan
Apartment AC
(accomplished)

1987 Novara
Sergio Tacchini showroom
(accomplished)

1987 Turin
Fitting out of the exhibition "Le Corbusier"
(accomplished)

1987 Genoa
Development project for the I.R.I. areas

1987 Bilbao, Spain
Coordinated image for the Metropolitana
(competition)

1987 Milan
Marisa shop on Via Sant'Andrea
(accomplished)

1987 Rapallo (Genoa)
S. Michele Pagano building (project)

1987–1988 Turin
Trademark for the exhibition "Civiltà della macchine" at the Lingotto
(accomplished)

1987–1990 Ancona
Headquarters of the Marche Region
(accomplished)

1987–1990 Ferrara
Exhibition center
(accomplished)

1987–1992 Cantù (Varese)
Sports arena
Partners: S. Cavalleri, F. Maffeis, E. Mantero, G. Medri

1987–1992 Darfo-Boario Terme (Brescia)
General Regulatory Plan

1987–1994 Sesto San Giovanni (Milan)
General Regulatory Plan

1987–1995 Padua
Service center in the San Carlo–Arcella area
(partially accomplished)

1987–1995 Turin
General Regulatory Plan

1987–2000 Bergamo
Gallery of modern and contemporary art at the Accademia Carrara
(accomplished)

1987–2001 San Giovanni Valdarno (Arezzo)
Valdarno hospital
(accomplished)

1987–2002 Lecco
Transformation of former SAE area
(accomplished)

1988–1998
GREGOTTI ASSOCIATI INTERNATIONAL
AUGUSTO CAGNARDI
PIERLUIGI CERRI
VITTORIO GREGOTTI

1988
Poster for the bicentennial of the French Revolution
(accomplished)

1988
Exhibition system for the publisher Electa
(accomplished)

1988
Tables for Fontana Arte (project)

1988
Coordinated image for the publisher Le Promeneur
(accomplished)

1988
Coordinated image for Pitti Image

1988
Exhibition system for car manufacturer Alfa Romeo
(accomplished)

1988 Barcelona, Spain
Fitting out of the exhibition "Le Corbusier" at the Fundaciò Joan Mirò
(accomplished)

1988 Bari
Study for the railway station

1988 Bilbao, Spain
Graphic image of the metropolitana
International competition by invitation

1988 Bologna
CNR research center
Competition

1988 Lecco
New hospital
Competition

1988 Milan
New Costa Crociere offices on Via Boccaccio
(project)

1988 London, United Kingdom
Fitting out of the exhibition "The FIAT Case" at the Science Museum
(accomplished)

1988 Milan
Fitting out of the exhibition "Razionalismo italiano" at the Salone del Mobile
(accomplished)

1988 Milan
Marisa shop
(accomplished)

1988 Milan
Fitting out of the exhibition "La fotografia" at the Triennale
(accomplished)

1988 Milan
Innovative transport system
Partners: Ansaldo Trasporti, S. Zorzi

1988
Graphics projects for:
· indoor signs for the Eurocucine fair
· Unifor
· Fontana Arte
· catalog of the exhibition "Paolo Deganello from 1973 till today" (Brinnen Gallery – Amsterdam)
· indoor signs for the Salone del Mobile
· trademark for the Consorzio Industriale Sardo (competition)
· monograph VIDAS
· image for Pitti Centro Moda Florence (competition)
· graphic image for *Leggere* magazine
· graphic image for publisher Le Promeneur
· book *Saras* Electa
· brochure for Zucchi fabric shop
· diary for the Cancer Research Association
· catalog for "I Fenici," Fabbri editori
· trademark for Finanziaria Fidis
· poster for Polaroid (competition)
(accomplished)

1988 Bari
Project for the station

1988 Turin
Alfa Romeo stand at the Motor Show
(accomplished)

1988 Portici (Naples)
CAMPEC building for ENEA
(accomplished)

1988 Genoa
Proposal for CAP Levante tourist facilities for "Impresit"

1988 Bologna
CNR research area (competition)

1988 Milan
Hotel on Via Pasubio

1988 Milan
Building on Via Valpetrosa

1988 Siena
Headquarters of Monte dei Paschi di Siena and the Chamber of Commerce
International competition by invitation

1988 Porto Marghera (Venice)
MONTEDIPE building and plant (project)

1988 Milan
Fitting out of the exhibition "Marcel Duchamp, la Sposa e i Readymade" at Brera Art Gallery
(accomplished)

1988
Exhibition system for Missoni (project)

1988 Milan
B&B ITALIA stand at the Salone del Mobile
(accomplished)

1988 Milan
Launch of the implementation phase of the Bicocca project:
· Studies on the road network system
· Building concessions assigned
· Collina dei Ciliegi
· Section 1S - Bdg. 120-334-45-262-46/66
· Building 43-1B-Section N-1B-Section HON
· Second University of Milan Section G
· Section 1S - Building 120-334
· Section H
· Section IL+1P
· Section IL - Tower U7-U8-U9-U1-U2-U3
· Section 1
· Section C - Headquarters of European Environment Agency
· Sections 1I and 1P - First proposal for Slemens Headquarters
· Section M - New offices AEM Building 157
· Building 222
· Section 1S-1B-43
· Variant of PRG Section GHN
(accomplished)

1988 Milan
Fitting out of the exhibition on rationalism at the Salone del Mobile
(accomplished)

1988 Milan
Fitting out of the exhibition "Forum del Design"
(accomplished)

1988 Venice
Pavilion of the Biennale (competition)

1988 Milan
Fitting out of the exhibition on chemistry at the Museum of Science and Technology
(accomplished)

1988 Lecco
Detailed plan of former SAE area

1988 Florence
Zucchi drapery stand at Pitti fair
(accomplished)

1988 Crema (Cremona)
Restructuring apartment D.
(accomplished)

1988 Ischia (Naples)
Sant'Angelo d'Ischia marina (project)

1988 Milan
Restructuring of a building on Via Valpetrosa-Via Torino
(accomplished)

1988
Lamp Tea for Fontana Arte
(accomplished)

1988 Venice
Graphics for the exhibition "I Fenici" at Palazzo Grassi
(accomplished)

1988 Venice
Italy pavilion at Sant'Elena Gardens
International competition by invitation

1988–1989
Recovery plan for the IRI areas in Genoa, Naples, Taranto, and Terni

1988–1989 Benidorm, Spain
Sports arena (project)

1988–1989 Brescia
Study for work on Cidneo Hill
With B. Albrecht, I. Tognazzi

1988–1989 Brescia
Transformation of the steelworks area (project)
Partners: Lombardi Associati

1988–1989 Milan
Proposal for transformation of the Motta area
(project)

1988–1990
Cruise ship *Costa Classica*
(accomplished)

Belém Cultural Center, Lisbon, 1988–1993

1988–1990 Genoa
**District heating power station
at Sampierdarena**
(accomplished)

1988–1993 Lisbon, Portugal
Belém cultural center
First prize in the international competition
by invitation
Partner: RISCO–Manuel Salgado
(accomplished)

1988–1997 La Spezia
Piazzale Kennedy urban center
(accomplished)

1988–2006 Milan
**Restructuring of the *Corriere della Sera*
headquarters**
(accomplished)

1989 Rome
**Fitting out of the Italian Communist Party
Conference at the Palaeur**
(accomplished)

1989 Estoril, Portugal
Conference center (competition)

1989 Hong Kong
Missoni sales outlet

1989 Birmingham, United Kingdom
Transformation of the Heartlands areas
International competition by invitation

1989 Florence
**Fitting out of the exhibition "L'idea Ferrari"
at the Forte di Belvedere**
(accomplished)

1989 Jesi (Ancona)
Restructuring of the Art Gallery

1989 La Spezia
Restructuring of A. Picco Stadium

1989 Marseilles, France
Concert hall
International competition

1989 Milan
Transformation of the Asea Brown Boveri areas
(project)

1989 Milan
Headquarters of Bayer Italia at il Portello
International competition by invitation

1989 Milan
Marisa shop
(accomplished)

1989 New York, NY / Venice
**Poster for the exhibition "Mario Merz"
at the Guggenheim Museum**
(accomplished)

1989 Reggio Emilia
Swimming center
First prize in competition

1989 Milan
Graphics projects:
· Salone del Mobile
· UNIFOR
· catalog for the traveling exhibition "Depero:
  Teatro magico," Electa
· coordinated image for Ferrari Auto and
  graphics project "Rivista Ferrari"
· book *Gregotti Associati*, Electa
· B&B ITALIA
· FIAT graphic atlas
· FIAT stand at Turin Motor Show
· AEM institution book
· signs for AEM
· catalog for the exhibition "Neoliberty e
  dintorni" for COSMIT
· graphic image for Fontana Arte
· graphic image for GFT Turin
(accomplished)

1989 Rome
Fitting out for the PCI conference at the Palaeur
(accomplished)

1989 San Benedetto del Tronto (Ascoli Piceno)
Plan for the urban spaces of the port area

1989 Scandicci (Florence)
Auditorium and music school (project)

1989 Milan
**B&B ITALIA showroom on Corso Europa
B&B ITALIA stand at EIMU**
(accomplished)

1989 Bologna
I Guzzini stand at SAIE
(accomplished)

1989 Brescia
B&B ITALIA sales outlet

1989 Frankfurt, Germany
Alfa Romeo stand at the Motor Show
(accomplished)

1989 Montelupo Fiorentino (Florence)
Colorobbia industrial complex (project)

1989 Novara
Fitting out of the exhibition "Arnaldo Pomodoro"
(accomplished)

1989
Chairs for B&B ITALIA

1989 Milan
New Marisa shop on Via Sant'Andrea
(accomplished)

1989 Frankfurt, Germany
FIAT stand at the Motor Show
(accomplished)

1989 Saturnia (Grosseto)
Project for a spa

1989 Tokyo, Japan
Catalog for the exhibition "Creativitalia"
(accomplished)

1989 Venice
**Fitting out of the exhibition "Arte italiana
1900-1945" at Palazzo Grassi**
(accomplished)

1989 Venice
Feasibility study for the port

1989
Furniture for Zanotta

1989 Turin
**Assolombarda pavilion for the exhibition
"Civiltà delle Macchine"**
(accomplished)

1989 Rome
Offices of the Italian Communist Party in Palazzo Valdina
(accomplished)

1989 Monticello (Varese)
House M. (project)

1989 Lecco
District Territorial Plan

1989 Arezzo
Auditorium (project)

1989–1991 Nîmes, France
Palais Omnisport
(accomplished)

1989–1993 Milan-Bicocca
AEM experimental power station
(accomplished)

1989–1994 Nîmes, France
Pavilion for trade fairs and expositions
(accomplished)

1989–1997 Sesto San Giovanni (Milan)
Plan for the transformation of the Falk Vulcano area

1989–1996 Cesena (Forlì)
Plan for the transformation of the former sugar refinery area
(accomplished)

1990 Aix-en-Provence, France
PAZ Zone Sud Stade des Costières
(competition)

1990 Lecco
Urban renewal plan

1990 Levallois-Perret, France
Le Plessis Robinson (competition)

1990 Barcelona, Spain
Project for the Pirelli factory in Villanueva y Geltru

1990 Milan
House A. and M.
(accomplished)

1990 Strasbourg, France
Gare de Kehl (competition)

1990 Redecesio di Segrate (Milan)
CISE workshops and offices (project)

1990
Graphics projects:
· UNIFOR
· AEM institution book
· catalog for the exhibition "Andy Warhol"
· poster "The Lion of Venice"
(accomplished)

1990 Singapore
Missoni Sport showroom–Malerba

1990 Paris, France
Cables Pirelli Saint Maurice (competition)

1990 Aix-en-Provence, France
Opération Sextius-Mirabeau
Second prize in the international competition by invitation

1990 Aix-en-Provence, France
Technopole de l'Arbois
International competition by invitation

1990 Berlin, Germany
Berlin Morgen
International consultation by invitation

1990 Jesi (Ancona)
Lift system for the historic town center (project)

1990 La Ciotat, France
Work on promenade (project)

1990 Milan
Davide Cenci shop on Via Manzoni
(accomplished)

1990 Milan
CISE workshops and offices

1990 Monza
Sports arena
First prize in competition

1990 Nairobi, Kenya
Times Kenya Complex
International competition by invitation

1990 Paris, France
Fila shop on Boulevard des Capucines
(accomplished)

1990 Paris, France
Alfa Romeo stand at the Motor Show
(accomplished)

1990 Spotorno (Savona)
Docks project in Serra area (project)

1990 Bastia (Corsica)
New Prefecture (competition)

1990 Milan
Fitting out of the exhibition "I popoli del sole e della luna"
(accomplished)

1990 Siena
Salvaging of the Santa Maria della Scala Hospital
International competition by invitation

1990 Stuttgart, Germany
Hewlett-Packard headquarters
International competition by invitation

1990–1991 and 1999 Paris, France
Salle des Etats and Aile Denon at the Louvre
Finalist in international competition by invitation

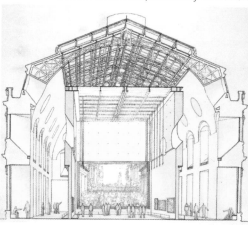

1990 Marseilles, France
Gare du Prado SNCF (competition)

1990 Cassinetta di Lugagnano (Milan)
Restoration of building P.

1990 Pordenone
Building on Via Garibaldi (project)

1990 Milan
Fitting out of the COSMIT exhibition
(accomplished)

1990 Geneva-Paris-Turin
Alfa Romeo stand at the Motor Show
(accomplished)

1990 Dubai, United Arab Emirates
National Bank of Dubai (competition)

1990 London, United Kingdom
Fitting out of the Alfa Romeo exhibition
(accomplished)

1990 Cameri (Novara)
General Regulatory Plan

1990–1993 Turin
Detailed plan Spina 2

1991 Berlin, Germany
Reorganization of Potsdamer and Leipziger Platz
International competition by invitation

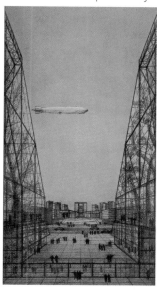

1991 Bonn, Germany
Fitting out and graphics for the exhibition "Erdsicht" at the Kunst und Ausstellungshalle (accomplished)

1991 Gargano
Gargano National Park
First prize in competition

1991 Lazise (Verona)
Naval Archaeology Museum (project)

1991 Lecco
Courthouse in former SAE area

1991 Lisbon, Portugal
Exhibition center at the airport
Partner: RISCO-M. Salgado

1991 Madrid, Spain
OS service station
(accomplished)

1991 Malaga, Spain
Plan for the Teatino district
Partners: M. Salgado, A. Siza

1991 Montreuil, France
Plan for transformation of the industrial area on Péripherique di Paris

1991 New York, NY
Fila shop
(accomplished)

1991 Potenza
Lift system to Parta Salza and Cucuzzo neighborhoods (project)

1991 Prague, Czech Republic
Workshop Prague 91
First prize in international competition by invitation

1991
Graphics projects:
· signs for the Museum of Ethnography, Frankfurt, Germany
· exhibition "L'arte americana" at the Lingotto (Turin)
· coordinated graphic image for the Lingotto
· coordinated graphic image for FIAT Group
· catalog for the exhibition "I Celti," Fabbri editori
· advertisement insert for *De Padova*
· coordinated graphics for the KAH Museum, Cologne, Germany
· catalog for the exhibition "Ori e argenti russi: Mille anni di storia," Electa
· trademark "Trony"
· brochure for Zucchi drapers
· brochure for Ferrari Auto
· FIAT institution book
· Guggenheim catalog
· Furniture Fair
· B&B ITALIA
· De Padova News
(accomplished)

1991 San Donato (Milan)
Multifunctional urban center
Idea competition by invitation

1991 Strasbourg, France
Place de l'Etoile
Partner: A. Rivkin
First prize in international competition by invitation

1991 Turin
Po project

1991 Treviso
Plan to salvage former Cerato area

1991 Milan
Fitting out of the exhibition "Mobili Italiani 1961–1991: Le Varie Età dei linguaggi" at the Triennale for COSMIT
(accomplished)

1991 Mantua
Work on Porta Pratella area (competition)

1991 Frankfurt, Germany
Alfa Romeo stand at the Motor Show
(accomplished)

1991 Milan
Fitting out for SMAU
(accomplished)

1991 Milan
Fitting out for Euroluce
(accomplished)

1991 Novara
Feasibility study for the salvage of former Perrone barracks (University)

1991 Rozzano (Milan)
Senior citizens' housing (project)

1991 Milan
Garibaldi-Repubblica Area (competition)

1991 Nîmes, France
Université Bipolaire Fort Vauban (competition)

1991 Spain
OS service stations (SARAS)
(partially accomplished)

1991
Fitting out of the exhibition "Erdschicht," KAH
(accomplished)

1991 Milan
Fitting out of the exhibition on Indonesia at the La Rinascente department store
(accomplished)

1991 Lisbon, Portugal
Bridge over the Avenida da India (competition)
Partner: RISCO-Manuel Salgado

1991 Milan
Fitting out of the fourth and fifth floors of the La Rinascente department store

1991 Montepulciano (Siena)
Revision of detailed plan

1991 Florence
Zucchi stand at Pitti fair
(accomplished)

1991 San Polo di Piave (Treviso)
Feasibility study for the historic town center

1991–1996
Coordinated graphic image for Fontana Arte

1991–1992
Coordinated graphic image for Valli & Colombo

1991–1992 Ca' del Bue (Verona)
Waste treatment plant
(accomplished)

1991–1992 Campegine (Reggio Emilia)
Coop headquarters and plants

1991–1992 Potsdam, Germany
Park for the Brandenburg Land (project)

1991–1995
Coordinated graphic image for Unifor

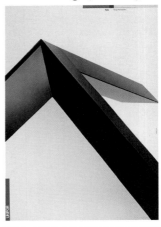

1991–1993
Cruise ship *Costa Romentica*
(accomplished)

1991–1993 Milan
CNR headquarters at Bicocca
(accomplished)

1991–1993 Portofino (Genoa)
Monte di Portofino Park (project)

1991–2007 Baruccana di Seveso (Milan)
Church and parochial buildings
(accomplished)

1992–1994
Exhibition system for Alenia factory
(accomplished)

1992
Graphics:
· Salone del Mobile
· graphics project and catalog for the exhibition "Leonardo a Venice," Palazzo Grassi
· forum for Salone del Mobile
· Zucchi drapers
· pocket dictionaries, Einaudi Edizioni
· Candle
· book *Ferrari Auto*
· KAH Bonn, Germany
(accomplished)

1992
Exhibition system for Lancia
(accomplished)

1992
Stand for I Guzzini
(accomplished)

1992 Turin
Fitting out and graphics for the exhibition on the new General Regulatory Plan
(accomplished)

1992 Erba (Como)
Project for the Northern Railways areas in Milan

1992 Mantua
Management center (project)

1992 Valdagno (Vicenza)
Allotment plan

1992 Lecco
Hotel (project)

1992 Berlin, Germany
Work on Leipzigerstrasse
First prize in international competition by invitation

1992 Lisbon, Portugal
Rector's office at the University
Partner: RISCO-M. Salgado

1992 Milan
Fitting out of the exhibition "1961–1991: Le varie età dei linguaggi" at the Triennale
(accomplished)

1992 Milan
Fitting out of the exhibition "Arte precolombiana" at Palazzo Reale
(accomplished)

1992 Como
Salvage for TICOSA (TIntoria COmense Società Anonima) area (project)

1992 Milan
Fitting out of fifth and sixth floors and reorganization of parking lot at La Rinascente department store

1992 Washington, D.C.
Italian Embassy
Competition by invitation

1992 Cadoneghe (Treviso)
Shopping center
(accomplished)

1992 Berlin, Germany
Rummelsburger Bucht (competition)

1992 Turin
Fitting out and graphics for the exhibition "Erdsicht" at the Lingotto
(accomplished)

1992 Setubal, Portugal
Work on urban center (project)

1992 Lisbon, Portugal
Salvage of a former military factory on the banks of the Tejio (project)

1992 Lille, France
Canal de Roubaix (competition)

1992–1993 Ukraine
Plan for a new city of 150,000 inhabitants
Partners: C.A. Barbieri, C. Bertelli, P. Gelmini, G. Martinotti, B. Secchi, D. Siniscalco, G.B. Zorzoli
First prize in international competition by invitation

1992–1995 Cameri (Novara)
General Regulatory Plan
Adopted

1992–1995 Lisbon, Portugal
Restructuring of building in historical city center
Partner: RISCO-M. Salgano
(accomplished)

1992–1996 Lisbon, Portugal
Residential complex in Leceia-Barcarena
Partner: RISCO-M. Salgado
First prize in competition
(accomplished)

1992–1998 Amadora, Portugal
Theater and film school
Partner: RISCO-M. Salgado
(accomplished)

1992–1999 Livorno
General Regulatory Plan
Adopted

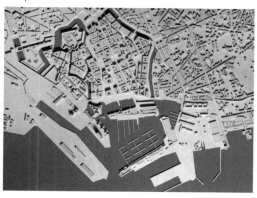

1992–1999 Turin
Doubling of the engineering school
(accomplished)

1993 Sesto Fiorentino (Florence)
Detailed plan

1993 Florence
La Rinascente department store (project)

1993 Venice
Graphic image of the exhibition "Palazzo Grassi al servizio di Marcel Duchamp," Palazzo Grassi

1993 Taranto
IACP (Istituto Autonomo Case Popolari) plan

1993
Graphic image for the publisher Einaudi
(accomplished)

1993 Amadora, Portugal
Public complexes in the railway area (project)
Partner: RISCO-M. Salgado

1993 Caparica, Portugal
University residences
Partner: RISCO-M. Salgado

1993 Berlin, Germany
Work on Spreeinsel
International competition by invitation

1993 Berlin, Germany
Work on Alemannkanal
International competition by invitation

1993 Berlin, Germany
Renovation of KaDeWe department store
(project)

1993 Moscow, Russia-Beijing, People's Republic of China-Singapore
ALENIA stand

1993 Milan
Fitting out of the exhibition "Gli ori di Prague" at La Rinascente department store
(accomplished)

1993 Dordrecht, Netherlands
New prison
International competition by invitation

1993–1994
Coordinated graphic image for "Schopenauer"

1993 Sondrio
Indoor swimming pool (preliminary project proposal)

1993 Lisbon, Portugal
ISCTE building
Partner: RISCO-M. Salgado

1993 Lisbon, Portugal
Extension of the headquarters of Banco di Santo Spirito
Partner: RISCO-M. Salgado

1993 Lausanne, Switzerland
Extension of the university (competition)

1993 Milan
I Guzzini stand at Euroluce
(accomplished)

1993 Roubaix, Belgium
Plan for work on Roubaix canal

1993 Stockholm, Sweden
Fitting out of the exhibition "Jorden Global Change" at the Moderna Museet
(accomplished)

1993 Vienna, Austria
Three towers in Donau City
Partner: Ove Arup Associates
International competition by invitation

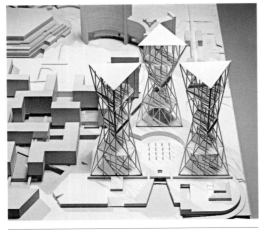

1993
Graphics project catalog and invitations for the exhibition of the Barilla Collection

1993 Rovellasca (Como)
New warehouse for Gabel factory
(accomplished)

1993 Paris, France
Project for a Pirelli technology hub (project)

1993 Milan
Unifor stand at EIMU
(accomplished)

1993
Office furniture for Unifor (project)

1993 Pordenone
Cristallo cinema and adjacent supermarket
(project)

1993 Bergamo
Fitting out of the exhibition on "Premio Bergamo" at the Accademia Carrara
(accomplished)

1993 Treviso
Allotment plan for the Viale Orléans-Via Verdi area

1993 Milan
Fitting out of the exhibition "I Goti" at Palazzo Reale
(accomplished)

1993
Restoration of the ship *Daphne*
(accomplished)

1993 Marseilles, France
Olympic stadium (competition, first place)

1993
Lamp Nota for Candle

1993 Milan
I Guzzini stand at Euroluce
(accomplished)

1993
Doorknobs for Fusital
(accomplished)

1993 Turin
Plan for the roofing of railway bypass

1993–1994 Hamburg, Germany
Building complex along the Holzhafen
International competition by invitation

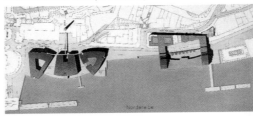

1993–1994 Lisbon, Portugal
Detailed plan for Expo 1998
Partner: RISCO-M. Salgado
First prize in international competition by invitation

1993–1996
Coordinated image for Ferrari Automobili
(accomplished)

1993–1995 Asiago (Vicenza)
General Regulatory Plan

1993–1995 Darfo-Boario Terme (Brescia)
Conference center
(accomplished)

1993–1995 Nîmes, France
Building in Place des Arènes–Îlot Grill
First prize in international competition by invitation

1993–1996 Lisbon, Portugal
Single-family house in Belém
Partner: RISCO-M. Salgado

1993–1996 Milan-Bicocca
Residences on Via Emanueli
(accomplished)

1993–1998 Berlin, Germany
Residential buildings in Spandau
(accomplished)

1993–2000 Iseo (Brescia)
Railway footbridge
(accomplished)
Detailed plan for the railway area

1993–2007 Jesi (Ancona)
Transformation of former SADAM area
(accomplished)

1993–2007 Pula (Cagliari)
Polaris technology and science park
(accomplished)

1994
Yacht *Blue Velvet*
(accomplished)

1994
Projects for Ferrari automobili:
- fitting out of the exhibition at the Nationalgalerie Berlin, Germany
- yearbook graphics project
(accomplished)

1994
Naòs office system for Unifor
(accomplished)
(Compasso d'Oro to Pierluigi Cerri)

1994 Berlin, Germany
Work on the Lehrter Bahnhof area
International competition by invitation

1994 Berlin, Germany
Transformation of the former military area at Biesdorf
Third prize in international competition by invitation

1994
Fitting out of the exhibition "Antico castello inglese" at La Rinascente department store
(accomplished)

1994 Paris-Le Bourget, France and Milan
ALENIA stand at Salon international de l'aéronautique et de l'espace de Paris
(accomplished)

1994 Cascais, Portugal
Work on promenade
First prize in idea competition

1994 Frankfurt, Germany
Poster for the exhibition "Ein Stück Grosstadt als Experiment" at the Deutsches Architektur Museum
(accomplished)

1994 Leipzig, Germany
Office block on the Goerdelerring
First prize in international competition by invitation

1994 Lisbon, Portugal
Residential complex Vila Garcia (project)
Partner: RISCO-M. Salgado

1994 Lisbon, Portugal
Single-family house on Avenida da Libertade
Partner: RISCO-M. Salgado
(accomplished)

1994 London, United Kingdom
Restoration and extension of the South Bank Center
International competition by invitation

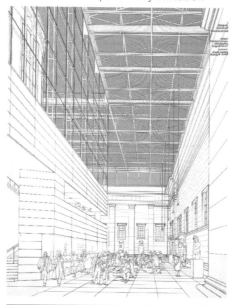

1994 London, United Kingdom
Work on the British Museum
International competition by invitation

1994 London, United Kingdom
Work on the Tate Gallery
International competition by invitation

1994 Milan
Graphic image for the Orchestra Sinfonica Giuseppe Verdi
(accomplished)

1994 Milan
Transformation of the former Redaelli industrial areas at Rogoredo
International consultation by invitation

1994 Milan
Fitting out for La Rinascente:
- exhibition "I tesori del Tibet"
- "Ori e ore-arte sacra e profana al tempo degli Zar"
- signs and ambient image coordination, fourth and fifth floors
(accomplished)

1994 Florence
Fitting out of the exhibition of the projects for the former FIAT industrial area in Novoli
(accomplished)

1994 Cologne
Stand for Indesit, Ariston, and Schöltes
(accomplished)

1994 Pavia
Science and technology park (project)

1994 Rimini
Funerary monument to Federico Fellini
With Arnaldo Pomodoro
(accomplished)

1994 Rozzano (Milan)
Headquarters of the Arnaldo Pomodoro Foundation
(accomplished)

1994 Berlin, Germany
Treptow Park

1994–1995
Cruise ship *Costa Victoria*
(accomplished)

1994–1997 Milan-Bicocca
Humanities Department of Bicocca University
(accomplished)

1994–1998 Milan
Residences on Via Sesto San Giovanni
(accomplished)

1994–1999 Milan
Science Department of Bicocca University
(accomplished)

1994–1999 Milan-Bicocca
Pirelli research center
(accomplished)

1994–2002 Milan-Bicocca
Tertiary towers
(accomplished)

1994–2003 Milan-Bicocca
Esplanade residences
(accomplished)

1994–2003 Tivoli (Latina)
Plan for the Piazza Matteotti area

1994–2004 Milan-Bicocca
Headquarters of the Siemens Group
(accomplished)

1995 Lisbon, Portugal
Waste treatment plant
Partner: RISCO-M. Salgado

1995 Lübben, Germany
New town hall (competition)

1995 Milan
Fitting out of the exhibitions at La Rinascente department store
• "Splendori dell'antica Cina"
• "Gli ori d'Africa"
(accomplished)

1995 Milan
Catalog for the exhibition "Anish Kapoor" at the Fondazione Prada
(accomplished)

1995 Milan
Salvage of the former DAC Chemical industries area (project)

1995 Milan
Fitting out of the exhibition on "Project Bicocca" at the Triennale
(accomplished)

1995
Graphics projects:
• Pirelli Portfolio—Madrid, Spain
• for Encyclomedia on "Il Seicento," by "Opera multimedia Olivetti" according to a project by Umberto Eco
• *Casamica* magazine
• book *I 50 anni della Ferrari*
• various for Ferrari (yearbook, posters of various cars, etc.)
• catalog for I Guzzini
• Graphics poster, leaflet, ticket, and banner for the exhibition "Palazzo aperto: Scene di vita Venicena di Gabriel Bella e Pietro Longhi della Fondazione Querini Stampalia," Palazzo Grassi
• T-shirt "Parole di cotone"
• collection book and illustrative sheet for fitting out of De Padova
• BT magazine *BTicino*
• concise catalog and brochure for I Guzzini
• exhibition "Magna Greece" at Palazzo Grassi
• catalog "Pedrag Matvejevic: Golfo di Venice," Consorzio Venice Nuova
• Graphics project signs multifunctional center—Lodi (With R. Piano Building Workshop)
• various for Olivetti
(accomplished)

1995 Berlin, Germany
Treptow Park (project)

1995
Four races sofa and photo shoot for Poltrona Frau
(accomplished)

1995 Paris-Le Bourget, France
Outdoor stands for ALENIA and Augusta at Salon international de l'aéronautique et de l'espace de Paris
(accomplished)

1995 London, United Kingdom
B&B ITALIA stand
(accomplished)

1995 Milan
Fitting out and graphics project, catalog, and poster for the exhibition "Arnaldo Pomodoro: Scene del Mediterraneo" at the Accademia di Brera
(accomplished)

1995 Milan
Shima Seiki stand at ITMA (international textile equipment exhibition)
(accomplished)

1995 Geneva, Switzerland
Pirelli stand at the "TELECOM 95" fair
(accomplished)

1995 Brussels, Belgium
Salvage of the Albert barracks (competition)

1995 Cassano d'Adda (Milan)
Salvage of the former flax mills area (project)

1995 Nîmes, France
Z.A.C. (Zone d'Aménagement Concerté) Ilot Grill
(project)

1995 Cadoneghe (Padua)
Square
(partially accomplished)

1995 Milan
Stand for Unifor at Salone del Mobile
(accomplished)

1995 Milan
Neglia shop
(accomplished)

1995
Cruise ship *Costa Olympia*
(accomplished)

1995 Genoa
Trussardi space at the International Nautical Fair

1995 Ischia (Naples)
Detailed plan

1995 Lecco
Residences and offices, Section 2/ED/B of former SAE area
(accomplished)

1995 Milan
Fitting out of the exhibition "Gli ori della steppa" at La Rinascente department store
(accomplished)

1995 Milan
Fitting out and graphics project for 75th anniversary exhibition of "Federchimica," Palazzo della Ragione
(accomplished)

1995 Paris, France
Schultes-Ariston-Indesit stand at "Confortec '95" fair
(accomplished)

1995 Milan
Orlandi shop I Guzzini

1995
Coffee table for Poltrona Frau

1995 Milan
Apartment on Via M. Bandello
(accomplished)

1995 Rome
Fitting out of the exhibition on the Italian Language at Palazzo del Quirinale
(accomplished)

1995 Lisbon, Portugal
Detailed plan of Pareda

1995 Venice
Technology and science park in Marghera
(competition)

1995 Vicenza
Salvage of former convent of San Biagio
(project)

1995 Venice
Fitting out of the exhibition "Magna Greece" at Palazzo Grassi
(accomplished)

1995 Milan–Bicocca
Building 1 P2 (executive)–Car park Ed 45
(accomplished)

1995–1997 Milan
Restructuring of former Hotel Marino alla Scala
(accomplished)

1995–1996 Rimini
Exhibition district (project)

1995–1997 Livorno
Detailed plan Porto Mediceo

1995–1999 Livorno
Detailed plan Porta di terra

1995–2000 Montreuil, France
Student housing and Decathlon department store on Périphérique di Paris
Partner: Atelier Bellet–de Pina
(accomplished)

1995–2001 Pavia
General Regulatory Plan

1995–2007 Livorno
D. Cestoni council aquarium
(accomplished)

1995–2007 Schio (Vicenza)
Plan for the transformation of the former Lanerossi area

1995–2007 Tivoli (Rome)
Plan for work on the Cartiere area—historical town center

1996
Yacht *MY47*
(accomplished)

1996 London, United Kingdom
Millennium Bridge
International competition by invitation

1996 Milan
Fitting out of the exhibitions at La Rinascente
• "Museo de Oro"
• "Gioielli Indiani"
(accomplished)

1996 Bergamo
Headquarters of 3V company (project)

1996 Portici (Naples)
New version of CAMPEC building for ENEA
(accomplished)

1996 Crema (Cremona)
Detailed plan for former "Everest" industrial area

1996 Turin
Plan for urban restructuring of Soperga area

1996 Jesolo (Venice)
General Regulatory Plan

1996 Milan
Trussardi shop on Via Sant'Andrea
(accomplished)

1996 Paris–Le Bourget, France
"Finmeccanica" chalet at Salon international de l'aéronautique et de l'espace de Paris
(accomplished)

1996 Milan-Naples
Fitting out of the exhibitions on "Carosello"

1996
Graphics projects:
• coordinated graphic image for I Guzzini
• coordinated graphic image for Olivetti
• coordinated graphic image for Pitti
• yearbook for Ferrari automobili '96
• calendar and book for Pirelli
• catalog for the exhibition "Michel Heizer" at the Fondazione Prada

1996 Piancastagnaio (Siena)
Industrial building "Pellettieri d'Italia" (project)

1996 Marghera (Venice)
Fitting out of exhibition "Federchimica"

1996 Milan
Fitting out of the exhibition "Gioielli da terre lontane dalla collezione di Colette e Jean-Pierre Ghysels," Palazzo Reale

1996 Milan–Bicocca
Buildings 1 P1, U2-U4 (executive), Section 1N, Car parks 1E Building 184, P5, P6 and P8, P Collina dei Ciliegi, and green V17
Urbanization works on Via Emanueli
(accomplished)

1996 Cologne, Germany
Unifor stand at Orgatec '96 fair
(accomplished)

1996 Portofino (Genoa)
Puny restaurant (project)

1996 Savona
Tramway (project)

1996 Como
Fitting out for "Idea Como," Villa Erba

1996 Rimini
Archaeological Museum (project)

1996 Milan
Fitting out of the exhibition "I Maestri," Cassina showroom
(accomplished)

1996 Orosei (Nuoro)
Guiso house-museum
(accomplished)

1996 Paris, France
Missoni shop
(accomplished)

1996 Rio de Janeiro (Brazil)–Geneva, Switzerland–Barcelona, Spain
Pirelli-Telecom stand
(accomplished)

1996 Rome
Fitting out for the PDS (Leftwing Democratic Party) conference at Palaeur
(accomplished)

1996–1997
Coordinated graphic image for:
• De Padova
• Prada
• Einaudi

1996–1997 Busto Arsizio (Varese)
SEA service center for Malpensa airport
(project)

1996–1998 Lisbon, Portugal
Signs for Expo 1998

1996–2001 Milan
Restructuring of residential building on Via Festa del Perdono
(accomplished)

1996–2002 Milan
Arcimboldi Theatre at Bicocca
(accomplished)

1996–2002 Gorizia
General Regulatory Plan

1996–2005 Brescia
Headquarters of Banca Lombarda
(accomplished)

1996–2014 Udine
Transformation of former Bertoli area
(partially accomplished)

1997
Scenography for the RAI broadcast "Quelli che il calcio"
(accomplished)

1997
Graphics projects:
• coordinated image for "Biennale di Florence: il tempo e la moda"
• catalog of the exhibition "La pittura fiamminga e olandese da Van Gogh, Ensor, Magritte, Mondrian ai contemporanei," Palazzo Grassi
• press Kit and poster for 550 Ferrari automobili

• Catalog for De Padova
• signs and trademark for Rome Auditorium

Banca Lombarda Headquarters, Brescia, 1996–2005

- brochure for Maserati
- trademark of the Venice Biennale 1997
- Ferrari auto technology and innovation
- Pirelli manual and yearbook '97
- balance sheet for Pellettieri d'Italia/Prada

1997 Singapore
Pirelli stand

1997 Milan
Cassina stand at Salone del Mobile
(accomplished)

1997
"Compasso" chair

1997
Exhibition system "Pirelli cavi" (project)

1997 Segrate (Milan)
Loft (project)

1997
Yacht *Orsi 2*
(accomplished)

1997 Brescia
Feasibility study for Magazzini Generali area

1997 Florence
Coordinated image for the Biennale della Moda
(accomplished)

1997 Geneva, Switzerland
La Praille stadium
International competition

1997 Venice
Fitting out of ecology conference

1997 Milan
Salvini shop on Via Montenapoleone
(accomplished)

1997 Milan
Headquarters of COSMIT on Foro Buonaparte
(project)

1997 Milan
Apartment T.

1997 Geneva, Switzerland
Ethnographic Museum
International competition

1997 Naples-Scampia
Transformation of a building in the "Le vele" district into the headquarters of Civil Protection
(project)

1997 Milan-Bicocca
Nursery school project
Green V11 Section 1C and 1D
Secondary urbaniZation works V14
Buildings 103 and 104 "Esplanade" (executive)
Church Esplanade Section 1Q (project)
Project for the former Ansaldo area

1997 Lecce
Project for the Buon Pastore area
(competition)

1997 Milan
Renovation of Marisa 1 boutique
(accomplished)

1997 Milan
COSMIT stand at Euroluce
(accomplished)

1997 Casale Monferrato (Alessandria)
Detailed Area Plan

1997 Cairo, Egypt
Cairo and Giza Museums (competition)

1997 Dubai, United Arab Emirates
Tower Hotel (competition)

1997 Marseilles, France
Municipal Library
Partners: Atelier Khelif, BET–SEEE
Méditerranée Ingérop
International competition by invitation

1997 Milan
Study for the redevelopment of the exhibition area

1997 New York, NY
Prada headquarters (project)

1997 New York, NY
Trussardi Sacks sales outlet
(accomplished)

1997 Viganò San Martin (Bergamo)
Neglia house (project)

1997 Milan
Fitting out of Poldi Pezzoli Museum (project)

1997 Guanzhou-Shenzen, People's Republic of China
Trussardi sales outlets (project)

1997 Florence
Trussardi shop (project)

1997 Venice
Fitting out for "Cinema" season at Palazzo Grassi
(accomplished)

1997 Potsdam, Germany
Lustgarten Altermarkt
International competition

1997 Thessaloniki, Greece
Work on promenade
International competition by invitation

1997 Venice
Catalog of the exhibition "Espressionismo tedesco: Arte e società" at Palazzo Grassi
(accomplished)

1997–1998 Abidjan, Ivory Coast
Business center (project)
Partner: SEEG

1997–1998 Aix-en-Provence, France
Redevelopment of Cours Mirabeau
Second prize in international competition by invitation

1997–1998 Strasbourg, France
Shopping center (project)

1997–1998 Valenza Po (Alessandria)
Exhibition center for Associazione Orafa Valenzana (project)

1997–2000 Ghemme (Novara)
General Regulatory Plan

1997–2002 Aix-en-Provence, France
Residential block in Sextius-Mirabeau
(accomplished)

1998–2014
GREGOTTI ASSOCIATI INTERNATIONAL
AUGUSTO CAGNARDI
VITTORIO GREGOTTI
MICHELE REGINALDI

1998 Florence
New access to the Uffizi Gallery
International competition by invitation

1998 Milan-Bicocca
Bridge over Viale Sarca
(partially accomplished)
Multiscreen cinema project
Project for the new headquarters of the Carlo Besta Neurological Institute
Section 1H public car park; Section P7 green; Section V13 (executive)
UrbaniZation works
Proposal for an exhibition Hall

1998 Milan
Fitting out of the exhibition "Falsi storici" at Poldi Pezzoli Museum
(accomplished)

1998 Bologna
Trussardi shops
(accomplished)

1998 Florence
Fitting out for the Leftwing Democratic Party conference
(accomplished)

1998
Renovation of apartment T. (now R.C.)
(accomplished)

1998 Venice
Fitting out of the exhibition "Picasso 1917–1924: il viaggio in Italia" at Palazzo Grassi
(accomplished)

1998 Geneva, Switzerland
Maserati stand at the Motor Show
(accomplished)

1998 Jesi (Ancona)
Multiscreen cinema (project)

1998 Cameri (Novara)
Family Chapel G.
(accomplished)

1998 Cameri (Novara)
Work on Bossi Spinning mill
(accomplished)

1998 Fatima, Portugal
Project for the Sanctuary (competition)

1998 Beijing, People's Republic of China
National Grand Theater
International competition

1998 Rome
Restructuring of the Palaeur (project)

Pirelli Real Estate Headquarters at Bicocca, Milano, 1999–2007

1998 Valdagno (Vicenza)
Residential plan Villa Favorita

1998 Verona
Work on Piazza della Stazione (project)

1998 Arezzo
Detailed plan for Garbasso area

1998 Paris, France
Fitting out of "Spazio Ungaro"
(accomplished)

1998 Hannover, Germany
Pirelli Cavi stand
(accomplished)

1998
Coordinated graphic image for Unifor

1998 Poggioreale (Trapani)
Old people's housing for Pie Raggruppate
(project)

1998 Riccione (Rimini)
Multiscreen cinema (project)

1998 Coriano (Rimini)
New buildings for San Patrignano (project)

1998 Giulianova (Teramo)
Kursaal building (project)

1998–1999 Livorno
Detailed plan for the new city center

1998–1999 Milan
Brera Newspaper Library in the former Cavallerizza
(accomplished)

1998–2001 Savona
Port Regulatory Plan for Savona–Vado Ligure

1998–2005 Venice
IUAV university offices in Campo della Lana
(accomplished)

1998–2006 Treviso
Complex of health care residences
Partner: E. Casagrande–AT&T Associati
(accomplished)

1998–2006 Venice
Physical/functional reorganization of the Island of San Giorgio Maggiore
(partially accomplished)

1998–2014 Civitanova Marche (Macerata)
Transformation of the Cecchetti area
(partially accomplished)

1999 Cattolica (Rimini)
Sports arena (project)

1999 Vimercate (Milan)
Salvage of the former Bassetti area (project)

1999 Milan-Bari
Salvage and transformation of the Central Stations (Grandi Stazioni competition)

1999 Milan-Bicocca
Student housing building H14
Detailed plan 1S1 and variant
Section 1I - Lot B (Siemens); Lot B-C
Executive project for the new headquarters of the Carlo Besta Neurological Institute
Piazza della Scienza underpass
Lecture hall/former porch/library, Sections (1U) U2 / U4
Tower 9 (building concession)

1999 Rome-Tormarancia
Numisia Park (project)

1999 Arezzo
Work on Viale Urbano area (project)

1999 Casablanca–Agadir Marrakech, Morocco
Football and athletics stadiums
Partner: S. Benkirane
International competition by invitation

1999 Frankfurt, Germany
Consultency for Deutsche Bank buildings

1999 Salerno
New judiciary offices (competition)

1999 Beijing, People's Republic of China
"Palazzo d'Italia" (project)

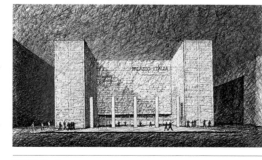

1999 Turin
Proposal for revision of use of the railway areas for Metropolis

1999 Potenza
Piazza with A. Pomodoro sculpture
(accomplished)

1999 Mozzo (Bergamo)
Detailed plan

1999 Rome
Contemporary Arts Center
International competition by invitation
Partner: F. Purini

1999 Caltagirone (Catania)
Detailed plan for southern entrance into the town

1999 Cameri (Novara)
Variant of the General Regulatory Plan

1999–2002 Venice
Guggenheim Museum at Punta della Dogana
(project)

1999–2003 Milan
Extension and redevelopment of the A4 Milan-Bergamo motorway (project)

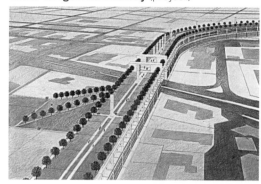

1999–2005 Milan
Generale headquarters of Pirelli Real Estate at Bicocca
(accomplished)

1999–2005 Venice
Ca' Foscari University library

1999–2006 Milan
Student housing at Bicocca
(accomplished)

1999–2013 Agadir, Morocco
Football and athletics stadium
Partner: S. Benkirane
First prize in international competition by invitation
(accomplished)

1999–2007 Bergamo
Beata Vergine di Loreto parochial complex
First prize in competition by invitation
(accomplished)

1999–2011 Marrakech, Morocco
Football and athletics stadium
Partner: S. Benkirane
First prize in international competition by invitation
(accomplished)

2000 Salerno
Feasibility study for the seafront

2000 Milan-Bicocca
Section 103 new solution
Tower 8: variant
Tower 7: building concession

2000 Milan
Apartment S.
(accomplished)

2000 Cesena (Forlì)
Bridge over the Savio River
(accomplished)

2000 Savona
Cruise terminal (project)

2000 Ghemme (Novara)
Street furniture (project)

2000 Cavriglia (Arezzo)
Salvage of a lignite quarry (project)

2000 Pula (Cagliari)
Palaceris Park (project)

2000 Mozzo (Bergamo)
Restructuring of house S.
(accomplished)

2000 Cesena (Forlì)
Multifunctional hall
(accomplished)

2000 Alba (Cuneo)
Miroglio Area (project)

2000 San Polo (Brescia)
Urban regeneration plan for San Polo area
(competition)

2000 Mestre (Venice)
Via Einaudi car park (competition)

2000 Riccione (Rimini)
Ceschina Area (project)

2000 Lyons, France
Building in Lyon Part Dieu (project)

2000 Oran (Algeria)
Holiday camp (project)

2000 Brescia
Crociera di San Luca cultural center
International competition by invitation

2000 Avellino
Detailed plan for Collina Liguorini

2000 Milan-Bicocca
Section 1H-Variant Car park P7-Green V13
Pirelli 1 headquarters (executive project)
Building concession variant Section H / U.I.
10-12
Public car parks P7 Section 1H
Building concession variant Section H / U.I.
11-13

2000 Cameri (Novara)
Variant of the General Regulatory Plan

2000 Turin
Roof for the railway bypass "Turin 2000"
(project)

2000 Perugia
Detailed plan for Ponte della Pietra area

2000 Ferrara
Structural plan for southern zone

2000 Brescia
Former Corn Market Area (project)

2000 Naples-Scampia
National Civil Protection Center (project)

2000 Vigevano
Advice on the reuse of Castello Visconteo

2000 Fabriano (Ancona)
Reuse of the Merloni area (project)

2000 Villaguardia (Como)
Restructuring of Villa Macciasca (project)

2000 Milan
Apartment on Via Ceradini
(accomplished)

2000–2001 Palermo
Redevelopment plan for the Arenella area

2000–2001 Paris, France
Restructuring of the Théâtre de la Gaîté Lyrique
First prize in international competition
by invitation (project)

2000 Pescara
Transformation of the De Cecco area
International competition by invitation

2000–2001 Milan
Detailed plan for the Porta Vittoria area

2000–2001 Nice, France
Town hall and new urban center
Partners: OTH, EDAW
International competition by invitation

2000–2003 Montreuil, France
Air France offices on Boulevard Périphérique di Paris
Partner: Atelier Bellet–de Pina
(accomplished)

2000–2004 Montreuil, France
Office building on rue Blanqui
Partner: Atelier Bellet–de Pina
(accomplished)

2001 Athens
Proposal for the International Olympic Broadcasting Center (project)

2001 Pordenone
Competition of ideas "Giannino Furlan"
With P. Val

2001 Brugherio (Milan)
Detailed plan for Bettolino Freddo Area

2001 Milan-Bicocca
Building 222 Headquarters National Research Council
Variant for university U9
Variant of building concession-Section H
Buildings 1, 2 and 4
Car parks and laboratories Building U5
New university building U10

2001 Ancona
Proposal for the Baraccola area (project)

2001 Pescara
Car park (project)

2001 Ferrara
Fitting out of the exhibition "Gregotti Associati" at MusArch
(accomplished)

2001 Turin
Reuse of FIAT AVIO area (project)

2001–2003 Avellino
General Regulatory Plan
Adopted

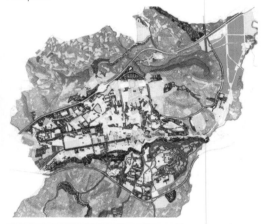

2001–2005 Bergamo
New section of the Gallery of Modern and Contemporary Art at the Carrara Academy
(accomplished)

2001–2007 Milan
Housing, shops, and university services on the central square of Bicocca
(accomplished)

2001–2014 Pujiang-Shanghai, People's Republic of China
New city of Pujiang for 100,000 inhabitants
Partners: Centro Studi Traffico–P. Gelmini, Ove Arup–J. Morgan, A. Cannetta, THAPE–X. Huang
First prize in international competition by invitation
In progress

2001–2002 Shanghai, People's Republic of China
Plan for the new city of Jiangwan for 100,000 inhabitants
Partners: Centro Studi Traffico–P. Gelmini, Sembenelli Consulting–P. Sembenelli, Manens Intertecnica–G. Viero, Ambiente Italia–M. Zambrini
Second prize in international competition by invitation

2002 Pujiang-Shanghai, People's Republic of China
Revision of the Master plan

2002 Senigallia (Ancona)
Preliminary proposal for the salvaging of the former Italcementi-Sacelit areas
With: Centro Studi Traffico (P. Gelmini)

2002 Tivoli
Detailed plan for Piazza Matteotti
(new adoption)

2002 Brussels, Belgium
Fitting out of the exhibition "Europalia 2003"

2002 Arezzo
Urban avenue in the Salvadori area (project)

2002 Shanghai, People's Republic of China
Waitanyuan Masterplan Review

2002 Florence
Museo dell'Opera del Duomo
Partner: C. Bertelli
International competition by invitation

2002 Moscow, Russia
Town hall and Duma
International competition

2002 Patras, Greece
Archaeological Museum
Partners: S. Digenis, A Digenis
International competition by invitation

2002 Turin
New high-speed railway station at Porta Susa
International competition

2002 Bologna
Fitting out of the exhibition "Gregotti Associati: Le architetture dello spazio pubblico" at the Esprit Nouveau Pavilion
(accomplished)

2002 Chia (Cagliari)
Detailed plan for S.T.I.M. area

2002 Milan-Bicocca
Executive Section 1H (monitoring) Buildings 10-12
Green V 14 and V15 – C.E.
Nursery school C.E.

2002 Fiorenzuola (Piacenza)
Feasibility study for a hydroelectric power station

2002 Cagliari
Commercial park for Elmas airport (project)

2002 Cotignola (Ravenna)
New I.B.L. offices (project)

2002–2003 Athens, Greece
Waterfront Open Space and Landscape Design
Partners: S. Digenis, A Digenis

2002–2003 Shanghai, People's Republic of China
Residential area of Pujiang Village
Partner: THAPE–X. Huang
First prize in international competition by invitation

2002–2003 Shanghai, People's Republic of China
Salvage and renovation of Waitanyuan area
Partner: THAPE–X.M. Huang
First prize in international competition by invitation

2002–2003 Trezzo sull'Adda / Capriate (Milan–Bergamo)
A4 motorway interchange area (project)

2002–2004 Castiglione delle Stiviere (Mantua)
Salvage of former hospital (project)

2002–2007 Casalbeltrame (Novara)
Plaster cast gallery of twentieth-century Italian sculpture
First prize in competition
In progress

2002–2007 Castiglione delle Stiviere (Mantua)
Salvage and transformation of the former psychiatric hospital area

2003 Shanghai, People's Republic of China
Shimao Riviera Garden (project)

2003 Fuzhou, People's Republic of China
Master plan "Fuzhou Shimao Bund Garden"

New City of Pujiang. Shanghai, China, 2001-2014. Master plan.

2003 Shanghai, People's Republic of China
Bund Central Business District
Partner: THAPE–X. Huang
First prize in international competition
by invitation

2003 Riccione (Rimini)
Transformation of the Dolphinarium area
(project)

2003 Vimercate (Milan)
**Salvage of the former industrial areas
of Via Milano** (project)

2003 Milan-Bicocca
**Proposal for administrative offices of Bicocca
University**
Pirelli 1 headquarters–Variant
**Multifunctional hall and laboratories internal
courtyard for Pirelli Tire Research Center**

2003 Shanghai, People's Republic of China
Chang Feng for "Fort" (project)

2003 Beijing, People's Republic of China
Salvage of Hutong area for "Fort" (project)

2003 Valdagno (Vicenza)
Exterior work on "La Favorita" flats (project)

2003 Valdagno (Vicenza)
New headquarters of Cooperativa Adriatica
(project)

2003 Arona (Novara)
Hotel "Villa Cantoni" (project)

2003
Theater chair for "Gufram"

2003 Tehran, Iran
Building for the tertiary "Casa Italia" (project)

2003 Shanghai, People's Republic of China
**Guidelines for the salvage and renovation
of the Waitanyuan area**
Partner: Shanghai Tongji Urban Planning and
Design Institute

2003 Shanghai, People's Republic of China
**Fitting out of the exhibition "Gregotti Assoiati:
New Pujiang Town" at Shanghai Urban Planning
Exhibition Building**

2003 Shanghai, People's Republic of China
Pujiang Town-Detailed Plan 6.7 km²

2003 Ponte della Pietra (Perugia)
Church (preliminary project proposal)

2003 Siena
New stadium (competition)

2003–2005 Perugia
International center for diabetes research
(project)

**2003–2005 Pujiang-Shanghai, People's Republic
of China**
Promotion Center and entrance to the new city
Partner: THAPE–X. Huang
(accomplished)

2003–2006 Caltagirone (Catania)
Work on the Verdumai slope (project)

2003–2007 Aix-en-Provence, France
Salle de Spectacles Sextius Mirabeau
Partners: Commins Acoustic Workshop, OTH
Méditérranée, Scene, Tribu
First prize in international competition
by invitation
(accomplished)

2003–2007 Milan-Bicocca
New university building (executive project)

2004 Brescia
Museum of industry and work (competition)

2004 Moscow, Russia
Renovation of GUM department store (project)

2004 Shanghai, People's Republic of China
New city of Pujiang: launch of initial phase

2004 Shanghai, People's Republic of China
Bund 15A building
First prize in international competition
by invitation

2004 Shanghai, People's Republic of China
Master plan for the Jian Guo Road East area
(competition)

2004 Shanghai, People's Republic of China
Plan for the Jiading district (competition)

2004 Shanghai, People's Republic of China
Salvage plan for the "Italian City" of Tianjin
Partner: THAPE–X. Huang

2004 Casalbeltrame (Novara)
Restructuring Villa G.
(accomplished)

2004 Milan-Bicocca
Project for reuse of former Wagon Lits area
**Central call center hall, Pirelli Tire Research
Center**
Project Headquarters 2 Pirelli R.E.
Building concession building 143

2004 Cologne, Germany
Fitting out of the exhibition "Project Bicocca"
(accomplished)

2004 Milan
**Feasibility study for hotel on Via Calderon
de la Barca**

2004 Venice
Cruise port at Bocca di Lido (project)

2004–2006 Turin
Urban park on central Spina
(accomplished)

2004–2007 Beijing, People's Republic of China
Study for the reform of the Italian Embassy

2004–2007 Rome
**New Urban Centrality of Acilia Madonnetta-
Municipio XIII** (project)

2004–2008 Arzignano (Vicenza)
**Guiding plan for the Poletto former industrial
area**

2004–2010 Trento
**Transformation of the Trento Nord industrial
areas** (project)

Grand Théatre de Provence (Salle des Spectacle Sextius Mirabeau), Aix-en-Provence, 2003–2008

2005 Novara
Feasibility study for the new Hospital della Carità

2005 Milan-Bicocca
Executive project building 143
Project section H–La Piazza
Car Park P7

2005 Lomello (Pavia)
Definitive project for old people's home
In progress

2005 Shanghai, People's Republic of China
Pujiang New Town: Gate S 12–Hypermarket

2005 São Paulo, Brazil
Fitting out of the exhibition on Gregotti Associati urban scale projects
(accomplished)

2005 Brescia
Allotment plan north of Via Cefalonia

2005 Acilia Madonnetta (Rome)
New headquarters of Rome Province
(competition)

2005 Beijing, People's Republic of China
Plan for the new urban hub of Tongzhou
Partners: Tianhua Ltd., Sistema project di A. Vettese, S. Cohen &C.
International competition by invitation

2006 Doha, Qatar
Plan for Area 1
Partners: Foa–F. Oliva Associati, Centro Studi Traffico, Arup, THAPE–X.M. Huang
International competition by invitation

2006 Rabat, Morocco
Headquarters of Telecom Maroc
International competition by invitation

2006 Trento
New judiciary hub
International competition by invitation

2006 Shanghai, People's Republic of China
Pujiang New Town: project Blocks 122/11 and 123/1

2006 Acilia Madonnetta (Rome)
Preliminary project proposal for the complex of the Scuola di Alti Studi of University of Rome 3

2006 Harbin, People's Republic of China
Reconversion of former industrial area (project)

2006 Udine
Variant of the detailed plan for former Bertoli industrial area

2006 Beijing, People's Republic of China
Participation in Architecture Biennial

2006 La Spezia
Seafront (competition)

2006–2014 Follonica (Grosseto)
Performance hall in former Leopolda Foundry (former ILVA area)
(accomplished)

2006–2007 Jesolo (Venice)
Tourist residence and hotel (project)

2006 Antibes, France
Salle de Spectacles (Second prize in international competition by invitation)

2006–2007 Milan-Bicocca
Extension of Pirelli Real Estate General Headquarters
(accomplished)
Building 143 for offices and services
(accomplished)
Preliminary project proposal ED - 120 - 95
Piazza della Scienza
Underground car park for Pirelli Tire Research Center

2006–2007 Naples-Scampia
Faculty of Medicine Federico II University
In progress

2006–2007 Ningbo, People's Republic of China
Detailed plan for East Ningbo

2006–2007 Reggio Calabria
Exhibition center in Arghillà (competition first prize)
In progress

2006–2007 Zhou Jia Jiao, People's Republic of China
Plan for the Citic Area

2007 Roseto degli Abruzzi (Teramo)
Redevelopment plan

2007 Cremona
New railway station (competition)

2007 Shanghai, People's Republic of China
West Shanghai (project)

2007 Udine
Trigeneration power plant (project)

2007 Stresa (Varese)
Salvage of Villa Palazzolo (competition)

2007 Dalian, People's Republic of China
Urban development plan

2007 Rabat, Morocco
Academy of Royal Arts (project)

2007 Turin
Study for Corso Marche and the area to the west of the city

2007 Verona
Trigeneration power plant in the former production area of Verona south (project)

2007 Rome
Capitol Two: the citizens' home (competition)
Partners: S. Dierna - M. Strickner

2007 Shanghai, People's Republic of China
Extension of Pudong financial district
Partner: THAPE–X. Huang

2007 Verbania
New theater (competition)

2007 Istanbul, Turkey
Zorlu Center (competition)

2007 Bolzano
Project for science and technology hub in the former Alumix industrial area (project)

2007 Alessandria
Salvage of Bertana G.L. farmhouse
(accomplished)

2007 Padua
Research Tower
(First prize in international competition)

2007 Lisbon, Portugal
Proposal for hotel and theater at Belém Cultural Center

2007 Brescia
Planovolumetrics for the SBIM area (project)

2007 Monza
Fitting out of the exhibition on Gregotti Associati projects in China
(accomplished)

2007 Shanghai, People's Republic of China
Pujiang New Town: project Block 122/10

2008 Istanbul, Turkey
Proposal for shopping center

2008 Milan-Bicocca
Block next to the Gronda Nord (former Besta Institute block) (project)

2008 Porto Tolle–Porto Viro (Rovigo)
Allotment plan for San Giusto village

2008 Rho (Milan)
Office tower in the new exhibition area
(competition)

2008 Casalbeltrame (Novara)
Salvage of shelter (fortified structure)
(project)

2008
Lamp Prisma

2008 Arzignano (Vicenza)
Guiding plan for Viale Vicenza

2008 Porto Viro (Rovigo)
Feasibility study for the salvaging of the former ENEL area

2008 Rho (Milan)
Salvage of the former FIAT-Rho area (project)

2008 Mortegliano (Udine)
Residential complex (project)

2008 Shanghai, People's Republic of China
Furnishings for the detached villas of Pujiang New Town (project)

2008 Shanghai, People's Republic of China
Pujiang New Town: project Blocks 122/8-9-12-13

2008 Milan-Bicocca
Variant of building U-10, student housing

2008 Nago-Torbole (Trento)
Residential complex (project)

2009 Kunming, People's Republic of China
Garden Residence District (project)

2009 Shanghai, People's Republic of China
Central Belt of Pujiang New Town (project)
Shopping center built
Partner: THAPE–X. Huang

2009 Paris, France
Plan for Paris urban area
Partners: G. Martinotti (sociological study),
M. Corajoud (landscape study)

2009 Aix-en-Provence, France
ZAC La Duranne (project)
Partners: Horizon, CFL Achitecture, IOSIIS
Méditerranée, IOSIIS Concept

2009 Aix-en-Provence, France
Gare Routiere (competition)

2009 Milan-Bicocca
Area of open spaces for U10 sports center
Infant school, Piazza Daini, completion
of Esplanade

2009 Zhuhai, People's Republic of China
Coast (competition)
Partner: THAPE–X. Huang

2009 Cairo, Egypt
Cultural hub of the new city of 6th of October
(project)

2009 Milan
Residence opposite the Colonne di San Lorenzo
(project)

2009 Brussels, Belgium
New Heysel stadium (competition)

2010 Shanghai, People's Republic of China
Revision of Waitanyuan Master plan

2010 Shanghai, People's Republic of China
Pujiang New Town: project Block 123/1

2010 Port Saint Louis, France
Urban Redevelopment Plan (competition)

2010 Milan-Bicocca
Headquarters Pirelli R.E: new entrance, operational center, library

2010 Ben Guerir, Morocco
New university (competition)
Partner: Sâd Benkirane

2010–2011 Langhirano (Parma)
Urban Redevelopment Plan and feasibility study for primary school

2010–2014 Turin
Detailed plan for Corso Marche

2011 Rabat, Morocco
National Archaeology and Earth Sciences Museum (competition)
Partner: Sâd Benkirane

2011 Suzhou, People's Republic of China
Suzhou West Eco City (project)
Partner: Tianhua Architecture Planning
& Engineering Limited (X. Huang)

2011 Milan-Bicocca
Green area V19 (U10)

2011 Ouled-Fayet, Algeria
Salle de Spectacle for 12,000 spectators
(competition)

2011 Mönchengladbach, Germany
Master plan (competition)

2011 Algeria
Modular city on the Trans-Saharan Highway
(feasibility study)
Partner: Ecosfera S.p.A.-F. Nissardi

2011 El Mènea, Algeria
Plan for the new city of El Mènea (competition)
Partner: Ecosfera S.p.A.-F. Nissardi

2011 Shanghai, People's Republic of China
Pujiang New Town: project Block 123/2

2011 Sidi Abdallah, Douéra, Algeria
Ministry of Land-use Planning and Environment–New city of Sidi Abdallah, Douéra
(competition, first place)

2012 Milan-Bicocca
Canopy for the escalator of the Piazza– Section H

2012 Algiers, Algeria
Regulatory Authority of Post and Telecommunications (competition)

2012–2014 Milan
South Park (project)

2012–2014 Livorno
Structural plan

2013 Florence
Feasibility study for the reorganization of Fortezza da Basso
Partner: Manens Intertecnica

2013 Aosta
Proposal of a detailed plan for the former football grounds

2013 Milan
Work on the Sala degli Scarlioni in Sforza Castle
(project)
Fitting out of the museum: Giovanni Agosti and Jacopo Stoppa

2013 Vaiano Cremasco (Cremona)
Salvage of Cazzaniga Farmhouse (project)

2013–2014 Shanghai, People's Republic of China
Research Program about the Preservation Methodology and Reuse of Historical Architecture in Shanghai
Partner: Guido Morpurgo

Building 143 for offices and services at Bicocca, Milan 2006–2007

PARTNERS

Vittorio Gregotti was born in Novara, Italy, in 1927 and graduated in architecture in 1952 from Milan Polytechnic. Between 1953 and 1968, he worked with L. Meneghetti and G. Stoppino. In 1974 he founded Gregotti Associati, of which he was the president. He has been a lecturer in architectural composition at the Istituto Universitario di Architettura in Venice, has taught at the Faculties of Architecture in Milan and Palermo, and has been visiting professor at the universities of Tokyo, Buenos Aires, São Paulo, Lausanne, Harvard, Philadelphia, Princeton, Cambridge (U.K.) and M.I.T. His work has been displayed at many international

exhibitions, and he was responsible for the introductory section of the 13th Milan Triennial (1964), for which he won the International Grand Prix. From 1974 to 1976, he was director of the visual arts and architecture sector of the Venice Biennial. He has been a member of the Accademia di San Luca since 1976 and Accademia di Brera since 1995. He was awarded an honorary degree by Prague Polytechnic in 1996, Bucharest Polytechnic in 1999, and Porto University in 2003. Since 1997 he has been a member of the BDA (Bund der deutschen Architekten) and since 1999 an honorary member of the American Institute of Architects. In 2000 he was conferred the Gold Medal of the Benemeriti della Scienza e della Cultura by the president of Italy. Between 1953 and 1955, he was an editor of the magazine *Casabella*; from 1955 to 1963 managing editor of *Casabella-Continuità*; from 1963 to 1965 editor-in-chief of *Edilizia Moderna* and editor of the architectural section of *Il Verri*; from 1979 to 1998, he was managing editor of *Rassegna*, and from 1982 to 1996 managing editor of *Casabella*. Between 1984 and 1992, he edited the architectural column in the news magazine *Panorama*, from 1992 to 1997 he wrote for the daily newspaper *Corriere della Sera*, and since 1997 he has written for *La Repubblica*.

Augusto Cagnardi was born in Milan, Italy, in 1937 and graduated from Milan Polytechnic in 1962. From 1962 to 1967, he was a researcher at the Istituto di Urbanistica in the same polytechnic. Then, from 1967 to 1973, he was a researcher at the Piano Intercomunale Milanese, involved in drawing up the area master plan and special projects such as the series of parks and the new organization of the transport systems. From 1974 to 1981 he worked in the fields of transportation, and environmental and urban planning, and, as a member of interdisciplinary groups, he won the competitions for the Bergamo railway project, the management center in Florence, and Pollino regional park. He joined Gregotti Associati as a partner and managing director in 1981, bringing with him specific skills related to city planning and project management. He was president of the Lombardy section of the INU (Istituto Nazionale di Urbanistica) from 1979 to 1985, president of the AIAP (Associazione Italiana degli Architetti di Paesaggio) from 1985 to 1988, and president of the Comitato Nazionale per le Scienze Ambientali e Territoriali in the same years. From 1987 to 1991 he edited *Terra*, a magazine dealing with environmental and territorial sciences. He has lectured and managed conferences in universities in Italy and abroad and continues to write on the subjects of politics and architecture for professional journals.

Michele Reginaldi was born in Teramo, Italy, in 1958 and graduated from the Istituto Universitario di Architettura in Venice in 1982. Since then, his professional life has been centered in Milan, where he founded the architectural firm Quattroassociati with Corrado Annoni, Stefano Parodi, and Daniela Saviola. He focused primarily on territorial planning, environmental recovery of disused industrial areas and plants, and the installation of new infrastructures for systems of transportation and production. On the subjects of his landscaping projects, which are documented in various publications, he has lectured and spoken at conferences in Italy and abroad. He has worked at Gregotti Associati International since 1982, and he became an associate in 1990 and a partner in 1998.

In addition to his professional work, he has taught at the Faculty of Architecture at Milan Polytechnic.

Books by Vittorio Gregotti

Il territorio dell'architettura, Feltrinelli, Milan, 1966

El territorio de la arquitectura, Gustavo Gili, Barcelona, 1972

Territorio da arquitectura, Perspectiva, São Paulo, 1975

Le territoire de l'architecture, L'Equerre, Paris, 1982

L'architettura dell'espressionismo, Fabbri, Milan, 1967

New Directions in Italian Architecture, George Braziller, New York, 1968

Nuove direzioni nell'architettura italiana, Electa, Milan, 1969

Il disegno del prodotto industriale: Italia 1860–1980, Electa, Milan, 1982

Questioni di architettura, Einaudi, Turin, 1986

Cinque dialoghi necessari, Electa, Milan, 1990

Dentro l'architettura, Bollati Boringhieri, Turin, 1991

Desde el Interior de la arquitectura. Un ensayo de interpretación, Península, Barcelona, 1993

Inside Architecture, MIT Press, Cambridge, Mass., 1996

La città visibile, Einaudi, Turin, 1991

Le scarpe di Van Gogh: Modificazioni dell'architettura, Einaudi, Turin, 1994

Recinto di fabbrica, Bollati Boringhieri, Turin, 1996

Venezia città della nuova modernità, Consorzio Venezia Nuova, Venice, 1998

Racconti di architettura, Skira, Milan, 1998

Identità e crisi dell'architettura europea, Einaudi, Turin, 1999

Sulle orme di Palladio, Laterza, Rome-Bari, 2000

В. Преготти, *По спедадм Паппадио. Рацио и праксис архитектуры*, Москва, MV, 2002

Diciassette lettere sull'architettura, Laterza, Rome-Bari, 2000

Dix-sept lettres sur l'architecture, Parenthèses, Paris, 2006

Architettura, tecnica, finalità, Laterza, Rome-Bari, 2002

Architecture, Means and Ends, Chicago University Press, Chicago, 2010 (translation by L.G. Cochrane)

Cinquanta domande a Vittorio Gregotti, CLEAN, Naples, 2002 (edited by A. Marotta)

L'architettura del realismo critico, Laterza, Rome-Bari, 2004

Autobiografia del XX secolo, Skira, Milan, 2006

L'architettura nell'epoca dell'incessante, Laterza, Rome-Bari, 2006

Contro la fine dell'architettura, Einaudi, Turin, 2008

L'ultimo hutong. Lavorare in architettura nella nuova Cina, Skira, Milan, 2009

Una lezione di architettura: Rappresentazione, globalizzazione, interdisciplinarità, Firenze University Press, Florence, 2009

Tre forme di architettura mancata, Einaudi, Turin, 2010

Cézanne e l'architettura, Skira, Milan, 2011

Architettura e postmetropoli, Turin, Einaudi, 2011

Incertezze e simulazioni, Skira, Milan, 2011

Il sublime al tempo del contemporaneo, Einaudi, Turin, 2013

Books by Augusto Cagnardi

La Riconversione Urbanistica, with M. Fabbri, Dedalo, Bari, 1978

Belice 1980: Luoghi, Problemi, Progetti, Dodici Anni Dopo il Terremoto, Marsilio, Venice, 1981

Strade, Piazze e Spazi Urbani (edited by), Milan, Angeli, 1983

Piano e Progetto, (edited by), Angeli, Milan, 1985

Un nuovo senso del Piano. Piani regolatori Gregotti Associati, Etas, Milan, 1995

Ritorni da Shanghai. Cronache di un architetto italiano in Cina, Allemandi, Turin, 2008

Books by Michele Reginaldi

Officina morfologica: Le costruzioni di Michele Reginaldi, edited by Bruno Pedretti, Bolis Edizioni, Azzano San Paolo (BG), 2001

Quaderni senza parole: Il disegno di Michele Reginaldi, edited by Bruno Pedretti, Bolis Edizioni, Azzano San Paolo (BG), 2004

Disegni e costruzioni, Oratorio della Passione, Bolis Edizioni, Azzano San Paolo (BG), 2005

PREVIOUS AND EXTERNAL PARTNERS COMPANY PROFILE

Gregotti Associati srl was founded in 1974 by Vittorio Gregotti together with Pierluigi Cerri, Pierluigi Nicolin, Hiromichi Matsui, and Bruno Viganò. Over the years the initial group has undergone some changes. Nicolin left the group in 1978, Viganò in 1981, Matsui in 1982, and Cerri in 1998, while August Cagnardi and Michele Reginaldi joined in 1981 and 1998 respectively.

In 1980 the group opened its second office, in Venice (Cannaregio 2179) and Carlo Magnani became a partner there from 1984 to 1988.

In 1984 a center of operations was opened in Lisbon with the company Risco, partner Manuel Salgado.

In 1988 the original company was transformed into Gregotti Associati International srl, with partners Augusto Cagnardi, Pierluigi Cerri, and Vittorio Gregotti, with whom a total of 16 architects have been affiliated since 1990.

Associate Architects between 1990 and 2014

Spartaco Azzola
Sergio Butti
Cristina Calligaris
Ilario Chiarel
Luciano Claut
Paoloemilio Colao
Michela Destefanis
Giuseppe Donato
Simona Franzino
Gaetano Gramegna
Tomaso Macchi Cassia
Augusta Mazzarolli
Guido Morpurgo
Maurizio Pavani
Carlo Pirola
Maurizio Trovatelli

GREGOTTI ASSOCIATI COLLABORATORS 1974–2014

Nicola Adami
Giuseppe Agata Giannoccari
Mario Agostini
Michele Alinovi
Franco Ancillotti
Alfonso Angelillo
Antonio Angelillo
Corrado Annoni
Sergio Antonini
Valeria Antonuccio
Adelina Aranaldi
Paolo Armellini
Alberto Aschieri
Paolo Asti
Annalisa Avon
Rocco Azzola
Spartaco Azzola
Mauro Bacchini
Franco Bader
Giorgio Baldissieri
Barbara Ballmer
Fabrizio Barbero
Stefano Baretti
Letizia Bassi Randi
Marta Bastianello
Francesca Battisti
André Sabastião Behncke
Mariella Belli
Stefano Bellinzona
Alessandra Bencich
Maria Benitez
Alberto Berengo Gardin
Anna Bettinelli
Giulio Bettini
Antonella Bergamin
Paola Bergamini
Valérie Bergeron
Pietro Bertelli
Fabio Bertoli
Franco Bertossi
Monica Bianchettin
Laura Bianchi
Marina Bianchi Michiel
Alberto Bianda
Alessandro Boccacci
Patrizia Boerci
Paola Bogoni
Paolo Bonazzi
Roberta Bonomi
Maddalena Borasio
Britta Bossel
Renzo Brandolini
Sebastiano Brandolini
Theo Brenner
Sonego Brenno
Stefano Bressan
Tatiana Brodatch
Giammarco Bruno
Donato Buccella
Luciano Bucci
Sergio Butti
Francesca Cadeo
Audrey Cadona
Vela Bianca Cagnardi
Claudio Calabrese
Ornella Calatroni
Cristina Calligaris
Maria Rosa Calmieri
Patrizia Cameo
Federica Campello
Giorgio Camuffo
Marina Candioli
Agostino Cangemi
Carlo Capovilla

Corinna Cappa
Diego Cappelletti
Piero Carlucci
Ginette Caron
Tomaso Carrer
Massimo Carta Mantiglia
Massimo Caruso
Elvio Casagrande
Stefano Casagrande
Vera Casanova
Gaetano Cassini
Cristina Castelli
Cristina Castello
Rita Cattaneo
Maria Teresa Cavagna
  di Gualdana
Annamaria Cavazzuti
Raffaello Cecchi
Alfonso Cendron
Emilia Ceribelli
Federica Ceschutti
Ilario Chiarel
Andrea Chiari Gaggia
Francesca Ciafrè
Luciano Claut
Graziella Clerici
Paoloemilio Colao
Laura Colini
Aldina Colombo
Alessandro Colombo
Barbara Colombo
Andrea Colonnello
Luisa Conte
Marco Contini
Davide Cornago
Luisa Corridori
Massimo Corsico
Maria Ludovica Costa
Silvana Costa
Claudio Costalonga
Samantha Cotterell
Andrea Cotti
Franco Croce
Luca Cuzzolin
Antonio D'Addario
Alessandra Dal Ben
Filippo De Filippi
Manolo De Giorgi
Stefano Degli Innocenti
Giuseppe Della Giusta
Marco Della Torre
Giulia Depero
Silvio De Ponte
Michela Destefanis
Jacopo Detti
Lorena Di Pietro
Carlo Donati
Giuseppe Donato
Sylvie Donnadieu
Luca Dotti
Carlotta Eco
Chiara Enrico
Anselmo Esposito
Alberto Faliva
Silvio Fassi
Marino Fei
Massimo Ferrari
Paolo Ferrari
Simone Ferrari
Rui Ferreira
Orietta Ferrero
Felicia Ferrone
Julia Fietz
Cinzia Francone

Simona Franzino
Francesco Fresa
Chiara Forti
Camilla Fronzoni
German Fuenmayor
Simona Furini
Sean Gaherty
Mauro Galantino
Federica Galbusieri
Giacomo Galmarini
Elena Galvagnini
Chiara Gamba
Gino Garbellini
Paola Garbuglio
Luisa Garlato
Carlotta Garretti
Claire Gazeau
Ambra Gerli
Michela Ghigliotti
Raffaele Ghillani
Rocco Giammetta
Concetta Giannangeli
Paola Giardina
Deirdre Gibson
Massimo Giordano
Valeria Girardi
Roberta Giudice
Graziella Giuliani
Susanne Glade
Attilio Gobbi
João Manuel Gouveia
  De Lacerda Moreira
Gaetano Gramegna
Salvatore Grande
Federico Graziati
Claudia Groenebaum
Ivana Guidi
Neil Gurry
Firuz Habibi Minelli
Heidi Hansen
Marion Hauff
Paul Honhsbeen
Silvia Icardi
Nobuko Imai
Sylviane Kellenberger
Antonio Lambertini
Andrea Lancellotti
Beatrice Lancini
George Latour Heinsen
Jacopo Livio
Ilaria Lombardi
Silvia Loreto
Elvira Losa
Lorenzo Lotti
Luca Lotti
Matteo Lualdi
Edoardo Lucchini Gabriolo
Alessandra Luzzato
Tomaso Macchi Cassia
Barbara Macedo
Franco Maffeis
Carlo Magnani
Chiara Majno
Stefano Malobbia
Andrea Mambriani
Stefania Mannironi
Giuseppe Mantia
Monica Marchesi
Francesca Marchetti
Lorenzo Marchetto
Stefania Martinelli
Laura Mascellani
Michela Mascia
Paola Masera

Laura Massa
Jun Matsui
Olivier Maupas
Cristiana Mazza
Maria Augusta Mazzarolli
Barbara Medini
Costanza Melli
Antoine Menthonnex
Filippo Messina
Elisabetta Michelini
Adria Minguzzi
Mariangela Moiraghi
Emanuela Monarca
Isidoro Montalbano
Luigi Montalbano
Claudia Montevecchi
Fabio Montrasi
Monica Moro
Guido Morpurgo
Leandro Murialdo
Paolo Musa
Jacopo Muzio
Clea Nardi
Daniele Nava
Federica Neeff
Francesco Nissardi
Walter Arno Noebel
Sue O'Brien
Lola Ottolini
Federico Pace
G.M. Padoan
Michela Pagan
Marcello Palazzo
Mariarosa Palmieri
Massimiliano Pani
Francesca Papis
Carla Parodi
Stefano Parodi
Marco Parravicini
Sergio Pascolo
Giovanna Passardi
Maurizio Pavani
Claudia Peducci
Anna Maria Penati
Anna Penco
Laura Peretti
Erica Pesaresi
Laura Pini
Martino Pirella
Carlo Pirola
Renza Pitton
Davide Pizzigoni
Peter Platner
Gianluca Poletti
Giulio Ponti
Ivana Porfiri
Giovanni Porta
Stefano Prina
Salvatore Provenzano
Emilio Puglielli
Isabella Quinto
Cristiano Ravizzotti
Michele Reginaldi
Salvatore Regio
Cecilia Ricci
Marcella Ricci
Sara Ricciardi
Daniela Rigamonti
Patrizia Ronchi
Maria Eleda Rosales
  Socorro
Silvia Ricca Rosellini
Franco Rosi
Martina Rossi

Paolo Rossi
Martina Rossini
Italo Rota
Eleonora Rovoletto
Gaetano Rubinelli
Gianbruno Ruggeri
Fabrizio Ruiu
Alejandro Ruiz
Umberto Saccardo
Nicola Saibene
Tomas Salgado
Christiane Sattler Zicari
Fortunato Scocco
Chiara Scortecci
Paul Seletsky
Paola Seria
Anna Serra
Donato Severo
Roberto Simoni
Susanna Slossel
Leila Smetana
Brenno Sonego
Frank Spadaro
Roberto Spagnolo
Stefania Spiazzi
Alessandra Spranzi
Elke Stauber
Christoph Stroschein
Aline Suares de Andrade
Margit Tappieiner
Matteo Tartufoli
Elena Terni
Paolo Tinelli
Ivan Tognazzi
Marcello Tomei
Elisabetta Torossi
Antonella Torre
Milena Tortorelli
Ada Myriam Tosoni
Gianfranco Trabucco
Monica Tricario
Vittorio Trombetta
Maurizio Trovatelli
Emanuela Uboldi
Pier Antonio Val
Monica Valdameri
Renzo Vallebuona
Marianna Vanoni
Carlo Vedovello
Isabella Vegni
Emanuela Venegoni
Claudia Ventura
Nico Ventura
Alessandro Verona
Barbara Veronesi
Bruna Vielmi
Paola Vignelli
Federica Vigo
Piero Vincenti
Chiara Vitali
Giovanni Vragnaz
Sandra Wenzel
Massimo Zancan
Tania Zaneboni
Dea Zanitoni
Dario Zannier
Flavio Zanon
Maurizio Zanuso
Mirko Zardini
Silvia Zauli
Uwe Zinkahn
Cino Zucchi

EXTERNAL PARTNERS WHO HAVE COLLABORATED ON SPECIFIC PROJECTS

B. Albrecht
Amman Progetti
F. Amoroso
Ansaldo Trasporti
Arnaud Fougeras
  Lavergnolle
Arup Italia
AT&T Associati
Atelier Bellet-de Pina
E. Battisti
L. Benevolo
S. Benkirane
BERIM
A. Bernardi
Bcv Progetti
Beterem
S. Bisogni
I. Bocci
C. Buxadé
Cabinet Casso
A. Calvesi, Campo
E. Casagrande
A. Castiglioni
P. Castiglioni,
S. Cavalleri
A. Cayatte
R. Cecchi, Centro
L. Celè

CentroStudi Traffico
Cepro
P. Cerri
Cfl Architecture
M. Chausse – R. Vayrat
B. Ciagà
A. Citterio
S. Cohen & C S.p.A.
Commins Acoustics
  Workshop
F. Correa
L. Corajoud, Y. Salliot
COSIDER Engineering
G. Creazza
Davis Langdon France
G. De Carli
A. Digenis
S. Digenis
Digierre 3
Ecosfera S.p.A.
ENCO Engineering
  Consulting
P. Erbetta
M. Federico
M. Felisatti
D. Ferretti
G. Franchini
R. Gabetti

GAD-Ing.G.P.D'Adda
M. Galantino
L. e M. Gemin
Global Project Developers
M. Goracci
J. Gutierrez, Inco
G14 Progettazione
Horizon
Intertecno
Iosiis Méditerranée –
  Iosiis Concept
Ismeri Europa
Ismes
A. Isola
Italprogetti
F. Landini
Laris
G. Lombardi
T. Lugli – M. Calzolari
F. Maffeis
P.P. Maggiora
F. Mancuso
Manens Intertecnica
E. Mantero
G.P. Mar
J. Margarit
G. Martinotti
F. Mascellani

H. Matsui
Mbm Arquitectes
  (J. Martorell, O. Bohigas,
  D. Mackay)
G. Medri
L. Meneghetti
A. Milà
G. Morandi
P. Nicolin, Noorami
  & Partners
Oth Bâtiments
Ove Arup & Partners
A. Paletti
P.En.T.A. Srl
PIG De Stefani
POOL Engineering Spa
Politekna Harris
G. Pollini
P. Portoghesi
G. Pravato
F. Purini
Ques.i.re, Reconsult
Risco - Manuel Salgado
A. Rivkin
C. Rusconi Clerici
SAGI Ingegneria
SCE
Scene

Sembenelli Consulting
R. Sha'ath
Sistema Progetto S.p.A.
SITI Istituto Superiore sui
  Sistemi Territoriali per
  l'Innovazione
STI Engineering Srl
Studio Bosi and Associati
Studio Cangemi
Studio Cappai e Mainardis
Studio Gpi
Studio Quaglia
SZ Sajni & Zambetti
Tekne
THAPE
Tianhua Architecture
  Planning & Engineering
  Ltd.
I. Tognazzi
J.P. Tohier
G. Trabucco
TRIBU, P.A. Val
N. Valle, N. Ventura
R. Vezzari
B. Viganò
Vrc
Zorzi

SELECTED BIBLIOGRAPHY

The following is a chronological selection of publications dedicated to the projects and creations of the Architetti Associati studio (Vittorio Gregotti, Lodovico Meneghetti, Giotto Stoppino), Vittorio Gregotti, and Gregotti Associati International. For a complete list, see the indices of specialist national and international journals which have published a steady stream of works and projects by Architetti Associati (V. Gregotti, L. Meneghetti, G. Stoppino), Vittorio Gregotti, and Gregotti Associati International.

Main reference works on Vittorio Gregotti and Architetti Associati 1954–1973

Samonà, G., *Architettura di giovani*, in *Casabella Continuità*, no. 206, 1954.

Rossi, A., *Il passato e il presente nella nuova architettura*, in *Casabella Continuità*, no. 219, 1959.

Tentori, F., *Quindici anni di architettura in Italia*, in *Casabella Continuità*, no. 253, 1961.

Canella, G., *Lo studio degli Architetti Associati*, in *Fantasia*, September 1963.

Portoghesi, P., *Tendenze degli Architetti Associati*, in *Comunità*, no. 115, 1963.

Tentori, F., *Lo studio Architetti Associati di Novara*, in *Casabella Continuità*, no. 259, 1963.

Filippini, E., *Appunti sopra un oggetto quasi sconosciuto*, in *Edilizia Moderna*, no. 82–83, 1964.

Tafuri, M., *Teorie e storia dell'architettura*, Laterza, Bari, 1968.

Santini, P.C., *V. Gregotti, L. Meneghetti, G. Stoppino, Architetture 1957–1968*, in *Ottagono*, no. 13, 1969.

Scolari, M., *L'architettura interrotta: tre progetti di Vittorio Gregotti*, in *Controspazio*, no. 3, 1971.

Traveaux d'equipes, in *L'Architecture d'aujourd'hui*, no. 170, 1973.

Main books on the works of Vittorio Gregotti and Gregotti Associati

Tafuri, M., *Vittorio Gregotti: Progetti e architetture*, Electa, Milan, 1982.

Crotti, S. (ed.), *Vittorio Gregotti*, Zanichelli, Bologna, 1986.

VV. AA., *Gregotti Associati: 1973-1988*, Electa, Milan, 1990.

Cagnardi, A., *Un nuovo senso del piano: Piani regolatori Gregotti Associati*, Etas, Milan, 1995.

Rykwert, J. (edited by Borasio, M., Colao, P., Hansen, H.), *Gregotti Associati*, Rizzoli, Milan, 1995.

Rykwert, J. (edited by Borasio, M., Colao, P., Hansen, H.), *Gregotti & Associates*, Rizzoli, New York, 1997.

VV. AA., *Progetto Bicocca 1985–1998*, Skira, Milan, 1999.

VV. AA., *La Bicocca abitata*, Skira, Milan, 2001.

Ceribelli, E., Morpurgo, G. (ed.) *Gregotti Associati, Frammenti di costruzioni*, Skira, Milan, 2001.

Ceribelli, E., Morpurgo, G. (ed.), *Fragments of Contructions*, Skira, Milan, 2001.

Morpurgo, G., *Gregotti Associati 1953–2003*, Rizzoli-Skira, Milan, 2004.

VV. AA., *Il teatro degli Arcimboldi*, Skira, Milan, 2004.

Morpurgo, G. (ed.), *Headquarters Pirelli Real Estate*, Skira, Milan, 2005.

Morpurgo, G. (ed.), *Un ordine comprensibile: Gregotti Associati, la nuova sede della Banca Lombarda/ An Intelligible Order: Gregotti Associati Banca Lombarda new Headquarters*, Skira, Milan, 2007.

VV. AA., *Gregotti Associati. La fabbrica del "Corriere della Sera,"* Skira, Milan, 2007.

Coppa, A., *Vittorio Gregotti*, Motta Architettura, Milan, 2007.

Morpurgo, G. (ed.), *Festschrift per gli ottant'anni di Vittorio Gregotti*, Skira, Milan, 2007.

Morpurgo, G., *Gregotti & Associati. L'architettura del disegno urbano*, Rizzoli, Milan, 2008.

Morpurgo, G., *Gregotti & Associates: The Architecture of Urban Design*, Rizzoli, New York, 2008.

Colao, P. (ed.) *Gregotti Associati: Grand Théâtre de Provence*, Flammarion-Skira, Milan-Paris, 2008.

Sartea, A., *I maestri dell'architettura: Gregotti Associati*, Hachette, Milan, 2010.

Reference works on Vittorio Gregotti, Gregotti Associati 1974–1988 and Gregotti Associati International 1988–2014

Bohigas, O., *Gregotti o una estructura teorica desde una pratica proyectual*, in *Arquitectura bis*, 4, 1974.

Montenagni, A., Sica P., *La politica urbanistica fiorentina e il concorso per la nuova Università*, in *Urbanistica*, no. 62, 1974.

Nicolin, P. L., *Nuovi dipartimenti di Scienze dell'Università di Palermo*, in *Casabella*, no. 394, 1974.

Rykwert, J., *La nuova Università della Calabria*, in *Domus*, no. 540, 1974.

Battisti, E., *Architettura, ideologia e scienza*, Milan, Feltrinelli, 1975.

Dal Co, F., Manieri Elia M., *La generation de l'incertitude*, in *L'Architecture d'Aujourd'hui*, no. 181, 1975.

Il quartiere ZEN a Palermo, in *Lotus International*, no. 9, 1975.

Berlin alt und neu, in *Lotus International*, no. 13, 1976.

Tafuri, M., Dal Co, F., *Architettura contemporanea*, Electa, Milan, 1976.

Special feature: Vittorio Gregotti, in *A+U*, no. 79, 1977.

Progetto per lo sviluppo integrato dell'Adda, in *Lotus International*, no. 14, 1977.

Huet, B., *Formalisme-Réalisme*, in *L'Architecture d'aujourd'hui*, no. 190, 1977.

Apartment in Milan, Italy, 1975–77; Architects: Gregotti Associati, in *GA Houses*, no. 5, 1978.

Università come fabbrica e fabbrica come Università: i nuovi Dipartimenti di Scienze dell'Università di Palermo, in *Parametro*, no. 67, 1978.

Burkhardt, F., *5 Architekten zeichen für Berlin*, Archibook Verlag, Berlin, 1979.

V. Gregotti, in *G.A. Documents*, special issue, 1970–1980, 1979.

Tafuri, M., (catalog edited by Rota I.), *Il progetto per l'Università delle Calabrie e altre architetture di Vittorio Gregotti*, Electa, Milan, 1979.

Case da vendere, in *Domus*, no. 611, 1980.

Frampton, K., *Città senza bandiere*, in *Domus*, no. 611, 1980.

Houses for sale, in *Architecture and Urbanism*, no. 12, 1980.

Il progetto per il Centro Ricerche Montedison a Portici, in *Domus*, no. 609, 1980.

Tafuri, M., *La sfera e il labirinto*, Einaudi, Turin, 1980.

Foster, H., *Pastiche/Prototype/Purity: "Houses for Sale" Leo Castelli Gallery*, New York, in *Artforum*, no. 7, 1981.

L'université industrialisée: nouveaux departements de scieces, Université de Palerme, Sicile, in *L'Architecture d'aujourd'hui*, no. 216, 1981.

Magnago Lampugnani, V., *Avant gardes architecturales 1970–1980*, in *L'Architecture d'Aujourd'hui*, no. 213, 1981.

Riti di fondazione, in *Domus*, no. 621, 1981.

Variation on a grid shape, in *Architectural Record*, no. 5, 1981.

Architecture de la terre, in *Le nouvel observateur*, 1982.

Dardi, C., *Un pensiero verde in un profilo verde*, in *Domus*, no. 628, 1982.

De Fusco, R., *Storia dell'architettura contemporanea*, Laterza, Bari, 1982.

Tafuri, M., *Vittorio Gregotti: Progetti e architetture*, Electa, Milan, 1982.

Aulenti, G., *La villa attraversata*, in *Casa Vogue*, no. 147, 1983.

Tretiack, P., *Concours international de la Tête-Défense. 424 projets dans l'axe*, in *Techniques et architecture*, no. 349, 1983.

Begegnung mit dem Ort, in *Daidalos*, no. 12, 1984.

VV.AA., *Gregotti Associati*, in *Process Architecture*, no. 48, 1984.

VV.AA., *Venti progetti per il futuro del Lingotto*, Etas-libri, Milan, 1984.

Boissiere, O., *Parigi per Parigi*, in *Domus*, no. 646, 1984.

Bohigas, O., *Juegos Olimpicos 1992*, in *Arquitecturas bis*, no. 37, 1984.

Bossi Factory's Extension, Novara, Italy, Design: 1980; Completion: 1983; Architects: Gregotti Associati, in *G.A. Documents*, no. 9, 1984.

Concurso de proyectos para el Anillo Olimpico de Montjuic, in *Arquitectura. Revista del Colegio Oficial de Arquitectos de Madrid*, no. 247, 1984.

La ville-territoire, in *Techniques Architectures, 1984*.

De Giorgi, M., Torricelli, A. (ed.), *Atlante comparato dell'architettura contemporanea: le otto posizioni emergenti e le loro teste di serie*, in *Modo*, no. 69, 1984.

Gregotti Associati 1981/83, in *Process Architecture*, no. 48, 1984.

Gregotti serves as first Tange Visiting Professor of Architecture and Urban Design, in *GSD News/ Harvard University Graduate School of Design*, no. 5, 1984.

Vittorio Gregotti & Gino Pollini: Science Departments at the University of Palermo, in *Architectural Design*, no. 11–12, 1984.

House in Oleggio, Italy, 1977–1983; Architects: Gregotti Associati, in *GA Houses*, no. 15, 1984.

Benevolo, L., *L'ultimo capitolo dell'architettura moderna*, Laterza, Bari, 1985.

Casciato, M., Muratore, G., *Annali dell'architettura italiana contemporanea*, Officina, Rome, 1985.

La fabbrica universitaria. Dipartimenti dell'Università di Palermo, in *Lotus International*, 4, 1985.

Neubau der Università della Calabria. Die Utopie des Zweifels, in *Bauwelt*, 46, 1985.

Territory and architecture, in *Architectural Design*, no. 5–6, 1985.

Architektur für das kollektive Gedächtnis. Universität von Palermo – neue wissenschaftliche Abteilungen am Parco d'Orleans, 1969-1984, in *Werk, Bauen + Wohnen*, no. 3, 1985.

Roda, R. (ed.), *Un progetto per Livorno: riflessioni e proposte del movimento cooperativo per una qualità urbana: laboratorio di progettazione, Consorzio Cooper Toscana, Cooper Livorno, Unicoopcasa, Abitcooper aderenti all'ARCAT/Lega con Gregotti Associati*, Alinea, Florence, 1986.

Bianchetti, C., Infussi, F., Ischia, U., Secchi, B. (ed.), *Progetto Bicocca: Concorso internazionale di progettazione urbanistica e architettonica ideato e realizzato per iniziativa della Industrie Pirelli S.p.A.*, Electa, Milan, 1986.

Boeri, S., *Alte Architektur für neue Technologien: Wettbewerb zur Umnutzung des Pirelli-Werk "Bicocca" in Mailand*, in *Bauwelt*, no. 46, 1986.

Concorso a inviti progetto Bicocca Milano, in *Domus*, no. 675, 1986.

Crotti, S. (ed.), *Vittorio Gregotti*, Zanichelli, Bologna, 1986.

De Michelis, M., *Nuovi progetti per la Giudecca: tipi di edificazione e morfologia dell'isola*, in *Lotus International*, no. 51, 1986.

Di Biagi, P., Bohigas O., Gabellini P., Secchi B., *Le occasioni del Progetto-Bicocca*, in *Casabella*, no. 524, 1986.

Frampton, K., *Edificio per abitazioni a Berlino: Gregotti Associati*, in *Casabella*, no. 525, 1986.

Magnago Lampugnani, V., *Gregotti Associati. Università della Calabria*, Cosenza, in *Domus*, no. 673, 1986.

Muri in mattoni e portali d'acciaio: Edificio per abitazioni a Berlino, Lützowstrasse, in *Lotus International*, no. 48–49, 1986.

Tebaldi, M., *Siviglia – concorso di idee per l'Esposizione Universale 1992*, in *Domus*, no. 677, 1986.

Architettura ed energia. Sette edifici per l'ENEA, De Luca, Rome, 1987.

Brandolini, S., Norri M-R., *Ajatuskia eurooppalaisesta regionalismista: kekustelu Vittorio Gregottin kansaa (On European Regionalism: Conversation with Vittorio Gregotti)*, in *Arkkitehti*, no. 3, 1987.

Bucaille, B., *Barcelone 92: les J.O. au stade du projet*, in *Architectes architectures*, no. 176, 1987

Football and Rugby Stadium, Nîmes, France, design: 1986, in *G.A. Document*, no. 18, 1987.

La ville dècline ses mémoires: O. Bohigas et J.A. Gotysolo à propos de Barcelone olympique, in *Techniques et architecture*, no. 373, 1987.

Neubau: Housing, Lützowstrasse (Southern Tiergarten) West Berlin, in *Architectural Review*, no. 1082, 1987.

Quatre stades de Gregotti, in *L'Architecture d'haujourd'hui*, no. 250, 1987.

Prächtiges Kaleidoskop gebauter Leidenschaften. IBA Berlin–eine Bilanz, in *Art*, no. 9, 1987.

Ranzani, E., *Gregotti Associati: Stadio "Luigi Ferraris,"* Genova, in *Domus*, no. 682, 1987.

Aldersey-Williams, H., *A Designer Olympics (1992 Olympics, Barcelona, Spain)*, in *Progressive Architecture*, no. 6, 1988.

Banlieue, in *L'Architecture d'aujourd'hui*, no. 259, 1988.

La costruzione della città e del territorio in Italia, Centro Edile, Milan, 1988.

Conti, S. (ed.), *Un'idea per le Murate*, Electa, Florence, 1988.

De Giorni, M., Spadaio, F., *Gregotti Associati: appartamento a Manhattan*, in *Domus*, no. 697, 1988.

Fortin, J.-P., *Milan La Bicocca*, in *L'Architecture d'aujourd'hui*, no. 259, 1988.

Housing on Lützowstrasse, Southern Tiergarten, Berlin, 1982–86, in *GA Houses*, no. 23, 1988.

Irace, F., *Berlino 1988*, in *Abitare*, no. 264, 1988.

Klaus Koenig, G., *Che lavoro porsi in Siena!*, in *Ottagono*, no. 91, 1988.

Progettare un edificio semplice è un problema. Centro di ricerche ENEA alla Casaccia, in *Lotus International*, no. 57, 1988.

Ranzani, E., Milano, *Progetto Bicocca: risultati finali del concorso*, in *Domus*, no. 698, 1988.

Sammartini, T., *Agenda Veneziana: costruire dove non sono ammesse periferie*, in *Parametro*, no. 167, 1988.

Secchi, B., *Il concorso per l'area di piazza Matteotti-la Lizza a Siena*, in *Casabella*, no. 552, 1988.

Skylight and Clerestory Center for Energy Research, Rome, in *Progressive Architecture*, no. 9, 1988.

Stucchi, S., *Edificio per abitazioni a Berlino*, in *Industria delle costruzioni*, no. 195, 1988.

Stucchi, S., *Edificio affidabilità e qualificazione dell'Enea alla Casaccia*, Roma, in *Industria delle costruzioni*, no. 205, 1988.

Secchi, B., *Il concorso per l'area di piazza Matteotti-la Lizza a Siena*, in *Casabella*, no. 552, 1988.

A Cannaregio, in *L'Architecture d'aujourd'hui*, no. 266, 1989.

Brandolini, S., *Off-shore Gregotti*, in *Architectural Review*, no. 1105, 1989.

Cadrages sur le ciel venetien: quartier d'habitation du Cannaregio, Venise, in *Techniques et architectures*, no. 383, 1989.

Catalano, P., *Streng: Showroom Marisa in Mailand*, in *Architektur*,

Innenarchitektur, Technischer Ausbau, no. 9, 1989.

Frascari, M., *Il Particolareggiamento in the narration of architecture*, in *Journal of Architectural Education*, no. 43, 1989.

Herzog, H.M., *Wohnquartier in Venedig-Cannaregio*, in *Bauwelt*, no. 28-29, 1989.

Krafft, A. (ed.), *Architecture contemporaine*, Bibliothèque des Arts, Paris-Lausanne, 1989.

Matsui, H., *International competition of invitation for new architectural solution of urbanization at the piazza Matteotti-La Lizza area in Siena*, in *Architecture and Urbanism*, no. 6, 1989.

Nicolin, P., *Tessuto e monumento: due interpretazioni al concorso per il centro culturale di Belém a Lisbona*, in *Lotus International*, no. 61, 1989.

Noebel, W.A., *Stadtplan oder Projekt*, in *Bauwelt*, no. 24, 1989.

Pirelli-Gelände "Bicocca" in Mailand, Italien, 2. Stufe, in *Architektur+Wettbewerbe*, no. 140, 1989.

Ranzani, E., *Gregotti Associati: quartiere residenziale area ex-Saffa*, Venice, in *Domus*, no. 704, 1989.

Bayne, G., *Barcelona und die Olympiade 1992-ein Zwischenbericht*, in *Bauwelt*, no. 4, 1990.

Brown-Manrique, G., *Architekturfürer Tessin und Lombardei. Die neunen Bauten*, Hatjie, Stuttgart, 1990.

Colao, P., Vragnaz, G. (ed.), *Gregotti Associati 1973–1988*, Electa, Milan, 1990.

De Giorni, M., *Vittorio Gregotti: La fatica del distacco teorico*, in *Domus*, no. 717, 1990.

Fortier, B., *Il concorso per il quartiere Sextius Mirabeau a Aix-en-Provence*, in *Casabella*, no. 572, 1990.

Genua. Eine Baubesschereibung, in "Stadtbauwelt," no. 106, 1990.

Graf, U., Blaser, W., *Gibellina Nuova. Ein Beispiel für den Widerstand gegen den Kulturkolonialismus*, in *Docu-Bulletin*, no. 4, 1990.

Ort und Stadion: neue Fussballstadien in Italien, in *Werk, Bauen +Wohnen*, no. 9, 1990.

San Pietro, S. (ed.), *1990 stadi in Italia*, L'Archivolto, Milan, 1990.

Stucchi, S., *Intervento residenziale nell'area ex-Saffa a Venezia*, in *Industria delle costruzioni*, no. 221, 1990.

Ullmann, G., *Der Glanze der Ringe. Neue Sportstadien in Barcelona*, in *Werk, Bauen +Wohnen*, no. 9, 1990.

Wettbewerbprofil des Architekten Vittorio Gregotti, Mailand, I., in *Architektur + Wettbewerbe*, no. 144, 1990.

Di Battista, N., *Gregotti Associati: riorganizzazione dell'area portuale di Venezia*, in *Domus*, no. 726, 1991.

Hamm, O., *Barcelona baut: Die Sportanlagen für die Olympischen Spiele 1992*, in *Deutsche Bauzeitung*, no. 5, 1991.

Mandolesi, D., *Berlino: idee per una metropoli*, in *Industria delle costruzioni*, no. 239, 1991.

Olympisches Stadion in Barcelona, Spanien, in *Architektur + Wettbewerbe*, no. 145, 1991.

Petruccioli, S., *Edificio per attività di interesse pubblico nella Repubblica di San Marino*, in *Industria delle costruzioni*, no. 236, 1991.

Strischein, C., *Ein Stadt-Umland-Ideal für Berlin-Brandenburg*, in *Bauwelt*, no. 48, 1991

Ullmann, G., *Zwitter: Umbau des Montjuic-Stadions in Barcelona*, in *Deutsche Bauzeitung*, no. 5, 1991.

Vuillermet, C., *Nîmes*, in *Abitare*, no. 300, 1991.

Zardini, M., *Il Corso negato: nel centro di Aix-en-Provence*, in "Lotus International," no. 70, 1991.

Centro culturale di Belém, Lisbona, in *Domus*, no. 738, 1992.

Fisher, T., *Stadium in the city*, in *Progressive Architecture*, no. 4, 1992.

Irace, F., *Una porta per la città*, in *Abitare*, no. 309, 1992.

Kush, C.F., *Le Arti Industriali*, in *Deutsche Bauzeitschrift*, no. 7, 1992.

La grande nave: Gregotti Associati, un progetto per la crociera / Pierluigi Cerri, in *Abitare*, no. 306, 1992.

Le renouvellement Strasbourgeois, in *Techniques et architecture*, no. 400, 1992.

Monninger, M., *Berlino: progetti per il Potsdamer/Leipziger Platz*, in *Domus*, no. 734, 1992.

Remodelacion del Estadio de Montjuic, Barcelona, in *ON diseño*, 1992.

Siza A., Gregotti en el estuario: Centro cultural de Belém, in *Arquitectura viva*, no. 27, 1992.

Stranieri in Francia, in *Abitare*, no. 309, 1992.

Torino: piano, struttura, progetto. Contributi di Gregotti Associati Studio, in *Casabella*, no. 592, 1992.

Delluc, M., *Montreuil*, in *AMC Moniteur architecture*, no. 40, 1993.

Experimentelles Kraftwerk in Mailand-Bicocca, in *Bauwelt*, no. 37, 1993.

Gazzaniga, L., *Gregotti Associati: Nuova sede della Regione Marche*, Ancona, in *Domus*, no. 754, 1993.

Ingersoll, R., *Il concorso per la nuova Cancelleria dell'Amasciata d'Italia a Washington D.C.*, in *Casabella*, no. 602, 1993.

Molinari, T., *Nuova Architettura*, in *Abitare*, no. 320, 1993.

Neugestaltung der Piazza Madrice in Menfi, in *Bauwelt*, no. 47, 1993.

Città di Torino, Assessorato all'assetto urbano, Piano Regolatore Generale di Torino, Ambiente urbano, tessuto edilizio e architettura nella zona centrale di Torino, Turin, 1994.

Cuatro propuestas residenciales para Teatinos, in *Geometria*, no. 17, 1994.

de Mendonça Raimudo, D., *Centro Cultural de Belém: Aspectos significativos da construçao*, Lisbon, 1994.

Faiferri, M., *La pietra mutevole*, in *Industria delle costruzioni*, no. 268, 1994.

Gregotti Associati, Manuel Salgado. Lisbona Centro culturale di Belém, in *Anfione Zeto*, no. 10, 1994.

Kulturfestung: Centro Cultural de Belém, Lissabon, in *Bauwelt*, no. 19, 1994.

Kusch, C., *Eine Architektur der grossen Dimensionen: zum Werk von Vittorio Gregotti*, in *Deutsche Bauzeitshrift*, no. 268, 1994.

Pollak, L., *The Visible City: Reflections on a Lecture by Vittorio Gregotti*, in *GSD News/Harvard University, Graduate School of Design*, 1994.

Rizzi, R., *Vittorio Gregotti: Belém*, Wien, Kiev, in *Lotus International*, no. 83, 1994.

Romanelli, M., *Nave da crociera Costa Romantica, Pierluigi Cerri (Gregotti Associati)*, in *Domus*, no. 760, 1994.

Secretaria de Estrado da Cultura, Centro Cultural e Belém, Lisbon, 1994.

Balfour, A. (ed.), *World cities: Berlin*, Academy Editions, London, 1995.

VV.AA., *Piani dello studio Gregotti Associati*, in *Urbanistica*, no. 104, 1995.

Bastianello, M., Colao P. (ed.), *Progetto Bicocca: Un contributo per Milano policentrica*, Triennale di Milano, Electa, Milan, 1995.

Emanuel, M., *Contemporary Architects*, St. James Press, New York-London, 1995.

Vittorio Gregotti. Context of Architecture, in *Gallery MA 1985–1995*, Toto, Tokyo, 1995.

Rykwert, J. (edited by Borasio, M., Colao, P., Hansen, H.), *Gregotti Associati*, Rizzoli, Milan, 1995.

Schröder, T., Berlin, *Berlin. Architektur für neues jahrhundert*, Nishen, Berlin, 1995.

Apollonio, F.I., *Architettura per lo spazio sacro*, Allemandi, Turin, 1996.

Curtis, C., Gates C., *The International Directory of Architecture and Design*, Volume 4, DID World Review, London, 1996.

Panizza, M., *Edifici per lo spettacolo*, Laterza, Rome-Bari, 1996.

Coppola Pignatelli, P., Mandolesi, D., *L'architettura delle università*, CDP, Rome, 1997.

Rykwert, J. (edited by Borasio, M., Colao, P., Hansen, H.), *Gregotti & Associates*, Rizzoli, New York, 1997.

M. Fuchigami, Europe. *The Contemporary Architecture Guide, Vol. 1*, Gallery MA, Tokyo, 1998.

VV.AA., *Progetto Bicocca 1985–1998*, Skira, Milan, 1999.

Cagnardi, A., *Nuovi piani, nuovi progetti: Livorno, Gorizia, Pavia*, in *Urbanistica*, no. 115, 2000.

Crespi, L., *Urban development in Milan*, in *Detail*, B2772, 1999.

Secchi, B., *Milano Berlino*, in *Domus*, no. 815, 1999.

Magnago Lampugnani, V., *Musei per un nuovo millennio. Idee, progetti, edifici*, Prestel, Munich–London–New York, 2000.

Santi, G., Crespi, G., *Nuove chiese italiane*, Electa, Milan, 2000.

Morpurgo, G., *"Dissimili scribendi genere" European Architecture, in "Mégalopole. Art, architecture, urbanisme,"* cahier 21, 2000.

VV.AA., *Progetto Bicocca. La Bicocca abitata*, Skira, Milan, 2001.

Gramigna, G., Mazza, S., *Milano. Un seco,lo di architettura milanese dal Cordusio alla Bicocca*, Hoepli, Milan, 2001.

Ceribelli, E., Morpurgo, G. (ed.), *Gregotti Associati Frammenti di costruzioni*, Skira, Milan, 2001.

Ceribelli, E., Morpurgo, G. (ed.), *Fragments of Contructions*, Skira, Milan, 2001.

Morpurgo, G., *La Bicocca-Milan: les villes visibles*, in Charre, A. (ed.), *Les nouvelles conditions du projet urbain. Critique et méthodes*, Mardaga, Sprimont, 2001.

Mulazzani, M., *Variazioni sul tipo: Due stadi della Gregotti Associati per Marocco 2006*, in *Casabella*, no. 694, 2001.

Raggi, F., *Sono un tipo ordinato, Intervista a Vittorio Gregotti*, in *Flare*, no. 28, 2001.

Baglione, C., *Teatro degli Arcimboldi: Architettura della normalità*, in *Casabella*, no. 699, 2002.

Caille, E., *Acoutisme à l'italienne*, in *Le Moniteur*, no. 5127, 2002.

Dai, Y., Zhao, Y., *Town of Pujiang, Shanghai*, in *Di Architecture & Design*, no. 100, 2002.

Irace, F., *Teatro degli Arcimbold:. Milano cambia centro*, in *Abitare*, no. 415, 2002.

Klüver, H., *Ausweichquartier: Mailands neue Scala*, in *Baumeister*, no. B5, 2002.

Kultermann, U., *Vittorio Gregotti, in 30 Years after: The future of the past*, Architecture and Art, Budapest, 2002.

La Biennale di Venezia, *Next: 8th International Achitecture Exhibition*, Marsilio-Rizzoli, Venice, 2002.

Marotta, A. (ed.), *Cinquanta domande a Vittorio Gregotti*, Clean, Naples, 2002.

Santa Maria del Fiore di Firenze, *Il nuovo Museo dell'Opera del Duomo: Quattro progetti*, Mandragora, Florence, 2002.

Pedretti, B. (ed.), *Gregotti Associati: La costruzione dello spazio pubblico*, Alinea, Florence, 2002.

VV.AA., *Forme e tracce dell'abitare. Una risposta sociale per la qualità urbana in Emilia-Romagna*, Editrice Compositori, Bologna, 2003.

Cagnardi, A., *Un'avventura affascinante: La nuova "città italiana" per 80.000 abitanti di Pujiang*, in *Urbanistica*, no. 122, 2003.

Dai, Y., Zhao, Y., *Urban Planning & Landscape Design of Pujiang Town*, in *Di Architecture & Design*, no. 104, 2003.

Durbiano, G., Robiglio, M., *Paesaggio e architettura nell'Italia contemporanea*, Donzelli, Rome, 2003.

Emulando a la Scala, in *Arkinka*, no. 86, 2003.

Ingersoll, R., *Teatro degli Arcimboldi*, in *Bauwelt*, no. 6, 2003.

Palazzolo, C., *Vittorio Gregotti: Principi di architettura*, in C. Quintelli (ed.), *Ritratti. Otto maestri dell'architettura italiana*, Celid, Turin, 2003.

Plan urbano para el área residencial de Pujiang Village, Shanghai, in *Archivos de Arquitectura Antillana*, no. 16, 2003.

Pujiang Village, in *Lotus International*, no. 117, 2003.

Sciascia, A., *Tra le modernità dell'architettura: Il caso del quartiere ZEN 2 di Palermo*, Andropolis, Palermo, 2003.

VV.AA., *Cesena_ex Zuccherificio_01*, Danilo Montanari Editore, Ravenna, 2003.

Inclined and curved glass wall. Arcimboldi Opera Theater, in *Details in Architecture*, no. 5, The Images Publishing Group, Victoria 2004. ,

Nuova sede generale Pirelli alla Bicocca, in *Abitare*, no. 439, 2004.

Il faro del villaggio. Chiesa di S. Clemente a Baruccana di Seveso (Milano), in *Chiesa oggi*, no. 63, 2004.

Lasagna, S., *Il borgo della fede*, in *Il nuovo cantiere*, no. 5, 2004.

Presbitero, S., *La Salle de spectacles du Pays d'Aix*, in *Progettare*, no. 14, 2004.

Polaris: Parco scientifico e tecnologico della Sardegna, in *Abitare*, no. 440, 2004.

Lighting box. Pirelli & C. Real Estate, in *Meeting*, Artemide Editoriale Lotus, 2004.

Pujiang New Town, in *Ibdi–Intelligent build & design innovations*, 2004/5.

Casotti, A., *Architetture di confine*, in *Modo*, no. 242, 2005.

Cagnardi, A., *Ispirazioni italiane in Cina*, in *Progetto & pubblico*, no. 18, 2005.

Pujiang New Town Promotion Center, in "A+U Architecture and Urbanism," *Beijing Shanghai Architecture Guide*, 2005.

Headquarters Pirelli Real Estate, in S. Brandolini, *Milano. Nuova architettura*, Skira, Milan, 2005.

Loggione, M., *Il midollo del regno Pirelli*, in *OFX Architettura*, no. 84, 2005.

Gamba, R., *Studio Gregotti Associati, Mauro Galantino, Centro scolastico ad Arezzo*, in *Costruire in laterizio*, no. 103, 2005.

Damiani, G., *Nuova luce per la storica sede di RCS*, in *Office layout*, no. 115, 2005.

Morpurgo, G., *Gregotti Associados: Planejamento urbano como modificação crítica da cidade/ Gregotti Associati: Urban Design as critical modification of the city*, in Cury P. (ed.), *6^ Bienal Internacional de Arquitetura de São Paulo–Viver na Cidade*, Fundação Bienal de São Paulo, Istituto de Arquitetos do Brasil, São Paulo, 2005.

Bondonio, A., Callegari, G., Franco, C., Gibello, L. (ed.), *Stop & go: Il riuso delle aree industriali dimesse in Italia*, Alinea, Florence, 2005.

Morpurgo, G. (ed.), *Headquarters Pirelli Real Estate*, Skira, Milan, 2005.

Morpurgo, G., *Orizzonti dell'intenzionalità: il disegno a pura linea nel progetto di Gregotti Associati*, in *Il disegno di architettura*, no. 31, 2005.

Pirelli & C. Real Estate Headquarters in Bicocca, in *A+U Architecture and Urbanism*, no. 420, 2005.

Sang Leem, L., *Vittorio Gregotti*, in *Space*, no. 460, 2006.

El Barrio de la Bicocca en Milán: Un centro histórico para la periferia, in *AAA Archivos de Arquitectura Antillana*, no. 025, 2006.

Boeri, S., Gregotti, V., *Gli enzimi dell'architettura*, in *Domus*, no. 895, 2006.

Bucci, F., *Direzione generale Pirelli Real Estate, Bicocca, Milano*, in *Casabella*, no. 747, 2006.

Teatro degli Arcimboldi, Centro culturale di Belém, Lisbona, in M. Narpozzi, *Teatri. Architetture 1980–2005*, Motta, Milan, 2006.

VV.AA., *Cesena: Il nuovo quartiere Ex Zuccherificio, testimonianze e immagini*, Cesena, 2006.

Headquarter Pirelli a Milano, in *Firenze architettura*, Il frammento, 2006.

Cube and Cooling Tower: Pirelli Real Estate Headquarters, in Boschetti J. (ed.), *Details in Design*, Images Publishing, Mulgrave, Victoria, 2006.

Vasumi, Roveri E., *L'architetto con la penna in mano: Conversazione con Vittorio Gregotti*, in *Parametro*, no. 267, 2007.

VV. AA., *Sopic-Architecture et citoyenneté. Six cas concrets pour décrire une éthique de promotion*, Transbordeurs, Marseilles, 2007.

Morpurgo, G. (ed.), *Un ordine comprensibile: Gregotti Associati, la nuova sede della Banca Lombarda/ An Intelligible Order. Gregotti Associati Banca Lombarda new Headquarters*, Skira, Milan, 2007.

Conforti, C., *Vittorio Gregotti, ristrutturazione della sede del Corriere della Sera*, in *Casabella*, no. 754, 2007.

VV.AA., *Gregotti Associati. La fabbrica del* Corriere della Sera, Skira, Milan, 2007.

Vittorio Gregotti. Ventiquattro disegni, "Antonia Jannone. Disegni di Architettura- Milano," Grafiche Milani, Segrate-Milan, 2007.

Morpurgo, G., *Festschrift per gli ottant'anni di Vittorio Gregotti*, Skira, Milan, 2007.

Morpurgo, G., *Gregotti & Associati: L'architettura del disegno urbano*, Rizzoli, Milan, 2008.

Morpurgo, G., *Gregotti & Associates: The Architecture of Urban Design*, Rizzoli, New York, 2008.

Morpurgo, G., *Concorso per la trasformazione delle aree Pirelli Bicocca, Milano 1985/1988; Sede del Gruppo Siemens, Bicocca, Milano 1985/1988; Tre torri per il terziario alla Bicocca. Milano*, in *I Beni Culturali. Tutela, valorizzazione, attività culturali, architettura contemporanea e bioarchitettura*, anno XVI, no. 4–5, July–October 2008.

Benevolo, L., *La sottile magia del lavoro d'equipe: I progetti dello studio di Vittorio Gregotti*, in *Corriere della Sera*, July 24, 2008.

Colao, P. (ed.) *Gregotti Associati: Grand Théâtre de Provence*, Flammarion-Skira, Milan-Paris, 2008.

Sartea, A., *I maestri dell'architettura: Gregotti Associati*, Hachette, Milan, 2010.

Gregotti Associati International. Città nuova di Pujiang, Shanghai 2001-09, in *Lotus International*, no. 141, 2010.

Gregotti Associati: Schema di assetto preliminare della centralità urbana di Acilia Madonnetta, Roma; Grand Théatre de Provenne, Aix-en-Provence, in Anfione e Zeto: Rivista di architettura e arti, no. 24, 2012.

Biraghi, M., Lo Ricco, G., Micheli, S., *Guida all'architettura di Milano 1954-2014*, Hoepli, Milan, 2013.

Biraghi, M., Micheli, S., *Storia dell'architettura italiana 1985–2015*, Einaudi, Turin, 2013.

INDEX BY LOCATION OF THE PROJECTS DESCRIBED IN THE TEXT

EXHIBITIONS

"Il progetto per l'Università delle Calabrie e altre architetture di Vittorio Gregotti," Milan, Barcelona, Berlino, Syracuse, NY, Palermo, 1980–1981

"Progetto per il Centro Montedison a Napoli," Naples, 1983

"Vittorio Gregotti," Harvard University, Cambridge, MA, 1984

"Comune di Modena, Piano particolareggiato della zona Corassori," Bologna, 1984

"Vittorio Gregotti: Architetture," MA Gallery, Tokyo, 1987

"Vittorio Gregotti: Architetture," ETH – Federal Polytechnic of Zurich, 1987

"Vittorio Gregotti: Architetture," Duom Gallery, Moscow, 1988

"Il Piano Regolatore Generale di Torino," Turin, 1992

"Gregotti Associati: Architetture 1974–2001," MusArc, Ferrara, 2001

"I progetti per il Teatro degli Arcimboldi," Teatro alla Scala, Milan, 2001

"Gregotti Associati: La costruzione dello spazio pubblico," Esprit Nouveau Pavillon, Bologna, 2002

Gregotti Associati "Next. 8. Mostra Internazionale di Architettura della Biennale di Venezia," Venice, 2002.

"Gregotti Associati: New Pujiang Town," Urban Planning Exhibition Building, Shanghai, 2003

"L'architettura di Vittorio Gregotti e Partners," Kévés Studio Gallery, Budapest, 2004

"Trasformazione delle aree Pirelli alla Bicocca," Istituto Italiano di Cultura, Cologne, 2004

"Gregotti Associati International," Sixth Architecture Biennial, São Paulo, 2005

"Gregotti Associati International," Second Architecture Biennial, Beijing, 2006

"La nuova città di Pujiang," in "Beijing, Shanghai, Nanjing," Galleria dell'Accademia di architettura, Mendrisio, 2007

Vittorio Gregotti "Ventiquattro disegni," Antonia Jannone Gallery, Milan, 2007

"Parco Nord, La città cresce," Palazzo Morpurgo, Udine, 2012

PHOTOGRAPHY CREDITS

Aaron/Esto
Amendolagine e Barracchia
Graziano Arici
Aldo Ballo
Gabriele Basilico
Dida Biggi, Ruggero Boschetti
Nello Brancaccio
Sergio Butti
Alessandro Cane
Mario Carrieri
Elvio Casagrande
Giorgio Casali
Vincenzo Castella
Cristina Castello
Lorenzo Castore
Leonardo Céndamo
Giovanni Chiaramonte

Alessandro Colombo
Antonio De Angelis
Carla De Benedetti
Donato Di Bello
Giuseppe Donato
Daniel Faure
Luigi Ghirri
F. Gorup de Besanez
Mimmo Jodice
Hero Lang
Walter Liaci
John Edward Linden
Saverio Lombardi Vallauri
Tomaso Macchi Cassia
Giorgio Maino
Maurizio Maniscalco
José Manuel
Jean Christophe Marmara

Andrea Martiradonna
Giovanni Mensi
Alberto Muciaccia
Antonia Mulas
Ugo Mulas
Stefan Müller
Toni Nicolini
ORCH, Peter Oszvald
Marco Parravicini
Filippo Piantanida
Pozzi & Romeo
Francesco Radino
Piero Raffaelli
Venanzio Raggi
M. Ramazzotti
Uwe Rau
Michele Reginaldi
Dirk Robbers

Ferdinando Rollando
Massimo Sacconi
Sandro Scalia
Roberto Schezen
Vaclav Sedy
Mark E. Smith
Luciano Soave
Rui Morais De Sousa
Studio Azzurro
Patrice Terraz
Onelio Ventura
Federico Villa
Paul Warchol
Dario Zannier
Marco Zanta

REALIZATION OF THE MODELS

Paola Andreoli and Roberto Rezzoli, Milan
Ornella Calatroni, Milan
Jianjin Model Co. Ltd., Shanghai
Luigi Morellato, Milan
Franco Quaglietta, Milan
Giovanni Sacchi, Milan

RENDERING

Stack Studios, Genoa
Strato Design, Milan